A Second Domesday?

A SECOND DOMESDAY?

The Hundred Rolls of 1279–80

SANDRA RABAN

OXFORD
UNIVERSITY PRESS

OXFORD
UNIVERSITY PRESS

Great Clarendon Street, Oxford OX2 6DP

Oxford University Press is a department of the University of Oxford.
It furthers the University's objective of excellence in research, scholarship,
and education by publishing worldwide in

Oxford New York

Auckland Bangkok Buenos Aires Cape Town Chennai
Dar es Salaam Delhi Hong Kong Istanbul Karachi Kolkata
Kuala Lumpur Madrid Melbourne Mexico City Mumbai Nairobi
São Paulo Shanghai Taipei Tokyo Toronto

Oxford is a registered trade mark of Oxford University Press
in the UK and in certain other countries

Published in the United States
by Oxford University Press Inc., New York

© Sandra Raban 2004

The moral rights of the author have been asserted
Database right Oxford University Press (maker)

First published 2004

British Library Cataloguing in Publication Data
Data available

Library of Congress Cataloging in Publication Data
Data available

ISBN 0–19–925287–4

1 3 5 7 9 10 8 6 4 2

Typeset in Sabon by
Cambrian Typesetters, Frimley, Surrey
Printed in Great Britain
on acid-free paper by
Biddles Ltd, King's Lynn, Norfolk

Preface

Like so many historians of medieval England, I first encountered the 1279–80 hundred rolls in search of evidence for a particular estate. By good fortune, this lay in Huntingdonshire where the rolls are beguilingly full and straightforward. At the same time I discovered the Huntingdon roll preserved in the Bodleian Library, perhaps the most intriguing of the texts associated with the inquiry. What began as a rich source for a doctoral dissertation on the estates of Thorney and Crowland Abbeys, ended by becoming a subject of study in its own right as I came to realize just how little interpretative material was available. This book is the fruit of more than fifteen ensuing years of work on various aspects of the inquiry, which have now been drawn together into a comprehensive account of its conduct, its background, the rolls themselves, and their later use.

During such a long period of gestation, I have acquired many debts, not least to Marjorie Chibnall who kindly read this text in its entirety. It was she who first introduced me to Domesday Book. Much of what I learnt from her and from the students with whom I explored it when I, in my turn, became an undergraduate teacher, has formed the background for this book. Paul Brand, whose unrivalled knowledge of thirteenth-century public records has been generously shared with me, as with so many others, is owed particular thanks for his unfailing response to requests for enlightenment and for commenting on the finished volume. Diana Greenway's enthusiasm for the project has been as valuable as her immaculate article on the Gallow hundred roll. Karen Attar, Stephen and David Baxter, Caroline Burt, Rosamond Faith, Harold Fox, Barbara Harvey, Rosemary Horrox, Junichi Kanzaka, and Andrew Lacey have all very kindly given me valuable assistance. I have also benefited from the help of Edmund King, Len Scales, and others involved in the Hundred Roll Project based at Sheffield University, which focused on the earlier inquiry of 1274–5. As always the comments of colleagues on papers read at Sheffield, the Institute of Historical Research, the Thirteenth Century England Conference at

Durham in 2001, and the Medieval History Seminar at Oxford have proved both illuminating and a means of escaping error. For mistakes which remain, I take full responsibility. With a subject as complex and unexplored as this one, some of the arguments hazarded in the following pages will inevitably come to be revised in the light of future investigation. Indeed I already revised some of my own earlier conclusions during the course of writing. For certain aspects of the rolls, there is no substitute for thorough topographical knowledge. I am aware that I have been considerably more sure-footed in parts of the country well known to me. If I have made statements elsewhere which appear crass to local readers, I can only apologize.

I have appreciated the help and expertise of staff at Cambridge University Library, the Bodleian Library, Oxford, the University of London Library, the National Archives, Norwich Record Office, and, especially, that of Tony Carr of Shropshire Archives. I would also like to thank Trinity Hall for a grant towards research expenses. Ruth Parr, the commissioning editor of Oxford University Press, has been unfailingly supportive of the book and I am particularly grateful to Andrew MacLennan for his timely advice and practical assistance in its early stages. Last, but certainly not least, I owe a huge amount to my husband Tony, for his constant encouragement and support.

Contents

List of Maps

List of Tables

Abbreviations

Ag. HR	*Agricultural History Review*
Bodl.	Bodleian Library, Oxford
BL	British Library, London
CAC Wales	*Calendar of Ancient Correspondence concerning Wales*
Cal. Close	*Calendar of Close Rolls*
Cal. IPM	*Calendar of Inquisitions Post Mortem*
Cal. Pat.	*Calendar of Patent Rolls*
Cart. Rames.	*Cartularium Monasterii de Rameseia*
CUL	University Library, Cambridge
EHR	*English Historical Review*
Ec. HR	*Economic History Review*
HR	Bodleian, Huntingdon rolls, 1
Norfolk Rec. Off.	Norfolk Record Office, Norwich
PRO	Public Record Office, London, now the National Archives
Rec. Comm.	Record Commission
RH	*Rotuli Hundredorum*
TRHS	*Transactions of the Royal Historical Society*
ULL	University of London Library
VCH	*Victoria County History*

Introduction

Beginning in spring 1279, the crown mounted a large-scale inquiry apparently designed to record land tenure and regalian rights throughout the country. Its returns are known today as the 1279–80 hundred rolls because the information was collected within the hundredal subdivisions of the county. They are some of the most enigmatic records to survive from medieval England. Although just one manifestation of an investigative culture that permeated thirteenth-century Europe, there is nothing else quite like them among the many other inquiries of the period. We know that they were commissioned for the whole country, but returns only survive for a handful of counties across middle England and East Anglia (see Map 1). It is therefore a matter for debate whether the enterprise was carried out as planned and the returns lost, or whether it was aborted part way through. Most intriguing of all is what Edward I really had in mind when he set his commissioners to work on 12 March.

A comparison with the Domesday inquiry of 1086 immediately comes to mind since, in both cases, information was amassed about countless estates, their demesnes, resources, and peasant tenants, as well as for a number of towns. The structure of individual estate entries in both the surveys is also very similar, even though the material in the hundred rolls has not descended to us in tenant-in-chief order like that of Domesday Book.[1] One of the questions to be addressed in this book is whether the 1279–80 inquiry was conceived with Domesday Book specifically in mind, but irrespective of the answer, there is a striking contrast in the way in which the two inquiries have been treated by posterity. One is a household name, the other scarcely known outside academic circles. The reasons for this, at least, are less of a mystery than other aspects of the inquiry. Domesday Book, and the inquest which lay behind it, achieved a symbolic importance derived initially from association

---

[1] See below, Ch. 2.

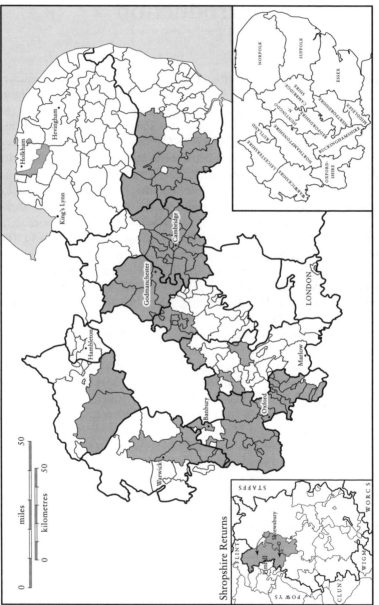

Map 1. Areas for which returns to the 1279–80 inquiry are known

with the Norman conquerors. The Peterborough continuator of the Anglo-Saxon Chronicle famously lamented that 'So very narrowly did he [the king] have it investigated, that there was no single hide nor virgate of land, nor indeed (it is a shame to relate but it seemed no shame to him to do) one ox nor one cow nor one pig which was there left out and not put down in his record'.[2] Within a few generations, Domesday Book itself had acquired such a hold on popular imagination that Richard Fitz Nigel, writing *c.*1179, observed that

This book is metaphorically called by the native English, Domesday, that is the Day of Judgement. For as the sentence of that strict and terrible last account cannot be evaded by any skilful subterfuge, so when this book is appealed to on those matters which it contains, its sentence cannot be quashed or set aside with impunity.[3]

This reputation was consolidated by subsequent appeals to its contents in pleas of ancient demesne. If an estate appeared as royal demesne in Domesday Book, its tenants enjoyed certain privileges. Chief among them were exemption from tallage and protection from an increase in rents by any subsequent lords. Thus, by the 1370s Domesday had come to represent, often unrealistically, a means to peasant freedom.[4]

The 1279–80 hundred rolls were born of very different circumstances. By the later thirteenth century, investigations of all sorts were a matter of routine. When the inquiry was begun, Edward I's new broom had already been sweeping vigorously for the best part of five years. Following so closely on the massive, if significantly different, hundred roll inquiries of 1274–5, and lacking the legal and administrative afterlife of Domesday Book, there was nothing to single out the 1279–80 hundred rolls or to propel them into enduring popular consciousness. Unlike the 'Ragman rolls' of 1274–5, so named because of the jurors' seals hanging at their foot in an untidy fashion, they did not even achieve the accolade of a nickname.[5] Most contemporary chroniclers failed to mention them

---

[2] *The Anglo-Saxon Chronicle*, ed. D. Whitelock, D. C. Douglas, and S. I. Tucker (London, 1961; repr; Westport, Conn., 1986), 161–2.

[3] *The Course of the Exchequer by Richard, Son of Nigel*, ed. and tr. C. Johnson (London, 1950), 64.

[4] R. Faith, 'The "Great Rumour" of 1377 and Peasant Ideology', in R. H. Hilton and T. H. Aston (eds.), *The English Rising of 1381* (Cambridge, 1984), 43–73.

[5] Although associated with the 1274–5 inquiry, the name was not unique to it. The same term was later used for other rolls with multiple seals, although they were

at all. Among the few who did was another Peterborough writer, but his laconic 'no-one was spared', appended to an extract from the royal commission, wholly lacks the passion of his predecessor's howl of outrage.[6]

A further reason for Domesday's greater modern fame lies in the nature and comprehensiveness of the final text. Essentially, it is Domesday Book rather than the inquest itself, however remarkable, which has earned lasting repute. The 1279–80 hundred rolls are not in the same class. Most particularly there is no finished product to compare with Exchequer (or Great) Domesday, due to the fundamental difference in the degree of editing to which the two sets of findings were subjected. With the exception of East Anglia, for which there are the fuller returns of Little Domesday, the 1086 material was so heavily and consistently edited that it is amenable to systematic analysis. This was undertaken in cartographic form in the major series of Domesday geographies published between 1952 and 1977, and more recently using computer technology and statistical techniques.[7] Escaping the hand of an equivalent editorial genius, the 1279–80 hundred rolls resemble something more closely analogous to the exceedingly complex collection of Domesday's so-called 'satellites' and associated texts.[8] Instead of a single finished compilation, they are a mélange of returns varying from the raw verdicts of hundredal jurors and

---

all political documents. H. M. Cam, *Studies in the Hundred Rolls: Some Aspects of Thirteenth-Century Administration* (Oxford Studies in Social and Legal History, 6; Oxford, 1921), 44.

[6] *Chronicon Petroburgense*, ed. T. Stapleton (Camden Soc. 47; London, 1849), 30. See also below, pp. 45–6.

[7] H. C. Darby, *Domesday England* (Cambridge 1977); idem, *The Domesday Geography of Eastern England* (Cambridge, 1952); H. C. Darby and I. B. Terrett (eds.), *The Domesday Geography of Midland England* (Cambridge, 1954); H. C. Darby and E. M. J. Campbell (eds.), *The Domesday Geography of South-East England* (Cambridge, 1962); H. C. Darby and I. S. Maxwell (eds.), *The Domesday Geography of Northern England* (Cambridge, 1962); H. C. Darby and R. Welldon Finn (eds.), *The Domesday Geography of South-West England* (Cambridge, 1967); J. McDonald and G. D. Snooks, *Domesday Economy: A New Approach to Anglo-Norman History* (Oxford, 1986); J. D. Hamshere, 'Regressing Domesday Book: Tax Assessments of Domesday England', *Ec. HR*, 2nd ser. 40 (1987), 247–51; R. A. Leaver, 'Five Hides in Ten Counties: A Contribution to the Domesday Regression Debate', *Ec. HR*, 2nd ser. 41 (1988), 525–42. There have also been a number of projects to make Domesday Book available in electronic form.

[8] For the most recent account of these, see D. Roffe, *Domesday: The Inquest and the Book* (Oxford, 2000), 94–112.

submissions of individual landlords to final, edited drafts. They thus reflect different stages of an elaborate process of compilation and consequently present a much more formidable obstacle to analysis.

The more we understand about eleventh-century society, the more difficult it becomes to take some of the Domesday information at face value. Nonetheless, since social and economic historians are almost entirely dependent on evidence pieced together from individual estate records, the importance of a source providing countrywide data cannot be overstated. This is quite apart from the intrinsic importance of such a wealth of information at a date when other evidence is very limited. A particular illustration of this is Robin Fleming's study of the rich leavening of legal material to be found among the more familiar data on manorial resources. Several thousand complaints are recorded, some in considerable detail. Nothing comparable is available before the late twelfth century.[9] It is therefore appropriate to describe Domesday Book as the foundation for our understanding of English society in the generation after the Conquest.

By the later thirteenth century, the situation had been transformed. The volume of record keeping both by government and private landlords had expanded hugely from the end of the twelfth century. An extraordinary number of these documents have survived to the present day, thereby reducing the importance of any single source, however voluminous. Even if this were not the case, the much more restricted geographical range of the 1279–80 hundred rolls would diminish their potential for providing a comprehensive picture. Domesday returns are available for the whole of England south of the Tees, albeit with a few important exceptions, notably London, Winchester, and Bristol. Against this, the limited returns of the 1279–80 inquiry look distinctly sparse. Had they covered the whole country, their profile would undoubtedly be much higher.

One should not exaggerate however. With all their limitations, the 1279–80 hundred rolls remain indispensable to historians. As with the subsidiary Domesday texts, documents belonging to the preliminary stages of an inquiry are more informative about its

---

[9] R. Fleming, *Domesday Book and the Law: Society and Legal Custom in Early-Medieval England* (Cambridge, 1998).

processes than a finished version could be. Furthermore, for all that the rolls are limited in their geographical scope, where they do exist, the amount of detail provided is far greater than in Exchequer Domesday. In a much quoted passage, E. A. Kosminsky hailed the 1279–80 hundred rolls as 'a general cadastral survey of all England—and one, moreover, incomparably fuller and more detailed than that carried out by the Conqueror', while more recently, Bruce Campbell called it 'the most ambitious survey ever attempted by medieval government'.[10] The full coverage of land-holdings within each hundred is particularly valuable for estates belonging to smaller lay landlords who, even in the thirteenth century, rarely left archives of their own. Such estates were as much a part of county society as those of the crown, church, and nobility. Indeed, in a county like Bedfordshire, they were the dominant group. Without the knowledge of such estates afforded by the hundred rolls, there would be little hope of understanding society as a whole.

Given this extraordinary wealth of information, the 1279–80 hundred rolls have received surprisingly little attention. Although there are modern editions of some of the otherwise unpublished returns and a few older editions of others, for most of the rolls scholars still depend on the Record Commission edition published in 1818. Furthermore, there remain a number of rolls which have never been published at all.[11] More than half a century ago, Kosminsky observed that 'It is, perhaps, time for the question of a new and full critical edition to be considered'.[12] It is still awaited. By good fortune, the Record Commission text is generally sound, but the lack of modern scholarly apparatus is a severe handicap. Apart from minor misreadings of the manuscript rolls and inconsistent, sometimes inaccurate, recording of membrane numbers, the chief shortcoming of this edition lies either in the omission of insertions and marginal symbols or, where they are included, failing to

---

[10] E. A. Kosminsky, *Studies in the Agrarian History of England in the Thirteenth Century* (Oxford, 1956), 13, quoted by J. B. Harley, 'The Hundred Rolls of 1279', *Amateur Historian*, 5 (1961), 9; B. M. S. Campbell, 'The Complexity of Manorial Structure in Medieval Norfolk: A Case Study', *Norfolk Archaeology*, 39/3 (1986), 236.

[11] *Rotuli Hundredorum*, 2 vols. (Rec. Comm., London, 1812–18), ii. 321–877. For a full list of texts, published and unpublished, see Appendix 1.

[12] Kosminsky, *Studies*, 28.

distinguish them from the main text.[13] Unavoidably, perhaps, a printed text also fails to do justice to the heterogeneous nature of the rolls, thereby creating a misleading appearance of uniformity. Anyone wishing to study the way in which the rolls were drawn up must refer to the manuscripts themselves. For other purposes, the most urgent need is for a translation. That such a rich source should continue to be inaccessible to anyone unfamiliar with record type and Latin is astonishing, although the size of the task would be daunting unless approached piecemeal. Surprisingly perhaps, the idea has not proved attractive to local record societies.[14]

The absence of a major study of the 1279–80 hundred rolls is harder to explain than the lack of a new edition. Most efforts to date have been concentrated on the 1274–5 inquiry. These rolls, mostly published in the same Record Commission edition, were the fruits of investigation into the usurpation of crown rights and maladministration. Unlike the 1279–80 rolls, they exist at least in part for most of the country, if sometimes only in the form of later extract rolls. Only Cheshire, Cumberland, Lancashire, Middlesex, Surrey, and Westmorland have no rolls of either type.[15] Pioneering work was done by Helen Cam in the 1920s in *Studies in the Hundred Rolls* and *The Hundred and the Hundred Rolls*. There then ensued a long fallow period before a project, funded by the Leverhulme Trust in the 1990s and based at Sheffield University, aimed to publish the hitherto unpublished rolls. So far this has resulted in texts for the Stamford inquiries and a study of the Cambridgeshire rolls.[16] Barbara English has also translated the

---

[13] For an example of a minor misreading of the text, see *et* for *ut* in the entry relating to Thomas Wyteman in the Bampton hundred roll (Oxon.) or *dono* for *domo* in returns for the NE ward of Oxford. *Oxfordshire Hundred Rolls of 1279*, ed. E. Stone and P. Hyde (Oxfordshire Record Society, 46; Oxford, 1968), 22, n. 7; *RH* ii. 797b, l. 4; 804b, l. 48. For the treatment of annotations, see below, Chs. 4 and 5. Examples of inconsistent or inaccurate membrane numbers are mm. 6, 7, and 9 of the Papworth roll (Cambs.) which have been omitted and m. 3 of the Ewelme roll (Oxon.) which is printed as m. 5. On the Wootton roll (Oxon.), m. 31 is transposed to read m. 13. *RH* ii. 473a–82a; 754a, 871b.

[14] An exception is *Oxfordshire Hundred Rolls*, ed. Stone and Hyde (Bampton hundred and Witney only).

[15] *RH* i. 1–19, 35–543, and ii. 1–37, 49–54, 87–113, 116–17, 125–229, 242–320; H. M. Cam, *The Hundred and the Hundred Rolls* (London, 1930), 48.

[16] *Stamford in the Thirteenth Century: Two Inquisitions from the Reign of Edward I*, ed. D. Roffe (Stamford, 1994); L. Scales, 'The Cambridgeshire Ragman Rolls', *EHR* 113 (1998), 553–79.

Yorkshire extract rolls in conjunction with the *Quo waranto* proceedings.[17]

The 1279–80 hundred rolls have not been wholly overlooked, but the most substantial study so far has been Kosminsky's analysis of the structure of estates recorded in the returns. This was undertaken as long ago as the 1930s, although not published in its revised form in English until 1956.[18] It shows the influence of the then burgeoning interest in social and economic history, and the material is now ripe for reworking, as Bruce Campbell has pointed out in his magisterial survey of English seigneurial agriculture.[19] Junichi Kanzaka's study of peasant rents employing a computer database represents the first step in this direction.[20] While rewarding, however, such analysis is no substitute for work on the texts themselves. For too long historians have been reliant on material which is imperfectly understood and therefore open to misinterpretation. Recent years have seen the first moves towards understanding the inquiry itself, so the time now seems ripe to remedy this deficiency with a comprehensive study.

The Record Commission edition of the rolls covers almost the whole of Huntingdonshire and much of Oxfordshire, together with parts of Bedfordshire, Buckinghamshire, and Cambridgeshire. As with the 1274–5 inquiry, a number of unpublished rolls have long been identified in the National Archives. Sixteen decrepit membranes from returns for Armingford hundred in Cambridgeshire were found among Chancery Miscellanea in 1928 and there are rolls for other Cambridgeshire hundreds, often in an equally poor condition.[21] This no doubt explains how they came to be separated from the main body of returns for the county and so failed to be included in the Record Commission edition. There is also a sizeable, if disappointing, group of thirty-four membranes of

---

[17] *Yorkshire Hundred and Quo Warranto Rolls*, ed. B. English (Yorkshire Archaeological Society, Record Series, 151; Leeds, 1996).

[18] Kosminsky, *Studies*, p. v.

[19] B. M. S. Campbell, *English Seigniorial Agriculture 1250–1450* (Cambridge, 2000), 57.

[20] J. Kanzaka, 'Villein Rents in Thirteenth-Century England: An Analysis of the Hundred Rolls of 1279–80', *Ec. HR* 55 (2002), 593–618.

[21] PRO, SC5/Cambs/Tower/15 (Radfield), 16 (Armingford), 17 (Cheveley). Small additions have also been found for Chesterton, Chilford, and to the printed roll for Northstow hundreds. SC5/Cambs/Tower/3, 4, and 6, as well as a membrane for Girton in Northstow hundred which is related to the main roll. SC5/8/5/5, m. 6.

returns from various London wards, as well as additional unpublished material for Cambridge, Oxford, Banbury, and the opening portion of Wootton hundred in Oxfordshire.[22] Several fragments have also been tentatively attributed to the inquiry. A single membrane relating to Hambleton and Normanton in Rutland is undated and somewhat different in ordering from other known texts, but could be a seigneurial submission.[23] Two membranes for the Worfield liberty in Shropshire are unlikely to belong, however, since its articles of inquiry refer to the Jews and the return of writs, neither of which featured in the 1279–80 proceedings. David Roffe identified them, together with a roll for Marlow (Bucks.), as belonging to the first hundred roll inquiry of 1255.[24] Two membranes relating to Middlesex hundreds also appear to belong to separate inquiries, although they are sewn together. The first, dealing briefly with six hundreds, concerns the inquiry into distraint of knighthood which was closely associated with the 1279 inquiry, but the second, relating to Ossulstone hundred alone, appears to refer to estates confiscated after the Battle of Evesham.[25]

Copies of returns which would otherwise have been lost have also surfaced both inside and outside the National Archives from time to time. Those for Warwick and the two Warwickshire hundreds of Stoneleigh and Kineton were discovered among the Miscellaneous Books of the Exchequer by Sir Paul Vinogradoff.[26] Extracts dealing with its own estates in these two hundreds, and the return for Coventry, were also copied by Coventry Priory into a fourteenth-century manuscript. Found among the Leigh collection held by the Shakespeare Birthplace Trust, they were recognized by Rodney Hilton as belonging to the inquiry.[27] Returns

---

[22] PRO, SC5/London/Tower/1–26; SC5/Cambs/Tower/1, mm. 36–40 (Cambridge); SC5/Oxon/Tower/part of 9b (Oxford), SC5/Oxon/Tower/16/1, m. 1 (Wootton), SC5/Oxon/Tower/17 (Banbury). The return for the borough of Witney was included in a translated edn. of the Bampton hundred roll. *Oxfordshire Hundred Rolls*, ed. Stone and Hyde, 91–105.

[23] PRO, SC5/8/5/7.

[24] PRO, SC5/8/5/4 and 6. D. Roffe, 'The Hundred Rolls of 1255', *Historical Research*, 69 (1996), 202 n. 4.

[25] PRO, SC5/Middx/Tower/1. I am grateful to Paul Brand for pointing the Evesham connection out to me. For distraint of knighthood, see below, Ch. 2.

[26] PRO, E164/15; P. Coss, *Lordship, Knighthood and Locality: A Study in English Society c.1180–c.1280* (Cambridge, 1991), 21; Kosminsky, *Studies*, 8.

[27] Shakespeare Birthplace Trust, Stoneleigh MS, DR 18/31/3. The returns are printed in *The Warwickshire Hundred Rolls of 1279–80: Stoneleigh and Kineton*

covering the interests of Bury St Edmunds in eight Suffolk
hundreds were copied into several of the abbey's medieval manuscripts.[28] That for Holkham in North Greenhoe hundred in
Norfolk also survives as a seigneurial copy.[29] It has also been
suggested that a late thirteenth-century survey of Sedgeford, in the
same county, belonging to the dean and chapter of Norwich, may
possibly have been a copy of the hundred roll verdict.[30] The King's
Lynn return may have been preserved in a fifteenth-century copy of
a survey listing tenants in Newland.[31] The existence of returns for
Leicestershire would be completely unknown but for the substantial transcriptions made by William Burton in the seventeenth
century, while without the transcript of returns from Shropshire
made by Joseph Morris in the nineteenth century, there would be
no clue that the inquiry reached as far as the Marches.[32]

One of the most interesting developments of recent years has
been the identification of original texts associated with the inquiry
outside the public records. The most notable of these is the
Huntingdon roll, of unknown provenance, now in the Bodleian
Library, Oxford. It consists of rolls for the two Huntingdonshire
hundreds of Normancross and Leightonstone, one of which is
almost identical to the printed roll, while the other is radically
different.[33] Other important discoveries are original returns from
the otherwise thinly documented survey of Norfolk. These consist
of fifteen membranes covering eight vills in Gallow hundred and a

---

Hundreds, ed. T. John (British Academy, Records of Social and Economic History,
NS 19; Oxford, 1992); 'The Coventry Hundred Rolls', ed. T. John, in P. R. Coss
(ed.), *The Early Records of Medieval Coventry* (British Academy, Records of Social
and Economic History, NS 11; London, 1986), 365–94.

[28] BL, Harl. MS 743, fos. 149ʳ–257ᵛ; CUL, Ee, iii, 60, fos. 234ʳ–319ᵛ, printed in
The Pinchbeck Register, ed. F. Hervey, 2 vols. (Brighton, 1925), ii. 30–282; CUL,
Add. MS 3395.

[29] *Lordship and Landscape in Norfolk 1250–1350: The Early Records of
Holkham*, ed. W. Hassall and J. Beauroy (British Academy, Records of Social and
Economic History, NS 20, Oxford, 1993), 215–30, no. 253, and commentary
524–32.

[30] Norfolk Rec. Off., DCN 4437; Campbell, 'Complexity', 233.

[31] King's Lynn borough muniments, Bc 1, printed in *The Making of King's Lynn*,
ed. D. M. Owen (British Academy, Records of Social and Economic History, NS 9;
Oxford, 1984), 156–81, no. 174; Campbell, 'Complexity', 232–3.

[32] Bodl., Rawlinson MS B, 350, partly printed in J. Nichols, *The History and
Antiquities of the County of Leicester*, 4 vols. (London, 1795, repr. Wakefield,
1971), i/1, pp. cx–cxxi; Shropshire Archives, 6001/28, 21–62.

[33] Bodl., Huntingdon rolls, 1. See below, Chs. 3, 4, and 6.

single membrane for Hevingham in South Erpingham hundred.[34] The identification of such strays adds considerably to our appreciation of the conduct of the inquiry, as well as raising questions about how far beyond the known returns it may originally have reached.

Although thorough investigation of the 1279–80 hundred roll inquiry is clearly long overdue, it is worth remembering that it is not so many years ago that the same could have been said of Domesday Book. Until the late 1980s, scholars were similarly dependent on an early edition of the text. The county translations in the *Victoria County Histories* and the Phillimore editions made Domesday Book more accessible to non-specialists, but it was only with the Alecto edition, published as part of the novocentenary celebrations, that historians were provided with a high-quality text and modern apparatus.[35] This anniversary also provided an enormous boost to Domesday studies in general, which had languished somewhat since the seminal work of F. W. Maitland and V. H. Galbraith.[36] Collections of essays edited by Sir James Holt and Peter Sawyer advanced understanding in many different aspects of the inquiry and the momentum has been maintained by further celebrations associated with the millennium as well as by Robin Fleming's study of the legal aspects of Domesday Book and David Roffe's recent and controversial book on the Domesday inquest and its relationship to Domesday Book itself.[37]

Sadly the seven-hundredth anniversary of the 1279–80 hundred rolls brought forth no comparable efflorescence of scholarship. Nevertheless, the extension of our understanding has been proceeding

[34] University of London Library, Fuller Coll., 7/5 (Gallow), discussed in D. E. Greenway, 'A Newly Discovered Fragment of the Hundred Rolls of 1279–80', *Journal of the Society of Archivists*, 7 (1982), 73–7; Norfolk Rec. Off., NRS 14761 29 D4 (Hevingham), discussed and printed in Campbell, 'Complexity', 225, 232–6, and app.

[35] *Domesday Book*, ed. A. Farley, 2 vols. (London, 1783); *Domesday Book*, ed. J. Morris *et al.*, 40 vols. (Chichester, 1974–86); *Great Domesday* gen. ed. R. W. H. Erskine (London, 1987–92). For an account of the Alecto enterprise, see H. Pearson, 'The Alecto Domesday Project', in E. Hallam and D. Bates (eds.), *Domesday Book* (Stroud, 2001), 151–8.

[36] F. W. Maitland, *Domesday Book and Beyond* (Cambridge, 1897, repr. 1987); V. H. Galbraith, *The Making of Domesday Book* (London, 1961).

[37] J. C. Holt (ed.), *Domesday Studies* (Woodbridge, 1987); P. Sawyer (ed.), *Domesday Book: A Reassessment* (London, 1985); Hallam and Bates, *Domesday Book*; Fleming, *Domesday Book*; Roffe, *Domesday*.

along a similar path, if at a slower pace. One has only to read J. B. Harley's useful introduction to the hundred rolls in the *Amateur Historian* of 1961 to appreciate how much has been achieved in the intervening years.[38] Moreover the insights gained through work on Domesday are also proving useful in interpreting its lineal descendant. They have taught us the questions to ask and alerted us to subtleties of textual interpretation. They also demonstrate vividly how the understanding of such large enterprises is cumulative. Roffe's work on Domesday shows that the benefits have not all been one-sided. His earlier studies of the hundred roll inquiries of 1255 and 1274–5 informed his understanding of the way in which the information was collected and led to his major re-evaluation of the Domesday inquest.[39]

This book aims to provide professional historians and the increasing ranks of amateur enthusiasts with a complete working tool based on such knowledge of the 1279–80 hundred rolls as is currently available. For students and those with a more general interest, it is designed to locate the inquiry in its political, social, and historiographical context. The following chapters will therefore begin by placing the inquiry in its historical setting. They will then assess its purpose and whether or not it ever extended further than the surviving returns would suggest. The inquiry itself will constitute the core of the book: its conduct, those who were involved in it, the way in which information was assembled, and how this massive harvest was then dealt with. Finally, the question of the subsequent fate of the findings and their value for later generations will be reviewed. Some of these aspects of the inquiry raise intractable problems and it would be unrealistic to expect the conclusions on any of them offered here to be definitive. As with Domesday Book, understanding will come gradually and from many quarters as historians build on the work of their predecessors. This study therefore, while intended for current users, also attempts to serve as a foundation, framework, and spur for work that is undoubtedly to come.

---

[38] Harley, 'Hundred Rolls', 9–16.

[39] D. Roffe, 'The Hundred Rolls and their Antecedents: Some Thoughts on the Inquisition in Thirteenth-Century England', *Haskins Society Journal*, 7 (1995), 179–87; idem, 'Hundred Rolls of 1255', 201–10; idem, *Domesday*, p. xi.

I

An Inquiring Culture

Within a few weeks of his return to England in August 1274, Edward I had embarked on a sustained programme of reform and legislation which, in the seventeenth century, earned him the title of 'England's Justinian'.[1] There was much to be done, given his father's long and often ineffectual reign, followed by more than a year and a half's delay between Henry's death and his own arrival to assume the throne. The restitution of crown rights, many of which had been usurped over time, was a major goal, but he also aimed to provide 'good government' for his subjects and an effective administrative machine to underpin his own ambitions. All this involved the exposure and punishment of wrongdoers and the enactment of legislation to deal with issues of wider moment. It was against this background that the hundred roll inquiry of 1279–80 was conceived.

The earlier hundred roll inquiry of 1274–5 had been Edward's first move in this drive for reform and was intended to reveal where remedial action was required. Another sizeable inquiry in 1285, known as 'Kirkby's Quest', sought information about crown debts and potential sources of revenue as part of exchequer reform.[2] There were also more specific investigations, such as the returns demanded of religious houses early in 1275 in order to provide information about their dealings with foreign merchants or the 1279 inquiry into distraint of knighthood, which checked on the efficiency with which officials carried out royal instructions.[3] A

---

[1] He was so called by Edward Coke, the great 17-cent. jurist. P. Brand, *The Making of the Common Law* (London, 1992), 135.

[2] M. Prestwich, *Edward I*, 2nd edn. (New Haven and London, 1997), 236–7; *Feudal Aids*, 1284–1431, 6 vols. (HMSO; London, 1899–1920), i, pp. viii–xvii.

[3] For examples of the 1275 returns, see PRO, SC1/14/130, SC1/19/113, SC1/19/115, SC1/21/55, SC1/21/62. For their context, see T. H. Lloyd, *The English Wool Trade in the Middle Ages* (Cambridge, 1977), 39. For the 1279 inquiry, see *Cal. Pat.* 1272–81, 342–3 and below Ch. 2.

remarkable series of statutes was enacted, many directly concerned with the findings of the 1274–5 inquiry. The ordinance known as the Statute of Ragman, probably dating from 1276, made provision for special judicial hearings to deal with those who had been indicted during the course of the Ragman inquiry, although the arrangements it laid down were soon superseded.[4] The First Statute of Westminster of 1275 and the Statute of Gloucester of 1278 were 'portfolio' statutes, focusing on a wide range of problems. Thus, Westminster I's fifty-one chapters addressed *inter alia* the commonest grievances revealed by the 1274–5 hearings, providing a definition of offences for which bail could be granted and penalties for those who failed to acquit debtors at the exchequer when they had in fact paid. They also embraced matters ranging from wardship and purveyance to significant legal reforms, foremost among which was an overhaul of the assize of novel disseisin, which was further refined in subsequent legislation.[5] This statute was concerned in large part with furthering the investigations into franchises begun in 1274–5, but included among its fifteen chapters were measures designed to curb malpractices affecting minors, widows, and landlords, as well as several chapters specific to London.[6] In contrast to these broad enactments, the 1279 Statute of Mortmain, the 1275 Statute of Jewry, and the so-called Statutes of the Exchequer of the same year, each introduced substantial measures within a single sphere. The 1279–80 hundred roll inquiry thus followed an unprecedented flurry of investigation and ameliorative action.

By January 1279, the most urgent problems facing the crown had been addressed, if not wholly resolved, but the king's reforming energy had not yet run its course, nor had it yet been deflected by military ventures elsewhere in his domains. The new inquiry was to be distinctive in its brief, but was nevertheless closely related to its predecessors in many respects and strongly rooted in two distinct but complementary traditions: those of England and the Continent.

The tradition rooted in native practice, originating in the pre-Conquest period, employed the inquest as a means of obtaining

---

[4] *Statutes of the Realm*, i. 44; D. W. Sutherland, *Quo Warranto Proceedings in the Reign of Edward I, 1278–94* (Oxford, 1963); 24–6 and below Ch. 5.

[5] *Statutes of the Realm*, i. 26–39.

[6] Ibid., 45–50; H. M. Cam, *Studies in the Hundred Rolls* (Oxford, 1921), 39–40.

information on myriad topics of concern to the crown and the community. By the thirteenth century, inquests held in the general eyre were the principal manifestation of this. In addition to hearing crown and civil pleas, justices were charged with receiving the verdicts of juries in response to specific questions framed in evolving articles of inquiry.[7] The hundred roll investigations adopted the same procedures and also shared a number of the eyre's articles of inquiry. In both types of hearing sheriffs were ordered to empanel jurors to whom the articles were given. Each of these juries consisted of twelve local knights or substantial freemen drawn from the hundred who, in turn, assessed information supplied by lesser juries from individual vills. Their verdicts, sealed in authentication, were then presented to the commissioners or justices as appropriate.

The inquiry of 1279–80 was preceded by two earlier hundred roll inquiries (three, if one counts the partial investigation ordered in January 1274). The main emphasis of these forerunners varied, but as well as similarities in procedure they shared considerable overlap in their remit. In broad terms, all were concerned either with regalian rights and liberties or the misconduct of officials or both.

The first hundred roll inquiry was carried out in 1255 and has been the subject of a study by David Roffe. Most of its extant returns are included in the Record Commission edition of the hundred rolls, although inconveniently interspersed among those of 1274–5.[8] On 22 June 1255 commissioners were appointed to six circuits covering the whole country, excluding only the palatinates of Chester and Durham and the counties of Cornwall, Middlesex, and Rutland.[9] They were charged with inquiring into:

---

[7] D. Crook, *Records of the General Eyre* (PRO Handbook, 20; HMSO; London, 1982), 1; Cam, *Studies*, 16–29 and Appendix 2.

[8] D. Roffe, 'The Hundred Rolls of 1255', *Historical Research*, 69 (1996), 201–10; *RH* i. 20–34 (Bucks.); ii. 38–45 (Oxon.); 55–86 (Salop.); 114–15 (Staffs.); 230–41 (Wilts.). Neither the return for the single Somerset hundred of Puriton (PRO, SC5/Som/Chapter/1) or the hundreds of Seisdon in Staffordshire (PRO, SC5/Staffs/Chapter/2) are printed in the Rec. Comm. edn., although the Seisdon roll is translated in *William Salt Soc.* 5/1 (1884), 110–17. A roll relating to Dole in Wiltshire (PRO, SC5/Wilts/Tower/37), formerly thought to belong to the 1255 inquiry, has more recently been attributed to an eyre, probably that of 1256. Roffe, 'Hundred Rolls of 1255', 202, n. 4. Returns for one Northamptonshire and one Worcestershire hundreds, and one of the two Staffordshire hundreds, survive in the form of copies only. *Book of Fees*, 3 vols. (HMSO; London, 1920–31), ii. 1287–91.

[9] Apart from the palatinates, where the nature of the jurisdiction might explain

TABLE 1. *Circuits for the 1255 hundred roll inquiry*

Commissioners	Counties
Henry of Bath, Richard de Shireburn	Notts., Derby., Yorks., Northumberland, Cumberland, Westmorland, Lancs.
Gilbert Preston, Roger Whitchester	Essex, Herts., Kent, Surrey, Sussex
Roger Thirkleby, Robert Shottenden	Hants., Dorset, Som., Devon, Wilts., Berks.
Master Simon Walton, William le Breton	Glos., Worcs., Heref.
Philip Lovel, Nicholas Hadlow	Northants., Beds., Bucks., Oxon., War., Leics., Salop., Staffs.
John le Frounceys,[a] John Wyvill	Lincs., Cambs., Hunts., Norf., Suff.

Source: From *Cal. Pat. 1247–58*, 438
[a] Replaced by Simon de Passelewe

those who owe suit at those counties and at the king's courts in those counties, and have withdrawn themselves from doing such suit, without warrant; and to enquire likewise touching keepers of castles and things belonging to those castles; and touching the state of woods, parks, hays and forests and all other things which seem expedient for the utility of the king and realm; and to extend the king's manors and demesnes and all profits belonging to the said castles.[10]

Material survives for some of the hundreds and liberties in the eight counties of Buckinghamshire, Northamptonshire, Oxfordshire, Shropshire, Staffordshire, Somerset, Wiltshire, and Worcestershire, with a strong bias towards the Midlands and west. It is not clear whether the small number of returns reflects their poor survival or a failure to carry out the investigations as planned. They represent only three of the six circuits and are unevenly distributed among them; five of the eight counties for which rolls survive belong to the Midland circuit for which Philip Lovel and Nicholas Hadlow were responsible, but any conclusions drawn

their omission, the random distribution of the missing counties suggests omission from the enrolment on the patent rolls. For the circuits, see Table 1.

[10] *Cal. Pat. 1247–58*, 438.

from this would be highly speculative. It is suggestive, however, that the only rolls remaining from Northamptonshire and Worcestershire, which belonged to different circuits, survive as transcripts in the *Book of Fees*, implying that the original returns cannot be relied upon as a guide to how much of the country was covered. Given the nature of the inquiry, it would be surprising if the rolls had not been returned to the exchequer once the work was complete, even though most of the commissioners were also justices, who were not always conscientious about returning their eyre rolls. Moreover, it was not until 1257, two years later, that a systematic attempt was made to recover such rolls and to store them in the treasury.[11] It is also possible that some of the 1255 rolls disappeared because they were subsequently issued to justices in the special eyre of 1260. The provisions for its conduct drawn up in 1259 required that 'the records of the inquiries made three or four years ago, in the autumn, concerning the king's rights' be taken along by the justices in order to assist them in dealing with the withdrawal of liberties and geldable vills. Certainly other rolls associated with this eyre failed to return into government keeping.[12]

The articles of the 1255 inquiry were not enrolled on the patent rolls, but have been reconstructed from the returns themselves by David Roffe. They formed two distinct groups. The first, consisting of twenty-nine articles, included ten common to the general eyre. Together they dealt with a broad range of royal interests, principally different kinds of jurisdiction and feudal incidents. Commissioners were also asked to extend the royal demesne in order to assess its annual value, although in practice this meant a summary valuation only. Among a small number of articles asking more general questions were those seeking information about Jewish chattels, Christian moneylenders, and lords who were abusing rights of ancient demesne. The king's principal aim appears to have been to conduct an audit of the crown's rights and dues. Such a goal is extremely plausible, given the limited information available to Henry III and the financial straits in which he found himself at that date. The second group of articles all related to the royal

[11] Crook, *Records*, 12.
[12] *Documents of the Baronial Movement of Reform and Rebellion, 1258–1267*, ed. R. F. Treharne and I. J. Sanders (Oxford, 1973), 162–3, clause 9.

forest. Roffe argues that they should be seen in conjunction with the sale of wood and investigation into forest misdemeanours which the king had authorized with the consent of his Council on 1 March 1255. The forest articles may thus belong to this initiative, which was later merged with the more comprehensive inquiry.[13]

The surviving rolls were not generally dated, but the abbreviated Wiltshire return records that the inquest was held at Wilton on 7 August 1255, suggesting that the proceedings there were briskly executed within seven weeks of the issue of the commission.[14] Speed was necessary since the circuits allocated to each set of commissioners were sizeable. Roger Thirkleby and Robert Shottenden, who conducted the Wiltshire hearings, were also responsible for Hampshire, Dorset, Somerset, Devon, and Berkshire, while Henry of Bath and Richard de Shireburn were required to cover virtually the whole of northern England.

Evidence for the subsequent use of the findings is elusive. Roffe suggests that they provided information for the increase in the increments to the county farms collected from sheriffs in 1256–7. The resumption of timber sales in autumn 1255, which had been brought to a halt because prices were too low, may also point to the role of the inquiry in resolving earlier problems.[15] The Wiltshire returns and entries for Doddingtree hundred in Worcestershire and Offlow hundred in Staffordshire, found in the *Book of Fees,* appear to be extracts from the original verdicts providing an inventory of royal interests hundred by hundred. That such summaries were made may indicate some practical afterlife in which they were used in routine administration.[16] The compilation of extract rolls could also be another reason why so few of the originals have been preserved; once the necessary details had been extracted, they had no further value.

There was no further hundred roll inquiry until 1274, but the investigations conducted at the instance of the baronial opposition to Henry III after it took control in 1258 were similar in all but name and were probably influential in determining Edward I's

---

[13] Roffe, 'Hundred Rolls of 1255', 204–6, 208–10. The articles, apart from those dealing with the forest, were recorded in the Burton Annals. *Annales Monastici,* ed. H. R. Luard, 5 vols. (Rolls Series; London, 1864–9), i. 337–8.

[14] *RH* ii. 230.

[15] Roffe, 'Hundred Rolls of 1255', 207.

[16] *RH* ii. 230–41; *Book of Fees,* ii. 1290–1.

course of action on assuming the throne in 1274.[17] Baronial interest centred primarily on the misconduct of officials, although the
eyre arranged for 1260 was also charged with investigating the
alienation of regalian rights.[18] In mid-1258, the Provisions of
Oxford had laid down that four knights in each shire would attend
the county court 'to hear all complaints of any trespasses and
injuries whatsoever, done to any persons whatsoever by sheriffs,
bailiffs or any other persons' and that 'the four knights shall have
all the complaints, with their attachments enrolled in order and
sequence, separately and severally for each hundred, so that on his
first visit the justiciar shall be able to hear and determine the
complaints separately for each hundred'.[19] Hugh Bigod, the justiciar, began his eyre at Oxford in June 1258 and continued with
hearings in southern England.[20] It soon became clear that it would
take far too long for the business to be completed in this way.
Arrangements were accordingly modified so that the knights would
bring their complaints to Westminster by 6 October 1258 in time
for the Michaelmas parliament.[21] Late in 1259 provision was made
for a special eyre, with the work now apportioned between seven
circuits covering much of the country.[22] Sheriffs were ordered to
summon twelve knights or 'law worthy' freemen from each
hundred before the justices who would then hand over the articles

[17] J. R. Maddicott, 'Edward I and the Lessons of Baronial Reform: Local
Government 1258–80', in P. R. Coss and S. D. Lloyd (eds.), *Thirteenth Century
England*, i (Woodbridge, 1986), 11–13; L. Scales, 'The Cambridgeshire Ragman
Rolls', *EHR* 113 (1998), 554–5.
[18] *Documents*, ed. Treharne and Sanders, 162–3, clause 9.
[19] Ibid. 98–9.
[20] R. F. Treharne, *The Baronial Plan of Reform, 1258–1263* (Manchester, 1932;
revised repr. 1971), 145–7.
[21] J. R. Maddicott, *Simon de Montfort* (Cambridge, 1994), 165; *Documents*, ed.
Treharne and Sanders, 112–15; *Cal. Pat. 1247–58*, 645–9.
[22] It is not easy to arrive at a clear picture of the circuits, owing to changes of
plan and confusion with other legal proceedings, but they appear to have been (1)
Norfolk, Suffolk, Cambridgeshire, and Huntingdonshire; (2) Wiltshire,
Oxfordshire, and Berkshire; (3) Gloucestershire, Herefordshire, and Worcestershire;
(4) London, Sussex, Hampshire, Essex, Hertfordshire, and Middlesex; (5) Somerset,
Dorset, and Devon; (6) Northamptonshire, Buckinghamshire, and Bedfordshire; (7)
Lincolnshire, Shropshire, Leicestershire, Staffordshire, Warwickshire, and probably
Rutland. A further circuit comprising Cumberland, Lancashire, Northumberland,
Yorkshire, and Westmorland had been planned, but was later dropped. Cheshire,
Durham, and Cornwall were omitted, as were Kent and Surrey where Bigod had
already been in action. Treharne, *Baronial Plan*, 196–7; Crook, *Records*, 189–91;
Documents, ed. Treharne and Sanders, 158–65; *Close Rolls, 1259–61*, 141–5.

of inquiry and set a date for them to return with the answers. Those accused were bidden to attend at the same time in order to be dealt with.[23] It was envisaged that the special eyre would begin on 7 January and be completed by Easter 1260.[24] Even with the greater manpower now available, however, the task still proved too onerous and the eyre was called off in the following June, ostensibly because of the famine then afflicting the country.[25]

Justices' rolls from this eyre survive for proceedings in Essex, Leicestershire, Oxfordshire, and Warwickshire but, in this instance, we can be sure that these do not represent the full scale of the hearings. The decision to prosecute those who were exposed as wrongdoers at the same time as the investigation itself, led to an account of amercements appearing on the pipe rolls. This evidence, together with allowances for the justices' expenses, makes it clear that otherwise undocumented hearings took place in other counties.[26]

On his return to England in August 1274, Edward I found a realm which had been administered remarkably well in his absence. The moment at which power is transferred from one ruler to the next tends to be a time of vulnerability and, in Edward's case, this should have been compounded by the weakness of a father whose subjects were rioting within earshot of his deathbed, as well as by his own long absence. As it turned out, Robert Burnell and others entrusted with government had served him capably, thereby enabling him to embark immediately on reform rather than take steps to secure his position. It is even suggested that the 1274–5 inquiry, in its inception, owed as much to the policies of these officials as to the initiative of the king himself.[27] Certainly an inquiry had been launched at the beginning of 1274, before his return to

---

[23] *Documents*, ed. Treharne and Sanders, 158–61; *Close Rolls, 1259–61*, 141–5.

[24] Treharne, *Baronial Plan*, 203; Crook, *Records*, 189; *Flores Historiarum*, ed. H. R. Luard, 3 vols (Rolls Series; London, 1890), ii. 437. The most recent survey of these arrangements is P. Brand, *Kings, Barons and Justices: The Making and Enforcement of Legislation in Thirteenth-Century England* (Cambridge, 2003), 20–41.

[25] *Documents*, ed. Treharne and Sanders, 190–3; E. F. Jacob, *Studies in the Period of Baronial Reform and Rebellion, 1258–1267* (Oxford Studies in Social and Legal History, 8; Oxford, 1925; repr. New York, 1974), 100–1.

[26] Crook, *Records*, 189–91; Treharne, *Baronial Plan*, 203.

[27] R. Huscroft, 'The Political Career and Personal Life of Robert Burnell, Chancellor of Edward I', London University, Ph.D. thesis, 2000, 75–6.

England, into 'liberties and rights belonging, in the time of Henry III, to the king's demesnes'.

This first inquiry covered some of the same ground as the one commissioned by Edward himself a few months later, but did not tackle the question of corruption which formed the main thrust of its successor. Evaluating its scope presents the usual problem of assessing what proportion of the original returns the few surviving rolls represent. On 28 January, Bartholomew de Yatingden and Guy of Taunton were commissioned to carry out investigations in eleven counties in the south and west of England.[28] The only surviving returns belong to Hampshire and Somerset. In so far as one can tell, the commissioners did not proceed county by county. The earliest inquests were in Somerset between 20 and 23 March, followed by others in the same county between 5 and 10 April, and in Hampshire on 12 June, before a return to Somerset between 22 and 27 July.[29] Given the fragmentary nature of the evidence, it is unlikely that these rolls represent the full scale of the work undertaken, but given too the rather desultory way in which the commissioners operated in Somerset, it is equally unlikely that they could have completed their full assignment by the time the much larger inquiry was commissioned in October.

How far the two inquiries can be seen as part of the same process is debatable. It has been suggested that the earlier investigation may have been a false start, hampered by an inadequate brief.[30] It seems more probable, however, that the two investigations were conceived independently. The aim of the January inquiry was to check on rights attaching to the royal demesne under the previous monarch. Neither a wider pursuit of regalian rights nor the pursuit of corrupt officials was envisaged. It was therefore closer in spirit to the audit undertaken in 1255 and, indeed, to the information sought by Edward a few months earlier in the recognitions of his vassals in Gascony.[31] Action to ascertain

---

[28] *Cal. Pat. 1272–81*, 65. The counties were Cambs., Dorset, Essex, Glos., Hants., Kent, Northants., Som., Surrey, Wilts., Worcs.

[29] *RH* ii. 118–24, 220, 223–4. In the Rec. Comm. edn. the returns for Hants. from the January inquiry are not distinguished from those commissioned later in the year. The returns are filed together in PRO, SC5/Soton/Chapter/1–5, where that for the inquest held at Wanstead (?) in Sothwick is misdated. The head of the roll is damaged, but since it was held before Yatingden and Taunton, there can be no doubt that it belongs to the earlier of the two investigations.

[30] Prestwich, *Edward I*, 92.   [31] See below, pp. 28–30.

the absentee monarch's rights would have been well within the power of his caretaker government, whereas it is harder to envisage it undertaking a wholesale assault on corruption and usurpations on its own initiative. It is more convincing to suppose that the limited January inquiry, which had nonetheless proved too large in its scope for Yatingden and Taunton alone, was aborted in the light of the more ambitious plans for reform instituted by the king on assuming personal control.

The commissioners appointed on 11 October 1274 were ordered to inquire into 'the deeds and the behaviour of sheriffs and bailiffs', as well as the 'rights, liberties and other things affecting the kings and the state of the commonalty'.[32] This became incomparably the largest of the hundred roll inquiries, whether in terms of its aims, the extent to which its findings survive or the use made of them in the following years. The country appears to have been apportioned between eleven circuits, six of which are recorded on the patent rolls and the remainder can be reconstructed from the returns themselves or subsequent eyre rolls.[33] Two commissioners were responsible for each circuit at any one time. Unlike the 1255 inquiry, few of the commissioners appear to have been royal justices. The majority, however, were royal officials already experienced in the king's service.[34] Lessons had been learnt from the earlier inquiries. The increased number of circuits was better geared to the size of the task and no attempt was made to deal simultaneously with matters raised by the findings.

As in 1255, the commissioners were issued with articles of inquiry, which in this instance were entered on the patent rolls.[35] The thirty-three articles which appear there are incomplete; there seem to have been thirty-nine questions common to all the circuits and further questions which were put to jurors on some circuits only. A total of fifty-one articles are known, printed, and translated by Helen Cam in *The Hundred and the Hundred Rolls* and Barbara English in *Yorkshire Hundred Rolls and Quo Warranto Rolls, 1274–1294*.[36] As in 1255, a number were the same as the articles

---

[32] H. M. Cam, *The Hundred and the Hundred Rolls* (London, 1930), 39; *Cal. Pat. 1272–81*, 59.
[33] Cam, *Studies*, 140–1.   [34] Cam, *The Hundred*, 40.
[35] Ibid. 39.
[36] Cam, *The Hundred*, app. 1, 248–57; eadem, *Studies*, 30–1; *Yorkshire Hundred Rolls*, ed. English, 3–4, 23–6.

TABLE 2. *Circuits for the 1274–5 hundred roll inquiry*

Commissioners	Counties
Richard de Fukeram,[a] Osbert de Bereford	Salop., Staff., Ches.
Bartholomew de Bryauncon, James de St Vigor	Kent, Surrey, Sussex, Middlesex, London
William de Brayboef, Guy of Taunton[b]	Wilts., Hants., Berks., Oxon.
Bartholomew le Juvene, Roger de Chenne	Som., Dorset, Devon, Cornwall
William de Sancto Omero, Warin de Chalcumbe	Northants., Rutland, Lincs.
Thomas de Boulton, William de Pereton[c]	Yorks.
Robert de Ufford, Ralph Sandwich	Herts., Essex (?), Suff., Norf.
Richard Creeping, Thomas Lewknor	Leics. (?), War. (?), Notts., Derby.
Sampson Foliot, Edmund Caldecote	Bucks., Cambs., Hunts., Beds.
Geoffrey Aguillon, Philip de Willoughby	Northumberland, Cumberland (?), Westmorland (?), Lancs. (?)
unknown	Glos. (?), Worcs. (?), Heref. (?)

Sources: From *Cal. Pat.* 1272–81, 59; Cam, *The Hundred*, 258.
[a] Replaced by Roger Lestrange, *Cal. Pat.* 1272–81, 116.
[b] Replaced by William Gerberd, *ibid.*
[c] One of whom was probably replaced by William de Chatterton. *Yorkshire Hundred Rolls*, ed. English, 1.7.

of the eyre or were expanded versions of such articles.[37] In general they faithfully followed the stated objectives of the inquiry. About half dealt with royal demesne, fiefs, and regalian rights, while most of the remainder covered abuse of administrative office. A few miscellaneous articles belonged to neither category. Article 39 sought information about the illegal export of wool during the recent dispute with Flanders, while article 49 addressed the perennial problem of weights and measures.

The commissioners appear to have begun work by 18 November

[37] Cam, *Studies*, 31–2.

and the latest known return is dated 21 March 1275. Taking just over four months, they accumulated an enormous amount of information with impressive speed. Procedure was superficially straightforward, in line with previous inquiries. Sheriffs were ordered to summon jurors to inquests at dates and places set by the commissioners. Their verdicts were to be returned under their own seals and those of the commissioners. Despite the homogeneous appearance given to them by the Record Commission edition, the returns as we have them are actually a mixture of preliminary verdicts and later revised versions.[38] Closer inspection of the unpublished Cambridgeshire rolls has shown how the initial hundredal verdicts were edited and supplemented when the jurors were summoned before the commissioners at Cambridge. Unusually, some private plaints were also added at this late stage, perhaps because vested interests among the jurors had made it difficult to include them earlier in the proceedings.[39]

Unsurprisingly, the invitation to accuse those who had abused their powers unleashed a huge volume of complaint. The Dunstable annalist's observation that 'nothing useful came of it' is over harsh.[40] As well as the most common abuses which were dealt with by reforming legislation in the first Statute of Westminster, others were tackled through the courts, albeit slowly.[41] There is no evidence that the arrangements for special hearings provided for in the so-called Statute of Ragman were ever implemented, but cases were heard in the London eyre of 1276 and after 1278 the Statute of Gloucester laid down that they should be dealt with in the general eyre and this indeed happened. The articles of the inquiry were added to those of the eyre, where they appear among the *nova capitula*.[42]

At some point between 1280 and 1294, most probably after 1290, four substantial extract rolls were drawn up from the original returns. Three summarized in standard form the verdicts of the jurors relating to the king's interests, each roll covering several counties.[43] For Bedfordshire, Berkshire, Cornwall, Huntingdonshire, Leicestershire, Northumberland, Somerset, Warwickshire,

[38] Ibid. 115–16; Scales, 'Cambridgeshire Ragman Rolls', 556–7.

[39] Scales, 'Cambridgeshire Ragman Rolls', 568–71.

[40] 'sed nullum commodum inde venit', *Annales Monastici*, iii. 263.

[41] See above, p. 14 and below Ch. 5.

[42] Sutherland, *Quo Warranto*, 24–5; Cam, *Studies*, 15.

[43] Cam, *The Hundred*, 48–9; *Yorkshire Hundred Rolls*, ed. English, 2–3. PRO, SC5/8/1–3. There was a further roll relating to Sussex alone. SC5/Sussex/Chapter/1.

Worcestershire, and Yorkshire, this is all that remains from the inquiry.[44] In counties where both original returns and extracts survive, most are printed together in the Record Commission edition, thereby disguising the way that counties were grouped together on the extract rolls.[45] The fourth largely unpublished roll, headed *De ministris*, comprised extracts dealing with accusations of administrative abuse.[46] It is easy to see why such rolls were compiled. Justices in eyre, accustomed to carting around the cumbersome original verdicts, festooned with their seals, must have welcomed more condensed and manageable working tools. Nevertheless, attempts to make their labours easier did not alter the fact that the task was ultimately too great for the creaking judicial system to accomplish. In such long-drawn-out proceedings, it was inevitable that many of the accused had either died or become untraceable. This was unfortunate, but would have been more so had punishment been Edward I's only objective. As it was, he was also signalling a new and better era to his subjects and, to his officials, his intolerance of corrupt behaviour.

The inquiry had revealed the murky origins of many franchises and the usurpation of others. Initially the king's intention seems to have been to deal with these in the Michaelmas parliament of 1275. The high status of offenders and the difficulty in proving title to many genuine privileges made proceedings more politically sensitive than the punishment of official misconduct. It was not the most urgent matter before parliament, however, and consideration of individual cases was continually postponed from one parliament to the next until it was overcome by the more pressing events of the first Welsh War. In 1278 therefore the king and council decided to convert these outstanding queries over franchises into a more searching examination of all such privileges, conducted by the justices of the King's Bench or the justices in eyre in the normal

---

44 Cam, *The Hundred*, 48

45 *RH* i. 35–48 (Bucks.); 63–96 (Devon); 97–103 (Dorset); 136–65 (Essex); 241–402 (Lincs.); 434–543 (Norf.); ii. 1–16 (Northants.); 49–54 (Rutland); 142–200 (Suff.). Only the extract roll for Staffordshire is printed in the Rec. Comm. edn., although there is a single short, unpublished, original roll for Totmonslow hundred. *RH* ii. 116–17; PRO, SC5/Staffs/Chapter/3.

46 PRO, SC5/8/4. This roll of eleven membranes covers the counties of Dorset, Essex, Herts., Norfolk, Northumberland, and Suffolk only. The Northumberland portion is printed in H. H. E. Craster, 'An Unpublished Northumbrian Hundred Roll', *Archaeologia Aeliana*, 3rd ser. 3 (1907), 188–90.

course of their business. This was duly provided for in the Statute
of Gloucester. In the event, with few exceptions, claims were only
heard before the justices in eyre, thus becoming part of the well-
known *Quo waranto* proceedings recorded in a separate section of
their rolls.[47]

Government had demonstrated its capacity to collect massive
quantities of information and complaint, but despite the varying
strategies employed since 1258, it had not succeeded in finding a
mechanism which would enable its findings to be dealt with effec-
tively. By 1278, the favoured solution to this dilemma had become
the institutionalization and perpetuation of the aims of the 1274–5
inquiry through the normal processes of the general eyre and its
nova capitula. This was no more successful than earlier measures,
however. Progress in hearing claims and cases was hampered
because no more than two sets of justices were in eyre at any one
time and the added weight of business proved too much for the
already overburdened system to bear.[48] In any case, the franchisal
claims fell victim to political expediency when they were called off
as a sop to magnate feeling in 1294. In the Michaelmas parliament
of that year, the king granted 'as a favour to his people and on
account of the instant war of Gascony that all his writs, as well as
of Quo Warranto as of plea of land should remain at present without day until he or his heirs wish to speak about them'.[49]

Such was the English context for the 1279–80 inquiry.
However, while Edward I was heir to the native tradition of the
inquest by virtue of his crown, he was equally steeped in continental practice by virtue of his French domains and lineage. It was this
inheritance which constituted the second and wider tradition out of
which the hundred roll inquiries grew. Some years ago Jean
Glénisson drew attention to 'une véritable fureur d'inventaire' on
the Continent from around the mid-thirteenth century. It was
largely a product of the growth of literacy in government circles
throughout Europe from the late twelfth century, enabling the
routine collection of information on a large scale. Rulers of all
sorts, popes and kings, dukes and counts, held inquiries into a wide

[47] Prestwich, *Edward I*, 258–63; Sutherland, *Quo Warranto*, 19–31; *Yorkshire
Hundred Rolls*, ed. English, 4–5; Crook, *Records*, 144–6.

[48] Crook, *Records*, 144.

[49] *Select Cases in the Court of King's Bench under Edward I*, ed. G. O. Sayles, 3
vols. (Selden Soc.; London, 1936–9), iii. 28.

variety of matters. Among the more notable were those of Louis IX of France and his brothers Alphonse de Poitiers and Charles d'Anjou, which showed many of the same concerns as those undertaken on the English side of the Channel. In 1247, before setting out on crusade, Louis investigated the misconduct of his officials in order to make amends for the good of his soul. Alphonse de Poitiers made similar inquiries throughout his domains during the 1250s and 1260s.[50] Rather different, but equally pertinent, was the survey of his rights undertaken by Charles d'Anjou in the county of Toulouse in 1252–6.[51]

Between 1236 and 1238, long before he commissioned the 1255 hundred rolls, Henry III, as duke of Aquitaine, had ordered a wide-ranging inquiry into 'the excesses and alienations of his *baillis* and into royal rights' in the Entre-deux-Mers.[52] In 1259 the Lord Edward ordered his seneschal Drue de Barentin to carry out an inquiry, part of which was intended to establish the 'rights, liberties and obligations' of his vassals, although it was never carried out.[53] Following his father's death, Edward showed the same enthusiasm for reform in Gascony as in England. Indeed, Gascony received his attention first, since he spent a considerable time there on the way back from his crusading expedition, between his accession in November 1272 and his return to England in August 1274. In the absence of the information which the 1259 inquiry should have provided, his most pressing problem was the need for basic facts about his possessions. Conditions prevailing in the duchy differed greatly from those in England. Demesne holdings were significantly fewer, leaving the king-duke at the mercy of his vassals to a larger extent than was the case in his kingdom. Poverty and the

---

[50] J. Glénisson, 'Les Enquêtes administratives en Europe Occidentale aux XIIIᵉ et XIVᵉ siècles', in W. Paravicini and K. F. Werner (eds.), *Histoire comparée de l'administration* (Munich, 1980), 19–23; *Enquêtes administratives d'Alfonse de Poitiers: Arrêts de son parlement tenu à Toulouse 1249–1271*, ed. P.-F. Fournier and P. Guébin (Paris, 1959), pp. xxiii, xxvi–xxxiii.

[51] J. Dunbabin, *Charles I of Anjou: Power, Kingship and State-Making in Thirteenth-Century Europe* (London, 1998), 48.

[52] Ed. J. Delpit, in *Archives Historiques du Département de la Gironde*, 3 (1861–2), 106–7, no. 36, 109–27, no. 38.

[53] M. Vale, *The Origins of the Hundred Years' War: The Angevin Legacy, 1250–1340* (Oxford, 1996), 64; J. P. Trabut-Cussac, *L'Administration anglaise en Gascogne sous Henry III et Edouard I de 1254 à 1307* (Société de l'École des Chartes, Mémoires et Documents, 20; Geneva, 1972), 17, 45; *Rôles Gascons*, ed. F. Michel and C. Bémont, 3 vols. (Paris, 1885–1906), i, supp., p. lxxxviii, no. 4.

right to private warfare also made Gascon vassals notably more bellicose and independent than their English equivalents who, whatever their grievances in the 1250s and 1260s, had been conditioned by two centuries of subordination to royal authority. As always, Edward was also driven by financial imperatives. He was in particular difficulty in 1273 when he was obliged to begin repaying Louis IX the 70,000 *livres tournois* which he had borrowed to fund his contingent of the crusading army. Under its terms, six monthly instalments of 5,000 *livres* became a charge on the Bordeaux revenues from March 1273.[54] The inquiry he set in motion between 1273 and 1274 was therefore designed to inform him of his rights and permit him to claim all that was his due.

Gaining a full picture of this and other Gascon inquiries presents even more problems than those carried out in England. The Bordeaux archives were largely destroyed during the course of their evacuation to England at the beginning of the war with France in 1294. Failure to pay the sailors hired to transport them led to them being deposited with the Franciscans on the Isle of Oléron. There they fell into the hands of the French and everything, except one register, was subsequently lost.[55] In consequence, historians are reliant either on letters emanating from the English chancery and entered on the Gascon rolls, or material originating in duplicates previously sent to London for information but which, in their turn, have now disappeared, leaving only limited transcripts. Unsurprisingly, the uneven character of this evidence often makes it easier to discover that an inquiry was commissioned than to know whether it was actually carried out.

Atypically, however, the reverse is true for the 1273–4 inquiry. No commission or articles survive and, since Edward was present in Gascony, it is likely that he issued his instructions orally. Our knowledge depends on the recognitions made by his vassals in response to questions put to them by the seneschal or his deputy. Unfortunately these have suffered in transmission. Copies or even copies of copies, they only survive in the form of a register

---

[54] *Réceuil d'Actes relatifs à l'administration des Rois d'Angleterre en Guyenne au XIIIᵉ siècle: Recogniciones feodorum in Aquitania*, ed. C. Bémont (Paris, 1914), p. xlvi; Prestwich, *Edward I*, 72; *Foedera*, i /1. 481.

[55] *Gascon Register A*, ed. G. P. Cuttino, 3 vols. (British Academy, London, 1975–6), i, pp. xii–xiii.

compiled in 1354 from records held in London.[56] Many of the texts are abbreviated and corrupt. The transcriptions are only in approximate chronological and geographical order, being grouped according to the notary public who was responsible for drawing them up. Miscellaneous documents dating from earlier in the thirteenth century, and unconnected business belonging to 1273–4, also lie scattered among them. There is no means of knowing how many recognitions may have been lost along the way, leaving our picture of the proceedings incomplete.

Despite these limitations, some deductions about the nature of the inquiry are possible. The king-duke's vassals were initially summoned to one of three gatherings to pay homage and fealty to Edward in person, after which they were required to declare their obligations before specially appointed jurors. The first of these gatherings was held at St Sever, on the southern edge of the Landes, in September 1273. The mundane business of questioning each vassal was delegated over the following twelve months to Peter Itier, castellan and prévôt of St Sever, acting on behalf of the seneschal, Luke de Tany.[57] A few months later, on the last day of February 1274, the town crier of Lectoure, south of Agen, called vassals from the Gers to assemble in the bishop's hall for the same purpose. No trace remains of these proceedings, although records survive of some other business transacted there.[58] It has been suggested, not altogether convincingly, that no vassal responded to

---

[56] Wolfenbüttel MS 2311, printed as *Recogniciones*, ed. Bémont. It is not known whether the scribes worked from originals, duplicates, or an existing register. Sacks of unrelated homages were recorded in the Tower in the early 14th cent. and perhaps those of 1273–4 were also stored there. It is likely, however, that a compilation had been made earlier, either in Gascony or London. Trabut-Cussac argued that the recognitions, as we have them, were copied from a lost Bordeaux exemplar which antedated the 1294 disaster. Registers of feudal recognitions are known to have been among the archives evacuated in 1294. *Gascon Register A*, ed. Cuttino, i, pp. xii–xvii. J.-P. Trabut-Cussac, 'Les Cartulaires gascons d'Edouard II, d'Edouard III et de Charles VI', *Bibliothèque de l'École des Chartes*, 111 (1953), 80–5; idem, *Le Livre des hommages d'Aquitaine: Restitution du second Livre noir de la connétablie de Bordeaux* (Société Archéologique de Bordeaux; Bordeaux, 1969), pp. xvi–xvii.

[57] *Recogniciones*, ed. Bémont, p. xlvii; 19–20, no. 23; 22–3, nos. 30–2; 47, no. 132; 49–52, nos. 138–73. For Itier's career, see Trabut-Cussac, *L'Administration anglaise*, 167–8.

[58] *Recogniciones*, ed. Bémont, 52, no. 174. For the other matters dealt with there in late Feb. and early Mar., see 52–3, nos.175–6; 180–3, nos. 452–4; 194–8, no. 468.

the summons in what was a border area between Edward's lands and those of the Agenais, which was still in the hands of Alphonse de Poitiers.[59] More probably the recognitions were omitted from the register. Finally, while still at Lectoure, the king had written to the mayor of Bordeaux commanding his presence, with twelve jurors, at Bordeaux in March.[60] There, between the 18th and the 24th, in the church of St Andrew, before Luke de Tany and in the company of lay and ecclesiastical notables, a large number of vassals and townsmen made their recognitions.

The first question put to those summoned was whether they held any land of the king-duke and, if so, what it was and what obligations their tenure entailed. In many recognitions, the evidence about tenure is followed by answers to questions about jurisdiction and alienations. In the Bordelais, questions commonly focused on the alienation of ducal jurisdiction.[61] In the south, it was more often whether anything had been alienated in mortmain.[62] Sometimes the type of alienation was unspecified and the question may have been framed to solicit information about any grant or sale.[63] Although there is no indication that the inquiry was designed to hear complaints, such a question inevitably brought to light the occasional grievance.[64] In general, however, the responses did not yield much to arouse ducal concern about encroachment on his rights, unless of course it was the very absence of findings. Relatively few vassals admitted to alienation of any kind and, where there were positive responses, they usually referred to alienations in mortmain. Even these often dated from earlier generations.[65]

Although no recognitions survive, similar hearings were ordered in 1276 in the dioceses of Poitiers, Limoges, and Cahors under the direction of the local seneschal and Master Bonet de Saint-

---

[59] Prestwich, *Edward I*, 301.

[60] *Recogniciones*, ed. Bémont, p. xlvii.

[61] *si alienavit aliquid de juribus domini regis.* This was also the case in a projected inquiry in the Lomagne in 1275. Trabut-Cussac, *L'Administration anglaise*, 45–6.

[62] *si aliquid est alienatum in manu mortua.*

[63] *si fuerat aliquid alienatum de hoc quod pertinet domino regi*: e.g. *Recogniciones*, ed. Bémont, 56, no. 185; 241, no. 521.

[64] e.g. in the course of making his declaration at St Sever, Amanieu de Benquet claimed that his brother had sold an estate at Lescun to a burgess of Mont de Marsan without his consent. Ibid. 48, no. 134.

[65] e.g. ibid. 31, no. 56; 39, no. 95.

Quentin.[66] Further recognitions and homages were received in the Agenais in 1286–7. A comparison with those of 1273–4 suggests that the earlier inquiries had been unusually searching. In 1286–7, vassals' acknowledgement of their holdings and obligations were recorded without incidental detail.[67] Such brevity probably reflects the greater degree of certainty about seigneurial rights in an area which, until the recent past, had been under the competent rule of Alphonse de Poitiers and which had seen similar inquiries in 1259 and 1272–3.[68] In 1273–4, Edward needed to make good the deficiencies of his less effective father.

Although maladministration was not his most pressing concern in 1273–4, it was already beginning to exercise Edward's mind. Veziano de Blazirt, an official of the vicomte de Lomagne, and Otto de Gontaud were each summoned on the first day of the recognition hearings at Bordeaux to answer accusations of corrupt and violent behaviour towards the king-duke and his subjects.[69] There was also the evidence of misgovernment which had emerged as a by-product of questions about jurisdiction and such exposure may have prompted an inquiry around Dax, on the southern edge of the Landes, in 1276.[70] In 1278 Robert Burnell and Otto de Grandison were sent to Gascony as what J.-P. Trabut-Cusac, the doyen among historians of Gascony, called 'enquêteurs-réformateurs'. However, their principal task appears to have been to deal with the political fall out from Luke de Tany's corrupt and over-abrasive rule.

---

[66] *Rôles Gascons*, ii. 17–18, no. 65. Vassals were required to justify their tenure and make full declarations. No further details are given.

[67] The proceedings were conducted by Raimond de Champagne, seneschal of the Agenais, Master Bernard de Saint-Loubès, and Bernard de Martin. *Archives Historiques du département de la Gironde*, 1 (1859), 349–87, no. 182.

[68] Bodleian Library, MS 917, *Le Livre d'Agenais, publié d'après le MS Bodley 917*, ed. G. P. Cuttino (Cahiers de l'Association Marc Bloch de Toulouse: Documents d'Histoire Méridionale, 1, Toulouse, 1956). It was copied by French scribes at Agen in 1283–6. A further copy, made by English scribes, was taken to London where it was recorded in the Gascon calendar. It survives in fragmentary form. *The Gascon Calendar of 1322*, ed. G. P. Cuttino (Camden Soc., 3rd ser. 70; London, 1949), 163; J.-P. Trabut-Cussac, 'Le Livre d'Agenais: A propos d'une édition récente', *Bibliothèque de l'École des Chartes*, 115 (1957), 180–6.

[69] *Recogniciones*, ed. Bémont, 52–3, nos. 175–6.

[70] Bernard Jourdain, of Larée near Condom, complained that he was unable to obtain justice under the present arrangements and requested that he might answer to a different court. Ibid. 40, no. 100; *Cal. Pat. 1272–81*, 140. Local officials were ordered to assist Robert son of John and Itier Bochardi who had been sent to make unspecified inquisitions.

Despite a hint in the Gascon rolls that they were charged with more general reform and a letter to Robert Burnell enclosing a return to an inquiry about the revenues of the provost of Barsac, there is no evidence of any broader investigation. Perhaps complaints were dealt with at the parliament they summoned in Bordeaux and for which virtually no record survives.[71]

Edward's approach to the vexed question of alienations in mortmain is an interesting reminder that he was vassal to the king of France just as much as king of England. Its chronology accords better with the policies of the French crown which had introduced legislation in 1275, four years ahead of the English Statute of Mortmain.[72] The problem was essentially the same in both countries; lords were losing feudal incidents because their tenants or subtenants were granting estates to the church in perpetuity. In France the situation was rendered even more chaotic by the scale and complexity of feudal tenures. For the sake of the church as well as lords, the introduction of ground rules by the French crown was welcome. The inquiries of 1273–4 had addressed the question of mortmain in southern Gascony, but not apparently elsewhere. The first substantive investigation into illicit grants to the church, with power to confiscate, was commissioned in Périgord, the Limousin, and Quercy at the same time as the feudal recognitions in 1276.[73] Other inquiries followed in the 1280s, in which Edward specifically ordered his officials to deal with alienation 'against the statute of the court of France'.[74]

Thus far Edward has been treated as heir to separate traditions in England and Gascony, but any sharp distinction between his English and Continental domains is artificial; they had much in common. In both, local jurors played a key role in information-gathering. Differences were those of practice rather than substance.

---

[71] PRO, SC1/18/35. A petition to the king mentions *nuncii a vobis missi in Vasconiam pro ballivorum et seneschallorum Vasconie forefactis et injuriis emendandis*, but the vice-regal powers as set out on the Gascon rolls were those of peacemaking and settling disputes. There is nothing explicitly to suggest the conduct of investigations. Trabut-Cussac, *L'Administration anglaise*, 56–8; *Rôles Gascons*, ii. 50, nos. 186–8.

[72] S. Raban, *Mortmain Legislation and the English Church 1279–1500* (Cambridge, 1982), 21–2; E. Miller, 'The State and Landed Interests in Thirteenth Century France and England', *TRHS*, 5th ser. 2 (1952), 124–5.

[73] *Rôles Gascons*, ii. 17, no. 63.

[74] Ibid. 183, no. 669; 214, no. 754; 222, nos. 790–1.

Officials responsible for hearings in Gascony might bear the less familiar titles of seneschal, prévôt, or mayor, but their procedure was very similar. The most significant difference was the use of local notaries public instead of royal clerks to record the recognitions. Occasionally historians have been tempted to push the parallels too far. Bémont saw a link between the Gascon hearings of 1273–4 and the first major English hundred roll inquiry which followed so shortly afterwards.[75] This cannot be sustained however. The fifty-one articles of the 1274–5 inquiry encompassed a far wider range of issues than the Gascon hearings, and their main thrust was maladministration rather than tenure. The questions were also targeted with a specificity made possible only by generations of centralized English government, which was lacking in Gascony. It would be more accurate to see them as the product of the same circumstances. Edward, faced simultaneously with the responsibilities of his new realm and full authority in Gascony, approached his need for basic information in broadly the same way and at much the same time.

This holds good for all his possessions, as is strikingly evident in his policy towards demesne holdings. His finances were already in their characteristically parlous state on his accession, dictating that he maximize income from all sources. It was, in any case, a sensible measure to establish the current value of his inheritance wherever it might be. Within the space of a year, steps were taken to this end in England, the Channel Islands, Gascony, and possibly Ireland. On 10 October 1274, John Wyger and Ralph de Broughton were charged with extending demesne lands and lands otherwise in royal hands in the Channel Islands.[76] In Gascony, in November, his seneschal, Luke de Tany, was ordered to summon jurors to extend all the ducal lands to which he had been assigned by Master John Dominici, as well as certain other land and forest in the Bordelais and the diocese of Cahors.[77] Perhaps similar surveys informed policy in Ireland where, in the same month,

---

[75] *Recogniciones*, ed. Bémont, pp. xlv, xlix–l. See Prestwich, *Edward I*, 301–3, for a discussion of this.

[76] *Cal. Pat.* 1272–81, 70; *Extente des Îles de Jersey, Guernesey, Aurigny et Serk; suivie des Inquisitions dans les Îles de Jersey et Guernesey, 1274* (Société Jersiaise, 2; St Helier, 1877), 3–4, 8–13; PRO, C47/10/5/1. The commission is dated 8 Oct. in the Société Jersiaise text.

[77] *Rôles Gascons*, ii. 1–2, no. 1.

'having learnt that the value of the king's demesnes and lands . . .
may be improved', Edward gave instructions for more remote
estates to be put at farm or exploited on a share-cropping basis.[78]
Finally, in England, late in 1275, changes in management of the
royal demesne led to the appointment of royal stewards to super-
vise its exploitation, who then undertook new surveys.[79]

   The same policy was followed with later accessions. In
December 1279, orders were given to Arnaud de Got, bishop of
Agen, Guitard de Burgo, and Master Adam of Norfolk to extend
ducal land in the Agenais, which had recently fallen to the English
crown under the terms of the Treaty of Amiens.[80] This was particularly urgent because of the agreement reached between Edward
and his mother, Eleanor of Provence, by which she was to receive
property in the Agenais in return for surrendering her claim to the
honour of Richmond, which her uncle, Peter of Savoy, had
bequeathed to her.[81] In Wales, too, following the wars of 1276–7
and 1282–4, he needed to discover what rights and dues he could
expect from his acquisitions. In 1280, a commission in
Carmarthenshire and Cardiganshire was charged with assessing
rents and customs on lands confiscated from Welsh lords.[82] In
1283, more extents were commissioned in north-west Wales and
completed by March the following year. Undated extents for
commotes in Merioneth probably belong to the same period.[83]

---

[78] *Calendar of Documents relating to Ireland, 1252–84*, 188, no. 1072.

[79] Maddicott, 'Edward I and Lessons', 21–2.

[80] *Rôles Gascons*, ii. 96, no. 363.

[81] M. Howell, *Eleanor of Provence: Queenship in Thirteenth-Century England*
(Oxford, 1998), 242–3, 292.

[82] As in Gascony, it appears that the king issued oral commands. R. A. Griffiths,
*The Principality of Wales in the Later Middle Ages: The Structure and Personnel of
Government* (Board of Celtic Studies, History and Law series, 26; Cardiff, 1972),
60–1.

[83] *Cal. Welsh Rolls*, 274. For the completion see R. R. Davies, *Conquest,
Coexistence, and Change: Wales 1063–1415* (Oxford, 1987), 367. 'Extent of
Merionethshire', ed. M. C. Jones, *Archaeologia Cambrensis*, 3rd ser., 51 (1867),
183–92. Internal evidence indicates a date between 1283 and 1300. A schedule
notes that the extents post-date the death of David ap Gruffudd in 1283 and an
interlineation in different ink adds that an estate is now held for life by royal grant
to Madoc ap Jereward, whose holding at will was converted to a life grant in April
1300. Ibid. 188; *Cal. Pat. 1292–1301*, 507. The known whereabouts of the officials responsible makes a date in 1284–6 possible. Richard of Abingdon was
appointed chamberlain of North Wales on 22 March 1284 and John de Havering
as justiciary under Otto de Grandison two days earlier. Both were in Wales in
1284–6 and John de Havering was still serving there in 1287 before going abroad

The extents ordered in the Channel Islands in 1274 were part of a larger enterprise. Articles for the Jersey inquiry survive. Commissioners were asked to identify usurpations of royal land, alienations of rights, and liberties without licence, and also to investigate various offences, together with the conduct of jurors and the king's bailiffs.[84] The extents were drawn up with the aid of grand juries, while, for the inquisitions, twelve jurors from each parish testified as to the king's tenants and their obligations. The parish jurors then joined the grand jurors in presenting their grievances against royal officials. The resulting rolls were then destined for the attention of the chancellor, Robert Burnell. The articles of inquiry echo those of 1274–5, having been drawn up within a day or so of the English inquiry, c.11 October, but as in Gascony, the precise tenor of questions reflected local conditions, in particular the maritime economy of the Channel Islands. As befitted a smaller society, some of the articles also had a rather domestic flavour. In addition to theft, homicide, and judicial corruption, the commissioners were bidden to investigate the frequenting of taverns and poaching of rabbits.[85] A further inquiry was commissioned in 1279. On 7 June, the king wrote to announce that Otto de Grandison, to whom he had granted the Channel Islands for life in 1277, would be coming to investigate and deal with exactions and grievances. It is unlikely that he did so in person; his only known visit was in 1323. However, in June 1280, Richard Creeping and Master John de Stroda received a more detailed commission ordering them to deal with complaints and Grandison was commanded to order his bailiffs to make full amends.[86]

John le Patourel saw the Channel Island inquiries of 1274 as an extension of the contemporary English inquiry and their close timing makes the idea attractive.[87] However, as with Bémont's

on the king's business. Neither is fully documented thereafter, although de Havering was in Gascony in 1289–92 and back in Wales for the rest of the 1290s. Griffiths, *Principality*, 36 n. 5, 94–5; *Cal. Welsh Rolls*, 284; *Cal. Close, 1279–88*, 496; *Cal. Pat., 1281–92*, 279, 283.

[84] *Cal. Pat. 1272–81*, 70; *Extente des Îles*, 6–7.

[85] *Extente des Îles*, 6–7 (articles), 8–48 (inquisitions); PRO, C47/10/1–3; Cam, *The Hundred*, 248–57. The Jersey inquisitions are endorsed *rotuli insularum tradendi Roberto Burnel.*

[86] J. H. le Patourel, *The Medieval Administration of the Channel Islands, 1199–1399* (Oxford, 1937), 53; *Rôles Gascons*, ii. 81, no. 305; *Cal. Pat. 1272–81*, 411.

[87] Le Patourel, *Medieval Administration*, 53.

view that the Gascon inquiries of 1273–4 were a precursor, such a judgement carries a connotation of the primacy of one inquiry over another. It would seem more appropriate to argue that policy in all of Edward's domains was informed by broadly the same needs and the same administrative machinery. This accounts for their similarities as well as the absence of slavish parallels. Local conditions varied, so did the scale of remedial action required. Commissioners in the Channel Islands were expected to deal at once with the alienations and abuses uncovered by their inquiries. In Ireland in September 1274, the justiciar was given authority to replace the sheriffs of Limerick, Waterford, and Tipperary as required. The Irish clergy and laity were exhorted to assist him in dealing with offences against the king and his subjects, and the power of seizure was clearly envisaged.[88] Such immediate action was not possible for the English commissioners of 1274–5, committed to a much more searching inquiry and the overwhelming number of issues it threw up.

What therefore emerges from the twin strands of Edward I's English and Continental inheritance is the essential interconnectedness of policy and administrative practice throughout Plantagenet domains. Although the evidence is often incomplete or even fragmentary, it is clear that he initiated a prodigious number of inquiries in the years immediately after his accession. Together they bear witness to his determination to obtain the information necessary for him to exploit his demesnes, defend his regalian rights, and punish those who abused the power they wielded in his name. At the same time, it is evident that ambition often outran administrative capacity. Few of the more wide-ranging inquiries seem to have been carried out in their entirety. Nor had solutions been found to the huge workload involved in acting on their findings. On the positive side, experience had been gained. In particular, there was a better understanding in England of what commissioners might reasonably achieve within a limited timescale and this was reflected in the smaller circuits of later inquiries. Nevertheless, on the eve of the 1279–80 hundred roll inquiry, the fact remained that it was easier to amass information than to act on it.

---

[88] *Cal. Documents relating to Ireland, 1252–84*, 175–6, nos. 1020, 1025. The power of seizure can be inferred from the order a month later not to make restoration without royal permission. Ibid. 184, no. 1050.

2

A Second Domesday?

As we have seen, the hundred roll inquiry of 1279–80 followed five years of intensive governmental activity throughout the whole of Edward I's domains and formed an intrinsic part of the inquiring culture which permeated the early years of his rule. In one important respect, however, it was distinctively different from anything which had gone before; the quest for detailed information about estates belonging to his subjects. It is the resulting surveys which invite comparisons with Domesday Book and raise questions as to the motives of the crown in commissioning such an ambitious undertaking.

Ink continues to be spilt over the purpose of the 1086 survey and how far Domesday Book itself was part of the original plan. The reasons for collecting the information recorded in the 1279–80 hundred rolls are equally, if not more, elusive. It is fortunate that the initial commission survives, although it does not throw much light on the question. The patent rolls preserve a copy, in association with the commission for the inquiry into distraint of knighthood dated 12 March 1279, addressed to Geoffrey Aguillon, John de Steingrave, and Godfrey de Hauterive in the following terms:

Because of various encroachments made on us and on others, rich and poor, within our kingdom, in demesne, fees, feudal rights, liberties, and other things of various kinds, we and other men are suffering, and will suffer, loss. In order that, in future, that which is and ought to be ours and that which is and ought to be theirs may be clear, we commission you, and those with whom you associate yourselves, to view all the cities, boroughs, and market towns in the counties of Warwick and Leicester,[1] both inside and outside the liberties of all men, rich or poor, to inquire into our demesnes, fees, feudal rights, escheats, liberties, and all things touching

[1] Although the commission refers to Warwickshire and Leicestershire, these counties were assigned to different commissioners in the list of addressees. See below, Ch. 3.

fees and tenements, and those of others, who holds them, to wit, demesne, villeins, serfs, cottars, then free tenants, woods, parks, chaces, warrens, riparian rights, fairs, markets, and any other tenures whatsoever, and held in whatever way and of whom, whether of mesne lords or of others, and from what fees and other tenures scutage was customarily given and is owed and how much from the fees of every honour, and who holds feudal rights, in what manner and of whom. So we wish that every vill, hamlet, and other tenure, in whatever name, be assessed separately and openly written in books to be delivered to us by you, in such a way that no one is spared and that everything about these things may be made clear to us and to others. Therefore we command you that on certain days and places etc. in every place in the above counties, you attend in person and that knights under oath etc., and also make faithful inquiry of others in those counties about the tenures and fees in the aforesaid form and to do it in such a manner that your faithfulness, industry, and circumspection may be perpetually commended and so that you may not be confuted by a fresh inquisition or attaint on account of negligence or insufficiency on your part in carrying out these matters . . .

The same instructions were given to other commissioners who between them were to cover all the counties in England, excluding only the palatinate of Durham.[2] The heart of the inquiry appears to have been a comprehensive survey of every holding throughout the realm. In this, it would have been a clear heir to Domesday Book. Nothing remotely comparable had been attempted since the eleventh century. The nature of the information sought for each manor was also very similar to that of the Domesday survey. Compare questions set out in the 1279 commission with some of those which, according to the late twelfth-century *Inquisitio Eliensis,* were asked in 1086: How many hides? How many ploughs in demesne? How many men? How many villeins? How many cottars? How many slaves? How many free men? How many sokemen? How much wood? How much meadow? How much pasture? How many mills? How many fish ponds? . . .'[3] The hundred roll returns contain a great deal more detail than Domesday entries, but the underlying structural similarity of the information provided in the two sources is evident, as the following example from Caldecote in Huntingdonshire illustrates.

[2] *Cal. Pat.* 1272–81, 342–3. For the Latin text of the commission see Appendix 2 and for the commissioners Table 3.

[3] *Inquisitio Comitatus Cantabrigiensis,* ed. N. E. S. A. Hamilton (London, 1876), 97.

[Domesday entry:]
In Caldecote Stric had 5 hides to the geld. Land for 6 ploughs. There is now 1 plough in demesne and 10 villeins and 2 bordars have 4 ploughs. There are 15 acres of underwood. In the time of King Edward it was worth £4, now £3. A knight of Eustace holds it.[4]

[Hundred roll entry:]
Lord William de Brus holds the manor and vill of Caldecote from Lord Robert de Brus for a third part of a knight's fee and it belongs to the honour of Huntingdon. And the whole vill consists of 3½ hides of land, each hide of which contains 5 virgates of land and each virgate contains 25 acres. Of these hides the said lord has 4 virgates in demesne with adjacent meadow of the same measurements. And the *curia* of the said manor, with its garden, contains 3 acres. And he has there private pasture containing 1½ acres. And he has there a windmill.

Free tenants
Alicia widow of Simon the clerk holds one messuage and half an acre of land measured as above by charter rendering to the above William one pound of pepper.
Thomas Faber holds one messuage and a quarter of a virgate of land by charter rendering from it per annum a quarter of a pound of pepper to the said Alicia.
Margery daughter of Nicholas de Morewyk holds one messuage and a quarter of a virgate of land by charter rendering from it per annum a quarter of a pound of pepper to the said Alicia.
Ivo Carter holds one messuage and a quarter of a virgate of land for his lifetime rendering from it per annum 10s. to the said Lord William de Brus.
John Faber holds one messuage with a curtilage containing a rod rendering from it per annum 6d. to the said Lord William.
The prior of Huntingdon holds there half a virgate of land measured as above in perpetual alms.
The Templars hold there ... acres of land in perpetual alms.

Villeins
Robert ad Portam holds one virgate of land in villeinage rendering from it per annum to the said Lord William 20s. for all the labour and services that his ancestors were accustomed to perform.
There are five other villeins there, namely Robert Spart, William son of Agnes, Gilbert son of Sarra, Henry de Rysle, Thomas son of Elena, each of

---

[4] Tr. from the 1783 text as reprinted in the Phillimore edn. (Chichester, 1975), 19: 2.

whom holds one virgate of land rendering from it for all labour the same as the aforementioned Robert and all give merchet and heriot.

In addition there are 9 other villeins there, namely Ralph son of Elena, Hugh son of Agnes, John Gode, Walter Cook, Walter le Lord, Alicia Fraunceys, Hugh Philip, John son of Agnes, each of whom holds half a virgate of land rendering from it 20s. per annum for all labour and services. And all these aforementioned villeins give merchet and heriot.

Cottars

Stephen son of Robert holds two cottages with crofts containing one acre, rendering from them per annum 5s. to the said Lord William.

And there are 5 other cottars, namely Symon Neel, Ivetta daughter of Matilda, Sarra Koc, Robert ad Portam, Gilbert son of Sarra, each of whom holds a cottage with a croft which consists of half an acre of land and each renders for himself 2s. 6d. per annum for all labour and services.

Warin de Dentone holds a cottage with a curtilage rendering from it 2s. per annum to the said Lord William.

Herberd Hebbe holds a cottage with a curtilage rendering from it 2s. per annum to the said Lord William.

William de Brus is patron of the church.

The rector of Caldecote church holds a messuage and one virgate of land in perpetual alms with which the church was anciently endowed.

The said rector has there one cottar, namely John Balle who holds a cottage and a croft containing half an acre, rendering from it 2s. per annum to the said rector.

A certain marsh belongs to the vill of Caldecote containing in length towards Whittlesey Mere two furlongs and in breadth one furlong and it lies between the marsh of Denton and the marsh of Stilton.[5]

Caldecote was chosen because it was in the hands of a single lord and because the hundred roll return is relatively brief, albeit demonstrably far fuller than that of Domesday. Both surveys begin with the demesne and then go on to record information about the tenantry. As on a number of other Huntingdonshire manors, free tenants had appeared since 1086, but villeins followed by small-holders constituted the basic peasant population at both dates. The absence of a church in the Domesday entry may indicate that, as yet, none existed, since they were recorded elsewhere in the county at the end of each entry, as they were in 1279. Making due allowance for changes over time as well as the considerable variety in the way in which estates were described across 1279 returns,

---

5 *RH* ii. 636b–7a.

essentially both sets of commissioners were required to assemble much the same categories of information in much the same order.

However, if the estate surveys constituted the core of the returns to both inquiries, thereafter the parallels between them have to be substantially qualified. Whereas the hundred rolls record information on a geographical basis, town by town, village by village, Domesday Book, with the exception of the associated text known as the *Inquisitio Comitatus Cantabrigiensis*, was ordered according to the holdings of tenants-in-chief. The 1279 commissioners were also ordered to investigate feudal obligations and franchises alongside particulars of estates and their tenants. In 1086, this was not an issue. With the exception of places connected with hunting and a few markets and fairs, any mention of liberties in Domesday Book was incidental, although it is possible that they featured more frequently in original verdicts which no longer exist.[6] Valuations were a striking component of the manorial entries in Domesday Book, and arguably central to its purpose. They were largely absent from the 1279–80 returns.[7] Moreover, while the minute details of the hundred roll returns contrast strikingly with the brevity of entries in Exchequer Domesday, there is no equivalent to the extensive lists of demesne livestock found in Little Domesday and Exon Domesday. It is evident that both inquiries expanded to accommodate concerns of the day, but they were not the same concerns. In 1086, questions regarding title to land were a major preoccupation; by 1279 the focus had shifted to the right to hold franchises, the erosion of tenurial obligations, and loss of feudal incidents.

The matter for debate here is whether the common ground between the two inquiries is sufficient to indicate a conscious attempt on the part of Edward I himself to create a second Domesday Book. There is no direct evidence to support such a proposition. Indirect evidence is however suggestive. The reason set out in the commission itself must carry some weight, namely that, because of all sorts of encroachments on the crown and others, 'in future that which is ours and ought to be ours and that which is and ought to be theirs [the king's subjects] may be made clear'. The author of the Dialogue of the Exchequer thought that Domesday Book was intended to fulfil a similar function, namely 'that every

---

[6] H. C. Darby, *Domesday England* (Cambridge, 1977), 195–207; 318–19.

[7] See below, Ch. 3.

man may be content with his own rights, and not encroach unpunished on those of others'.[8] The command in the commission that findings be 'written in books to be delivered to us' is unusual. Returns to previous inquiries had always been recorded on rolls, as indeed they were in this one, despite the king's express instructions. The intention could, however, indicate that the king had Domesday Book in mind. Alternatively, the sheer impracticability of the 'Ragman rolls', with their dangling seals, may have suggested that books would be more convenient for everyday use. With all its ambiguity, this is the only reference in the official record which might reveal a specific link with Domesday Book. It is therefore necessary to seek evidence elsewhere in order to reach a conclusion.

There is no doubt that Domesday Book was both known and used in the later thirteenth century. Moreover Edward I's weakness for grandiose allusions to the past makes a deliberate attempt to replicate it credible. He and his court were much preoccupied with the Arthurian legend, an equally potent symbol of past glory. In 1278, accompanied by Queen Eleanor, he visited Glastonbury where he ordered the opening of what was reputed to be Arthur's tomb. At Michaelmas in the following year, he participated in the glittering 'round table' held at Kenilworth by his friend Roger Mortimer and subsequently held his own 'round table' at Nefyn in 1284.[9] In an even grander conceit, Roman might was evoked by the banded masonry and polygonal towers of Caernarfon Castle, modelled on the Theodosian walls of Constantinople, complete with imperial eagles on the turrets of its main tower.[10] To a monarch who identified with Arthur and Roman emperors, the idea of following in the footsteps of the Conqueror would not be out of place, especially as Edward was himself riding on the crest of a wave of conquest. Only the previous year, he had apparently brought Llywelyn ap Gruffudd to heel following the first Welsh War of 1276–7 and had also received the homage of Alexander III

---

[8] *The Course of the Exchequer, by Richard, Son of Nigel*, ed. C. Johnson (London, 1950), 63. My tr.

[9] R. S. Loomis, 'Edward I, Arthurian Enthusiast', *Speculum*, 28 (1953), 115–17. Such 'round tables' were not unprecedented. Ibid. 117. R. R. Davies, *The First English Empire: Power and Identities in the British Isles 1093–1343* (Oxford, 2000), 31–2.

[10] I. Rowlands, 'The Edwardian Conquest and its Military Consolidation', in T. Herbert and G. E. Jones (eds.), *Edward I and Wales* (Cardiff, 1988), 52–5; Davies, *First English Empire*, 32.

of Scotland before a great throng at Westminster. That neither submission was to prove enduring could not affect the aura of outstanding achievement surrounding him at this point in his reign.

At a more mundane level, the importance of archival evidence was also well understood both by Edward and his subjects. The king's own awareness is best seen in the famous inquiries of 1291, when he asked monastic houses to search their chronicles and other records for information to justify his claims to the Scottish throne.[11] It was not a new phenomenon, however. In 1280, he had ordered a trawl among past treasury and memoranda rolls in support of his legal dispute with Llywelyn, while in 1282, the seneschal of Ponthieu was commanded to search his own records and, if necessary, make application to see those of the king of France in order to establish liability for military service in respect of the county.[12]

By Edward's reign, searches in government archives to clarify lesser matters had become routine, so much so that in 1279 deputy chamberlains were allowed to charge for this service and for the issue of transcripts.[13] The frequency with which private landlords made copies of Domesday entries relating to their own estates and the sizeable energies devoted to drawing up abridgements of its whole contents, testify to its pre-eminence among royal records and its role as a living authority. The illuminated exchequer *Abbrevatio*, probably made in the mid-thirteenth century, has been described as 'a document fit for a king' and may even have been presented to Henry III.[14] From the 1270s Domesday Book became the principal source of proof in claims to hold land in ancient demesne, but annotations to the exchequer *Abbrevatio* show that it was also consulted on broader matters of tenure and obligations.[15] Inevitably the passage of time limited the usefulness of a

[11] E. L. G. Stones, 'The Appeal to History in Anglo-Scottish Relations between 1291 and 1401', *Archives*, 9 (1969), 11–16; *Edward I and the Throne of Scotland, 1290–1296*, ed. E. L. G. Stones and G. G. Simpson, 2 vols. (Oxford, 1978), i. 7, 138–43.

[12] *The Welsh Assize Roll, 1277–84*, ed. J. Conway Davies (Cardiff, 1940), 27–9, 62–3, 68; *CAC Wales*, 59–60, no. XIII; 124; *Rôles Gascons*, ed. F.-Michel and C. Bémont (Paris, 1885–1906), iii. 565–6, no. 5046; H. Johnstone, 'The County of Ponthieu 1279–1307', *EHR* 29 (1914), 444.

[13] N. J. Williams, 'The Work of Peter le Neve at Chapter House, Westminster', *Journal of the Society of Archivists*, 1 (1955–9), 127 n. 16.

[14] E. M. Hallam, *Domesday Book through Nine Centuries* (London, 1986), 42.

[15] Ibid. 42–4, 50–1, 77, 95–7.

survey compiled in the late eleventh century for this type of question. It is therefore quite possible that either the king or his officials saw the need for a more up-to-date record and one which would include information about the vexed issue of franchises.

There is nothing in the immediate political context of 1279 to throw light on how the inquiry was conceived, although there is plenty to suggest that its findings would have been useful. The *Quo waranto* proceedings provided for in the Statute of Gloucester had begun in the Hertfordshire eyre by the end of 1278. The onus was on those claiming liberties to produce proof that they held them legitimately. Twenty-eight lords, including a galaxy of prominent religious led by the abbots of St Albans and Westminster, the bishop of London together with the chapter of St Paul's, and the military orders, each proffered their evidence.[16] An official record which would have enabled officials to ensure that all claimants were cooperating would have been useful. Other needs may also have been drawn to the attention of the government. At about the same date, John Wyger, the escheator of Cornwall, wrote to Robert Burnell suggesting that a survey of lands held in chief or from others would enable him to deal with the many usurpations in the county. At the same time he protested about the state of the coinage.[17] The latter problem was indeed pressing and was addressed in January 1279, when a decision was taken to embark on an innovative recoinage in which round halfpennies and farthings and the groat were introduced for the first time.[18] This was only one of the financial worries facing Edward I in the late 1270s. Perennially in debt, he still needed to repay money borrowed from merchants of Lucca to finance the first Welsh

---

[16] There are no records of *Quo waranto* hearings in the Westmorland and Cumberland eyres conducted simultaneously. D. Crook, *Records of the General Eyre* (London, 1982), 146–7, 158; *Placita de Quo Warranto* (Rec. Comm.; London, 1818), 275–86. An undated letter from Burnell to John de Reigate suggests that proceedings had also begun in Kent by the beginning of 1279. PRO, SC1/32/17. See *List of Ancient Correspondence of the Chancery and Exchequer* (PRO Lists and Indexes, 15; revised edn., repr. London 1968), 486, for the date. Piece numbers cited in this list are those for the dorse of letters.

[17] M. Prestwich, *Edward I*, 2nd edn. (New Haven and London, 1997), 234, 245; PRO, SC1/24/199. The letter is undated, but refers to the fifteenth of 1275 and must antedate the recoinage of Jan. 1279. It is dated 1277–8 in Lists and Indexes, 15, 376.

[18] Seminar paper given by Martin Allen at the Department of Coins and Medals, Fitzwilliam Museum, Cambridge, 31 Jan. 2003.

War.[19] It would not be out of place therefore to ask whether, as in 1086, the inquiry might have been planned, in part at least, as an aid to the raising of taxes.

The presence of valuations in some returns is suggestive, but they are not sufficiently common to indicate that they were central to the inquiry as a whole.[20] Moreover, the only mention of taxation at that time is an unsubstantiated claim in the Hagnaby Chronicle that the king had bid unsuccessfully for a grant of 4d. from every bovate in the whole of England at a meeting in London in 1280.[21] The strongest case for a fiscal purpose rests on the particular attention paid to scutage obligations in some of the returns, taken in conjunction with a clear change of crown policy just before the inquiry was commissioned. In February 1279, in a break with previous feudal custom, scutage payments were levied on tenants-in-chief for all knights' fees, in addition to military service or fines for non-performance calculated on the reduced *servitium debitum* established earlier in the thirteenth century.[22] Up-to-date information about knights' fees and scutage obligations would have been helpful in this and it is possible that the inclusion of scutage in the commission reflects this.

Other chronicles have little helpful to add. Indeed, very few mention the inquiry at all. The Dunstable annalist, who was so dismissive of the 1274–5 inquiry, completely ignored its successor.[23] The fullest account is given in the *Chronicon Petroburgense*. The author was probably William of Woodford, sacrist and later abbot of Peterborough. Deeply involved in the abbey's legal affairs, his chronicle is dominated by accounts of law suits, incorporating extensive quotations from relevant documents. When it came to describing the 1279–80 inquiry, he seems to have drawn on a copy of the commission, adding only 'and no-one was spared' at the end of his extract.[24] This echoes the passage in the commission imme-

---

[19] M. Mate, 'Monetary Policies in England, 1272–1307', *British Numismatic Journal*, 41 (1973), 43.   [20] See below, Ch. 3.

[21] BL, Cott, Vesp. B xi, fo. 27ᵛ; Prestwich, *Edward I*, 236.

[22] See below, Ch. 5. H. M. Chew, 'Scutage under Edward I', *EHR* 37 (1922), 327–8; M. Jurkowski, C. L. Smith, and D. Crook, *Lay Taxes in England and Wales 1188–1688* (PRO Handbook, 31; London, 1998), pp. xix–xxi.

[23] *Annales Monastici*, ed. H. R. Luard (London, 1864–9), iii. 263. See above, p. 24.

[24] *Chronicon Petroburgense*, ed. T. Stapleton (London, 1849), 30; *The White Book of Peterborough*, ed. S. Raban (Northants. Rec. Soc.; Northampton, 2001), pp. xvi–xviii.

diately following his quotation and may be no more than common form, but it is perhaps worth noting that it was also the phrasing chosen by the annotator to a passage about Domesday Book in Matthew Paris's *Historia Anglorum*. In recounting the tradition about how it acquired its name, the scribe noted 'it is called Domesday; and it is called this because no-one was spared, just as on the Great Day of Judgement'.[25]

Bartholomew Cotton shared Woodford's predilection for copying archival material. He too mentions the inquiry, albeit briefly and in such a way as to suggest that he may have had a text of the commission to hand: 'In the same year [1279] King Edward ordered an inquiry into the size (*de quantitate*) of all the tenements in the kingdom of England, of arable, meadow, woodland, pastures, homages'.[26] The absence of comment in other late thirteenth-century chronicles is frustrating. Most concentrated on matters of local and domestic interest. Very few wider events caught their authors' attention. The commonest topics were the death or election of prelates, several of which occurred in 1279. A good many also recorded the king's visit to France to perform homage for Ponthieu, which Queen Eleanor of Castile had recently inherited, the prosecution and hanging of the Jews for coin clipping, and the subsequent recoinage. Surprisingly, given that it affected them directly, few mentioned the Statute of Mortmain enacted on 14 November 1279.[27] This being the case, perhaps the omission of one more government inquiry should not be regarded as significant, whether or not it was intended to be a new Domesday Book.

Given the tenuous nature of the evidence, the question of Edward's intentions must remain open, but if he had hoped to

---

[25] *Historia Anglorum*, ed. F. Madden, 3 vols. (Rolls Series; London, 1866–9), i. 27 n. 1, where it appears under 1083.

[26] *Historia Anglicana*, ed. H. R. Luard (Rolls Series; London, 1859), 158.

[27] *The Chronicle of Bury St Edmunds, 1212–1301*, ed. A. Gransden (London, 1964), 67–73; *Annales Monastici*, ii. 391–2 (Waverley Annals); iv. 280–4 (Thomas Wykes); *The Chronicle of Pierre de Langtoft*, ed. T. Wright, 2 vols. (Rolls Series; London, 1866–8), ii. 174–7; *Flores Historiarum*, ed. H. R. Luard (London, 1890), iii. 52–3 (Westminster Flores); *Chronica Johannis de Oxenedes*, ed. H. Ellis (Rolls Series; London, 1859), 252–5 (St Benet Holme); *Chronicon ex Chronicis*, ed. B. Thorpe (London, 1849), ii. 220–3 (Peterborough Abbey version of the Bury chronicle); *Chronicon de Lanercost*, ed J. Stevenson (Edinburgh, 1839), 102–3; *Annales F. Nicholai Triveti*, ed. T. Hog (London, 1845), 293, 299–301 where the Statute of Mortmain is recorded under 1275.

emulate Domesday Book, his plan was overtaken by events. The process of translating an already wide-ranging commission into articles which the sheriffs and commissioners could put to jurors caused the project to swell to unmanageable proportions. No end product analogous to Domesday Book was ever achieved. Indeed, even if the terms of the commission had been more narrowly interpreted, it is doubtful whether its successful execution would have been feasible.

No enrolled copy of the articles survives, but they are rehearsed in some detail in some of the Cambridgeshire returns, notably those for Cambridge itself and for the vills of Kingston and Toft in Longstow hundred.[28] There were thirty-five main articles, comparable in number to the thirty-nine articles of the 1274–5 inquiry.[29] Like the earlier inquiry, there were also a handful of other questions which crop up in a few places only. Such were those asking about the identity of patrons of churches in the borough of Cambridge or the precise dimensions of purprestures at Waterbeach.[30] Only articles 4 to 6 were closely modelled on the commission itself. Those parts of its text which relate to tenures were copied into the articles more or less word for word, but various details were spelt out more fully. The commission had listed different types of peasant, while those of higher rank were merely described as holders of liberties 'rich or poor'. These were now specified as archbishops, bishops, abbots, priors, earls, barons, knights, freemen, and burgesses. The order to investigate landholdings was now extended to cover fee farms and land held for life or fixed terms as well as hereditary tenures. Manorial appurtenances were similarly expanded to include fisheries, mills, gardens, heathland, marshes, turbaries, and alder groves.

The precise form of the Cambridgeshire articles was coloured by local conditions. The marshland and turbaries seem suspiciously redolent of the Fens and are unlikely to have featured in questions put to the country at large. This is borne out by the thirty-two articles set out in the somewhat problematic nineteenth-century copy of the return for the borough and liberty of Shrewsbury. Here the

---

[28] For the Latin text and translation of the articles, see Appendix 3A.
[29] See above, p. 22.
[30] Appendix 3A, arts. 36 and 39.

question about boundaries between Shropshire and Wales was
clearly unique to the Marches, while, as one would expect from the
terrain, encroachment within the royal forest features in place of
alder groves and turbaries.[31] Even allowing for some corruption in
transmission, however, these articles differ so much in expression
and, to some extent, content from those found in the
Cambridgeshire returns that one cannot account for it by local
circumstances alone. Whereas the first article in Cambridgeshire
asked about demesne manors in the king's hand, in Shrewsbury it
was fees and feodalia.[32] Striking among articles not found in
Cambridgeshire were those asking about the conduct of the sheriff
and escheator; issues which do not seem peculiar to Shropshire.[32]
The last of the thirty-two articles also asked about those 'having
twenty pounds worth of land', an interesting indication that in
Shrewsbury the two inquiries, commissioned on 12 March 1279,
were dealt with at the same time.[34] While some of the remaining
articles, such as that dealing with scutage, are substantially the
same or close to the Cambridgeshire articles, others are materially
different. In particular, there is no equivalent in Cambridgeshire for
article twenty-nine which asks about valuations.[35]

London also had a different set of articles, better suited to the
distinctive conditions found there. These are listed in an abbreviated form in a few returns permitting their partial reconstruction.[36]
For the most part they are unremarkable, although there is no trace
of any questions about tenants, their holdings, and obligations. It
is apparent that, as in Shrewsbury, the inquiry into knighthood was
conducted simultaneously since the first three articles usually ask
about those who held land worth £20, those who were distrained
to bear arms, and the whereabouts of their lands. This was not

---

[31] *Ad xxxi articulum ubi inquirendum est de divisionibus metis et bundis inter
comitatum Salop' et Walliam etc.* Shropshire Archives, 6001/28, 52; *Ad viij articulum ubi inquirendum est si aliquis appropriavit quoquo modo de foresta domini
regis sive in bosco vasto bruariis, quis sit ille et quantum occupavit.* Ibid. 49, and
also 50, art. 20. For the problematic nature of this text, see below, Chs. 4 and 6.

[32] Appendix 3A, art. 1; Shropshire Archives, 6001/28, 21.

[33] Shropshire Archives, 6001/28, 50–1, arts. 12, 23, 25–6.

[34] *Ad xxxij articulum ubi inquirendum est si aliquis habens xx^{ti} libratas terre etc.*
Ibid. 52.

[35] *Ad xxix articulum ubi inquirendum est de hiis qui tenet terras (?) et quantum
valent per quod servicium etc.* Ibid.

[36] For the Latin text and translation of the articles, see Appendix 3B.

invariable however. The articles listed for Queenhithe ward, for example, appear to begin with questions about land and escheats.[37]

What is one to make of these divergent texts? There was a precedent for separate articles for London in the earlier eyres, where only fifty-one of the seventy 'national' articles were used and a number of articles unique to London introduced.[38] The Shrewsbury articles are harder to explain. It is just possible that they represent a free rendering of the same set of articles found in Cambridgeshire, together with a few additional ones. More probably they imply that there was no standard set of articles circulated to all commissioners, which may perhaps explain why no articles for this inquiry are to be found on the patent roll.

Verdicts from other circuits, none of which mention the activities of sheriffs and escheators, as well as the unimpeachable authority of original returns, suggest that the Cambridgeshire articles should generally be taken as a better guide to the inquiry as a whole. Most had antecedents in previous inquiries or *capitula* of the eyre or were drawn directly from the commission itself. Faced with the king's instructions, it appears that either exchequer officials or commissioners turned to tried and tested tools. Twelve articles from the 1274–5 inquiry were recycled in this way, some verbatim, others in broadly the same terms.[39] There were also more distant echoes of the articles used in 1255 and the *vetera capitula* of the eyre, notably articles 18 and 23–5, which were designed to check on infringements of the king's feudal incidents, of marriage and escheat. In Cambridgeshire, as in the commission itself, the thrust of the inquiry was away from administrative abuses and towards land tenure, feudal incidents, and franchises. The adaptation of existing articles was a practical response to the huge and ill-defined task which the commissioners had been set. It preserved the spirit of the commission, but by introducing articles which had been created in other contexts, it inevitably introduced a measure of distortion.

The commission was framed in terms of providing a solution to

---

[37] SC5/London/Tower/1, m. 1.

[38] *The London Eyre of 1276*, ed. M. Weinbaum (London Rec. Soc., 12; London, 1976), p. xx and appendix A, pp. xxxiii–xxxv.

[39] Arts 1–3, 10, 12–14, 16–17, 19–22, and 33 are either identical or very similar to the articles of 1274–5, which were incorporated into the *nova capitula* of the general eyre. See Appendix 3A and above, p. 24.

the losses suffered by the king and 'other men' by means of a definitive record of who held what and where. This wider dimension
was lost, however, as the borrowed articles shifted the emphasis
away from his subjects towards detailed questions about alienations from the crown alone. That the effect is not more noticeable
is largely due to the bulk of information collected in response to
articles 4–7. Another consequence of using old articles was the
spotlight they threw on mortmain tenure, which had not been
mentioned at all in the commission. Article 17 asked about advowsons acquired by churchmen and appropriated to their own use to
the prejudice of the crown, while articles 19 and 33 focused on
lands and tenements which the religious had bought or been given,
whereby the king was deprived of his incidents of wardship and
marriage. Article 41, which only appears in a couple of
Cambridgeshire village returns, simply asked about lands held in
free alms. A good deal of information was collected under these
heads and annotations to the rolls suggest that these findings were
subsequently singled out for attention.[40] To that extent, the original aims of the inquiry were subverted.

Only article 7 in the Cambridgeshire returns was without parallel in either previous articles or the wording of the commission. The
question 'How many lands and tenements each free tenant, villein
or serf or cottar holds in market towns or all other vills and
hamlets and from which lords and for what services and for rendering what customs?' had profound consequences. The commission
had limited itself to asking for information about the holders of
land and the different types of tenant found there, not how many
lands or tenements these tenants themselves held or what their
obligations were. Even in 1086, the more limited goal of recording
lords and the number of their tenants without further elaboration
had run into difficulties, especially in East Anglia and the north-
ernmost counties. By 1279, an ever more intricate web of sub-
infeudation meant that the situation was too complex throughout
the country to be easily captured in writing. With the added burden
of information imposed by article 7, the hundredal returns were
weighed down by descriptions of peasant tenements and rents,
time-consuming to record and of questionable practical value. It
must have been this, more than anything else, which prevented the

---

[40] See below, Ch. 5.

inquiry from being successfully completed in book form as the commission had envisaged.

The most outstanding feature of the 1086 survey had been the way it covered almost the whole of England. We know that Edward I had intended his inquiry to be equally comprehensive because commissioners were appointed to every county. We do not know to what extent his orders were carried out. Even the returns which survive from London and eleven Midland and East Anglian counties are far from complete in their coverage. The nine hundreds of Bedfordshire are represented only by Stodden and Willey (including the half hundred of Bucklow). Moreover, verdicts survive for just five of the fourteen vills in Stodden hundred and one of those appears on the roll for Leightonstone hundred (Hunts.).[41] Huntingdonshire, which has rolls for each of its four hundreds and the borough of Godmanchester, and is therefore the best documented county, nonetheless lacks anything for Huntingdon itself.[42] What is one to make of this? Did fuller returns once exist? Was the inquiry carried out in its entirety, but the rolls subsequently lost? Did the whole enterprise prove too unwieldy and grind to a halt, or was it deliberately abandoned when the problems involved in implementing it became manifest?

There are good reasons to suppose that the inquiry extended further than the extant returns would suggest. The fate of the returns to the previous hundred roll inquiries and hearings of the baronial reform period amply demonstrate that surviving rolls are not a reliable guide to those which once existed. If it were not for the extract rolls, we would know nothing of the 1274–5 returns for a vast swathe of the country on which they were based: those for Bedfordshire, Berkshire, Cornwall, Huntingdonshire, Leicestershire, Northumberland, Somerset, Warwickshire, Worcestershire, and Yorkshire exist in extract form only. Nor would we know about the Northamptonshire and Worcestershire inquiries in 1255 if returns had not been transcribed into the *Book of Fees*. In exactly the same way, we would know nothing about most of the East Anglian inquiries nor that for Coventry in 1279–80 but for

---

[41] *RH* ii. 321a–33b, 622b–3a. See also Map 1. The four vills of Clapham, Milton Ernest, Riseley, and Melchbourne appear on the Stodden roll, while Swineshead is recorded with other parts of the earl of Hereford's fee in Leightonstone hundred.

[42] *RH* ii. 591a–687b. Several vills are also missing from the rolls for individual hundreds.

seigneurial copies of the original returns and the Leicestershire and Shropshire returns would have been lost but for the zeal of local antiquarians.[43] With such a haphazard record of preservation, it is anyone's guess as to how far any of the 1279 inquiries may originally have stretched.

Many fates could have befallen missing rolls in the seven hundred years after they were compiled. We know that some of those for Cambridgeshire, while remaining in official custody, subsequently became separated from the main body of the returns, probably because they were damaged. Stitch marks on the final membrane of the rolls for Mursley and Stodfold hundreds in Buckinghamshire suggest that other membranes once existed for that county too.[44] Storage conditions may have been poor, so that some returns simply decayed. The first membrane of a roll was particularly vulnerable and could render the whole hard to identify. It could also lead to the loss of material without this being otherwise obvious, especially where the membranes were later sewn end to end. This happened to the roll for Hurstingstone hundred in Huntingdonshire where the return for King's Ripton has only survived by chance in a sixteenth-century copy associated with Ramsey Abbey.[45]

It is also possible that rolls were thrown away as redundant, either because they belonged to an early stage in the drafting process or because they had been transcribed into a more convenient format. The fragmented tenures of some circuits may have presented such a challenge that the efforts of the commissioners were discarded as useless. It is also conceivable that, like the 'Ragman' rolls, the returns later accompanied justices on eyre, occasioning both damage and loss. It is equally probable that some of the commissioners failed to return their rolls. This would have been all the more likely if the inquiry was discontinued before its business had been completed. We know that a William Gerberge, who may have been the commissioner for Hampshire and Wiltshire, was guilty of just such dereliction of duty in another capacity towards the end of his career. Appointed as keeper of the writs and rolls for Cressingham's circuit in the general eyre of

---

[43] See above, pp. 9–10 and below, Ch. 6.
[44] See below, Ch. 6. PRO, SC5/Bucks/Tower/1, m. 3; SC5/Bucks/Tower/2, m. 4.
[45] PRO, SC12/8/56; *RH* ii. 598a–b.

1292–4, he still had the rolls in his possession at his manor of Chedgrave in Norfolk in 1305 on the grounds that the eyre remained unfinished. Even though some of them were surrendered to the treasury in that year, his successor to the property reported that others had been abandoned there and Gerberge was not prepared to take any further responsibility for them.[46] Such a casual attitude could also explain the escapees from the Huntingdonshire and Norfolk inquiries now found in the Bodleian and University of London libraries.[47] Against this, is the rarity of such rolls. Given that each of the commissioners probably had his own copy, one might have expected a higher rate of survival both inside and outside the public records if they had ever been compiled.[48]

Had there been chronicle accounts from those parts of the country for which there are no returns, this might have been regarded as prima-facie evidence that the commissioners had been at work there and their findings lost. As it is, only the chronicle of Bartholomew Cotton, monk of Norwich, even remotely falls into this category, reinforcing the probability that the remains for Gallow hundred, Holkham, Hevingham, and possibly Sedgeford, were once part of a more comprehensive survey for Norfolk. Even Cotton's testimony cannot be relied upon however. It is likely that writing *c.*1292, he drew on an earlier account, which was itself derivative and therefore not necessarily a good guide to Norfolk affairs.[49]

As we have seen, the commission was issued on the same day and to the same commissioners as the order to investigate how well sheriffs had executed earlier instructions about distraint of knighthood and to fine those who had not complied, unless they had already paid for respite.[50] In London and Shrewsbury the investigation into those with land worth twenty pounds became part of the wider inquiry.[51] There is also some evidence from the Oxfordshire rolls that the two inquiries were conducted in parallel.

---

[46] Crook, *Records*, 27. [47] See above, pp. 10–11.
[48] For multiple copies of the returns, see below, Ch. 4.
[49] A. Gransden, *Historical Writing in England*, 2 vols. (London, 1974–82), i. 444.
[50] *Cal. Pat. 1272–81*, 342–3.
[51] See Appendix 3B; PRO, SC5/London/Tower/1–26, particularly mm. 8(6), 10(8); Shropshire Archives, 6001/28, 52.

There are references at the end of the Bullingdon roll to inquisitions 'outside the articles' (*extra capitula*) into the royal forest and distraint of knighthood ordered by Sampson Foliot, commissioner for both inquiries. This implies that the two inquiries were merged. On the other hand, another entry about distraint, on the dorse of the Pyrton roll, refers to 'the first inquisition', while a third, on the dorse of the Bampton roll, notes distraints but is otherwise uninformative.[52] Taken together, these references suggest that in Oxfordshire the two inquiries were closely associated, but not necessarily fully integrated.

Establishing a close link between the two inquiries is important in interpreting ambiguous references to the activities of the commissioners or where there is evidence that distraint proceedings took place and which might therefore prove that the larger inquiry had been carried out as well. In November 1279, William de Hevere was replaced by Stephen de Baketon 'to make inquiry in Kent' alongside Hamo de Gatton and Robert le Blund.[53] The names make it clear that the order was connected with the March inquiries, but there is nothing to show whether one or both was intended. In Yorkshire, where William of Beverley replaced Ralph le Botiler as a commissioner alongside Geoffrey Aguillon and John de Steingrave in the same month, it was to make inquiries 'as to distraint of persons having land to the value of £20 yearly who ought to take up knight service and have not done so, and as to other matters contained in the letters directed to the latter'. We cannot be sure that these 'other matters' referred to the hundred roll inquiry, but the chancery clerk might well have preferred to make a brief reference rather than rehearse the lengthy details of the commission. An undated letter from Aguillon and Steingrave to the king refers to inquiries into 'fees, feodalities and other things contained in your writ and into knights' fees and the making of knights as in your letters patent'. This letter not only associates the two inquiries, but it also asks the king to abandon them because Ralph le Botiler had not turned up. The fact that he was replaced in November argues that in Yorkshire, as in Kent, the crown still intended that the inquiries should be carried out some eight months

---

[52] *RH* ii. 689a, 725b; PRO, SC5/Oxon/Tower/1, m. 2[d]; SC5/Oxon/Tower/3, m. 21[r]; SC5/Oxon/Tower/12, m. 8[d].

[53] *Cal. Pat. 1272–81*, 406.

after they had been launched.[54] If the two inquiries were indeed conducted simultaneously, then the chances are greater that the hundred roll inquiry reached out beyond the Midlands to northern and southern England and that it was still being actively pursued there eight months after the initial commission.

It has to be admitted that the evidence for countrywide hearings remains largely indirect and threadbare, resting on hints such as these and the demonstrable loss of original returns from every other hundred roll inquiry. However, the survival of Shropshire returns, although in a late copy, greatly enhances the possibility that the inquiry extended beyond its previously known limits.[55] One is on still firmer ground in suggesting that undocumented hearings were likely to have been held in the East Midlands and East Anglia. Mention of liberties in vills for which there are no manorial surveys in Bunsty and Lamua hundreds (Bucks.) reinforce the impression given by the stitch marks on the manuscript rolls that returns for this county were at one time more extensive.[56] Undated verdicts from an inquiry into those with land worth more than twenty pounds per annum from South Greenhoe hundred in Norfolk and the Suffolk hundreds of Hoxne, Blything, Claydon, Samford, and Wangford offer a hint, if not incontrovertible proof, that some action was taken on the March inquiries in hundreds for which there are no hundred rolls.[57] The identification of Norfolk returns in recent years shows how quickly the picture can be transformed by chance discovery. The heading to one text of the Holkham return implies that it was taken from an otherwise unknown roll for North Greenhoe hundred, further extracts from which could yet surface.[58] The Gallow hundred roll was thought to be a rental until it was identified by Diana Greenway.[59] It is possible that what have been assumed to be rentals or surveys elsewhere may equally be transcripts of hundred roll returns. Where lords copied returns for their own estates only, such misclassification would be easy. Northamptonshire, for which there are no known

---

[54] *Cal. Pat. 1272–81,* 351; PRO, SC1/14/153.

[55] Shropshire Archives, 6001/28, 21–62.

[56] For separate returns for liberties, see below, Ch. 3.

[57] PRO, E198/3/12–14. I am grateful to Paul Brand for these references.

[58] *Lordship and Landscape in Norfolk,* ed. W. Hassall and J. Beauroy (Oxford, 1993), 524. See also below, Ch. 6.

[59] ULL, A. Mace, '*Handlist of Documents in the Fuller Collection*', i. (1977), 48.

rolls, makes a particularly tempting target for investigation, surrounded as it is in the most striking manner by extant returns.[60] If the single membrane for Hambleton and Normanton in Martinsley hundred in Rutland, on the same circuit, belongs to the inquiry, then the likelihood that some Northamptonshire rolls once existed is the greater. Unfortunately this cannot be proved. Although jurors are named, the membrane is undated. Moreover, the entry for the demesne is placed atypically after the Normanton material at the end of the return.[61] This book will have achieved an important part of its purpose if it leads to the recognition of even one more hitherto unrecognized roll.

As with Edward's intentions *vis-à-vis* Domesday Book, the question as to whether the inquiry ever began in some parts of the country or whether it was aborted at a comparatively early stage, must remain open. One might argue that work could well have started in counties closer to the heart of government and failed to reach the extremities of the realm. Such was frequently the pattern of royal administration throughout the Middle Ages and well into the seventeenth century. However, with commissioners appointed for twenty-six circuits, far more than ever before, and with more distant counties each forming a circuit on their own, there was no inherent reason for this to happen.[62] Most of the incomplete inquiries of the baronial period were due to the small number of circuits, leaving justices overwhelmed by their task. In 1279 work should have started in parallel throughout the realm. It is more likely therefore that the project foundered in the face of difficulties encountered by the commissioners as soon as they attempted to carry out their brief. It is probably no accident that the counties for which the fullest and most finished rolls exist were also those with some of the most straightforward tenurial structures. Huntingdonshire in particular, dominated as it was by large monastic houses, had a substantial number of vills comprising single estates whose lords were likely to have their own surveys to hand.

One should not forget either that justices in eyre were also at work in a number of counties in the summer and autumn of 1279. Indeed, in late July, the king of Scotland sent envoys to complain about their activities in Cumberland, Westmorland, and

---

[60] See Map 1.   [61] PRO, SC5/8/5/7.   [62] See below, p. 59.

Yorkshire.[63] Any attempt to conduct two major government undertakings at the same time would have placed a very heavy burden on local officials. It is also evident from the patent rolls that within a short time commissioners were being assigned to other tasks. As early as the end of March 1279, Adam de Chetewynd, one of the Shropshire commissioners, was asked to hold an inquest concerning a Derbyshire manor.[64] Several commissioners were appointed to commissions of *oyer and terminer*, again not always, in the county for which they had been commissioned. Alexander Threekingham was so engaged in Lincolnshire by August 1279, while Thomas Folejambe was appointed to three commissions of *oyer and terminer* before the end of the year. Only one of these, a case also involving Ralph Arnhall, his fellow commissioner, was in Nottinghamshire.[65] Thomas de St Vigor similarly found himself assigned to three commissions of *oyer and terminer* concerning the West Country in the same period.[66] Unless the hundred roll hearings were expected to be over in a few weeks, such commitments would have been a distraction.

For others, their additional duties were more than a mere distraction; they involved substantial work. By November 1279, Leon son of Leon, one of the Cheshire commissioners, was engaged alongside Bogo de Knovill in Powys, extending all the waste belonging to Montgomery castle, together with lands illicitly rented out by former constables. They were then charged with the task of making fresh arrangements or exchanges of land as expedient.[67] Earlier in the year, on 15 May, Oliver Ingham and John de la More, commissioners for Norfolk and Suffolk, had been appointed to audit the murage accounts of Great Yarmouth, where the bailiffs and burgesses stood accused of embezzlement, as a result of which the building of the walls had not even begun. On the following day, they were further appointed to inquire into the misconduct of the king's bailiffs and others and 'certain conspiracies against justice in those parts'.[68] The subject of their investigations was reminiscent of the 1274–5 inquiry and may even indicate a broadening of their

---

[63] Crook, *Records*, 147–8 (Westmorland, Northumberland, Yorkshire), 159 (Sussex, Surrey); PRO, SC1/20/157.

[64] *Cal. Pat. 1272–81*, 344.

[65] Ibid. 326, 346–9, 406. The other two cases involving Folejambe were in Staffordshire and Lancashire.

[66] Ibid. 346, 349, 406.   [67] Ibid. 350.   [68] Ibid. 315, 344.

remit. Even if this were not the case, such a major additional
responsibility would have been more than enough to divert their
attention from collecting surveys in a county already characterized
by its complicated lordship. Thomas of Wymondham would have
been prevented from carrying out his commission by a different,
but unequivocal commitment. He was physically removed from
Lancashire by October 1279, when he received a safe conduct in
order to carry jewels from Edward to the king of Norway.[69] For
whatever reason, it must have been difficult to assemble, and keep
together, teams of commissioners for any length of time.

Had the hundred roll commission of March 1279 been implemented as planned, not only would it have resulted in a second
Domesday, but the first Domesday would have been wholly
eclipsed. It is hard to overestimate the importance that a countrywide survey containing such a wealth of detail would have had
both for contemporaries and for future historians. However, like
many a latter-day bespoke computer system, the specifications
swelled to cover all eventualities, until it was too vast and complex
to be brought to a successful conclusion. The very fact that so
many of the rolls preserved by central government were only
partially edited points strongly in the same direction. Almost
certainly, the crown failed to understand the magnitude of the task
it had set, even without its subsequent embellishment. Efforts to
bring the inquiry to fruition may nevertheless have stretched
further than we currently appreciate. The unsystematic way in
which the commissions and articles of earlier inquiries were
enrolled and the arbitrary way in which many of their returns have
survived, as well as the identification in recent years of fragments
of the 1279–80 inquiry outside the national archives, make it possible, even probable, that commissioners began work in some other
counties and achieved more than we realize in those for which rolls
exist. If it is also plausible, though equally beyond proof, that
Edward I had Domesday Book in mind when he commissioned the
inquiry, there can be no doubt the scope of the inquiry would have
justified such an association.

---

[69] *Cal. Pat.* 1272–81, 328.

3

Collecting the Information

On 12 March 1279, in recognition of the immense task in prospect, seventy-seven commissioners were appointed to carry out the inquiry on twenty-six circuits, more than had ever been assigned to a previous inquiry. Most of the circuits comprised two counties, but the more distant shires of the North, West Midlands, and West Country, as well as Kent and Lincolnshire, formed circuits on their own.[1] Everywhere except Cheshire, where there were only two commissioners, each circuit was allocated three commissioners, one of whom was a clerk, presumably to service the proceedings. The anomalous position of Cheshire may owe something to the special nature of its administration. The two commissioners were Guncelin de Badlesmere, justice of Chester and Leon son of Leon, its chamberlain.[2] Such heavyweights may have been expected to draw on their own clerical establishment.

The names of the commissioners are derived from the list of those appointed on the same day for the inquiry into distraint of knighthood. The patent roll entry following the enrolment of the commission for the hundred roll inquiry is explicit that they were the same men: 'all the aforementioned assigned in the same way to make like inquisitions in each and every one of the aforesaid counties'.[3] The commission itself is addressed to Geoffrey Aguillon, John de Steingrave, and Godfrey de Hauterive and appoints them

---

[1] See Table 3.

[2] Leon had been appointed chamberlain in 1278 with instructions that he apply all the revenues he received to the king's works at the abbey of Vale Royal. He already had a track record in financial administration. In 1275 he had been sent round the kingdom in the company of Luke, merchant of Lucca, on business associated with the new wool custom. He later received money from Luke and his fellow merchants as expenses for work on the king's service. In 1277, he was engaged in preparations for Otto de Grandison's expedition directed at Anglesey. *Cal. Pat. 1272–81*, 97, 185, 197, 252.

[3] PRO, C66/98, m. 21[d]; *Cal. Pat. 1272–81*, 343.

to conduct their investigations in Warwickshire and Leicestershire. The list of commissioners, however, shows that Geoffrey and John were appointed to Yorkshire, while Godfrey had no ascertainable connection with the inquiry at any stage. This raises the unwelcome possibility that the commissioners for the distraint proceedings cannot be relied upon to identify those charged with the larger inquiry. Such fears appear to be groundless however. The Warwickshire and Leicestershire returns make it clear that the list is correct in naming Henry of Nottingham, Henry de Sheldon, and John of Arundel as the appointees for those counties, rather than the trio named in the commission itself.[4] Where returns for other counties name the commissioners, they too prove the list to be accurate. Sampson Foliot and Fulk de Rycote appear in the Oxfordshire returns, William Muschet, Geoffrey de Sandiacre, and Nicholas of Bassingbourn in those for Cambridgeshire and Huntingdonshire, and Roger de Bacheworth in those for Cripplegate ward in London.[5] The most plausible explanation for the discrepancy between the commission and the list is that the commission was enrolled from a draft, and that subsequently details of personnel and the counties to which they were assigned were altered without the scribe feeling obliged to update his exemplar. Other appointments made on 12 March reinforce the idea that initial arrangements were somewhat fluid. Nicholas of Cogenhoe, commissioner for Northamptonshire and Rutland, was assigned to a gaol delivery before apparently being replaced in that duty by John de Lovetot, while Thomas de St Vigor, commissioner for Somerset and Dorset, was also appointed to a commission of *oyer and terminer* for a Wiltshire case.[6]

Although known to modern historians as commissioners, contemporaries commonly referred to these appointees as justices or 'inquisitors of the lord king'. Perhaps surprisingly, only three of them had served in the earlier inquiry of 1274–5 and then for

---

[4] *The Warwickshire Hundred Rolls of 1279–80*, ed. T. John (Oxford, 1992), 25, 58; J. Nichols, *The History and Antiquities of the County of Leicester* (Wakefield, 1971), i/1, pp. cx, cxix.

[5] *RH* ii. 402a, 446b, 483b, 542b, 554b, 607b, 665b, 782a, 822a; PRO, SC5/London/Tower/14, m. 22 (20).

[6] I am grateful to Paul Brand for his advice on this point. *Cal. Pat. 1272–81*, 341.

TABLE 3. *Circuits for the 1279–80 hundred roll inquiry*

Commissioners	Counties
Laurence de Plumberegh, William de St Clair, German of Colchester	Essex, Herts.
Alan de Orreton, Robert de Molecastre, Stephen de Houeden	Cumberland
Henry de Stavele, John de Rossegill, Master Adam de Crokedayk	Westmorland
John de Aulton, William de Middelton, Roger of Doncaster	Northumberland
Geoffrey Aguillon, John de Steingrave, Ralph le Botiler[a]	Yorks.
Alexander Threekingham, Hugh de Boby, William of Luton	Lincs.
Robert Banastre, Adam de Hoghton, Thomas of Wymondham	Lancs.
Guncelin de Badelesmere, Leon son of Leon	Ches.
Thomas Folejambe, Ralph Arnhall, Roger de Drayton	Notts., Derby.
Henry of Nottingham, Henry de Sheldon, John of Arundel	Warwicks., Leics.
William Bagod, Adam de Chetewynd, Master Adam de Botindon	Salop., Staffs.
William de Colevill, Giles de Berkele, William de Plumpton	Glos.
Roger de Burghull, Roger de Pywelesdon, Thomas de Thorp	Heref.
Paulinus of Cardiff, William le Blund, William le Rus	Worcs.
Sampson Foliot, Fulk de Rycote, Henry de Gildeford	Oxon., Berks.
Thomas de St Vigor, Richard de Coleshull, William of Beverley	Som., Dorset
Henry de Rale, Malger de Sancto Albino, William Fauiler, clerk	Devon
John de Bello Prato, Ralph of Arundel, Richard Brendesworth	Cornwall

TABLE 3. *Continued*

Commissioners	Counties
John de Bottele, William Gerberge, Roger de Lecford	Hants., Wilts.
John de Abbernun, Ralph de Berners, Hugh Oyldeboef	Surrey, Sussex
Oliver de Ingham, Richard Creeping, John de la More	Norfolk, Suffolk
William Muschet, Geoffrey de Sandiacre,[b] Nicholas of Bassingbourn	Cambs., Hunts.
Peter Loreng, Edmund de Wedon, Flurus, parson of Blettesho	Bucks., Beds.
Nicholas of Cogenhoe, Ralph de Ardern, William de Boyvill	Northants,[c] Rutland
Hamo de Gatton, William de Hevere,[d] Robert le Blund	Kent
Roger de Bacheworth, Henry de Boneley, William de Birle	Middlesex, London

Sources: PRO, C66/98, m. 21d; *Cal. Pat.* 1272–81, 342–3.

[a] The patent roll commission is addressed to Aguillon, Steingrave, and Hauterive, but assigns them to Warwickshire and Leicestershire, whereas Aguillon and Steingrave, together with Ralph le Botiler are subsequently listed for Yorkshire. William of Beverley replaced Ralph le Botiler later in the year. *Cal. Pat.* 1272–81, 343, 351.
[b] John Avenel replaced Geoffrey de Sandiacre in the inquiry 'touching knight service due as well in the fees of the king as of others' in Oct. 1279. *Cal. Pat.* 1272–81, 329.
[c] Mis-calendared as Northumberland. Both the MS and geography make it clear that Northamptonshire is the correct reading.
[d] Stephen de Baketon replaced William de Hevere to make inquiry in Kent alongside Gatton and le Blund in Nov. 1279. *Cal. Pat.* 1272–81, 406.

different counties.[7] Few of them were in fact professional lawyers, but most were well versed in administrative duties. While not of the highest rank, they were drawn from the next tier down and were very similar in kind to those employed in the 1274–5 inquiry.[8]

---

[7] Sampson Foliot for Bucks., Cambs., Hunts. and Beds.; Richard Creeping for Notts., Derby. and probably Leics. and War.; Geoffrey Aguillon for Northumberland and probably Cumberland, Westmorland, and Lancs.
[8] H. M. Cam, *The Hundred and the Hundred Rolls* (London, 1930), 40.

Mostly knights, eleven had either served earlier, or were currently serving, as sheriffs and a twelfth, John de Bottele, was appointed sheriff of Hampshire, although he never acted in that capacity.[9] William de Boyvill followed his stint as sheriff of Northampton with a short spell as escheator north of the Trent.[10] Adam de Chetewynd was escheator for Chester before handing over to Guncelin de Badlesmere in September 1275 and Sampson Foliot is recorded as having seized the manor of Ramsbury (Wilts.) while escheator in 1271.[11] Stephen de Houeden and Geoffrey de Sandiacre were successively custodians of the castle and honour of Tickhill (Yorks.) and the manor of Gringley (Notts.).[12] Sandiacre also seems to have spent a year in the Channel Islands on the king's business between 1276 and 1277.[13] Thomas de St Vigor had also been abroad on the king's business. When he was appointed to the hundred roll inquiry he was newly returned from the papal court in Rome.[14] As one might expect, given the plethora of accusations brought forth by the 1274–5 inquiry and the nature of their previous experience, several commissioners featured among those accused of maladministration. Sandiacre, Creeping, Bagod, Boyvill, Hevere, Folejambe, and St Vigor were all subject to some form of complaint, chiefly concerning the usual sorts of extortion and bribery.[15]

Caroline Burt has very kindly shared with me the fruits of her research into crown servants in Shropshire, Warwickshire, and Kent.

[9] William Bagod (War. and Leics.), Giles de Berkele (Heref.), William de Boyvill (Northants.), Roger de Burghull (Heref.), Richard de Coleshull (Som. and Dors.), Richard Creeping (Cumberland), Sampson Foliot (Oxon. and Berks.), William de Hevere (Kent, Sussex), Fulk de Rycote (Oxon. and Berks.), William de St Clair (Essex and Herts.), Thomas de St Vigor (Oxon. and Berks.; Som. and Dors.). *List of Sheriffs for England and Wales* (PRO, Lists and Indexes, 9, repr. London, 1963), 26, 43, 54, 59, 67, 92, 107, 122, 135, 144; *RH* i. 13b; *Cal. Pat. 1272–81*, 7, 109; C. Moor, *Knights of Edward I*, 5 vols. (The Harleian Society, 70–4; London, 1929–32), i. 127, 223, 247; ii. 78, 228; iv. 161, 171, 197.

[10] Between April and Sept. 1274. *Cal Pat. 1272–81*, 47 (2), 57.

[11] Ibid. 105; *List of Escheators for England* (PRO, Lists and Indexes Society, 72, compiled 1932, issued London, 1971), 21; *Cal. Pat. 1272–81*, 105; *RH* ii. 266b.

[12] *Cal. Pat. 1272–81*, 30, 98–9.

[13] Ibid. 155.

[14] Ibid. 303.

[15] *RH* i. 16a, 60b, 110a, 114a, 124a, 164a, 204a–b, 209b, 212b, 225b, 228b, 232a–b, 235a, 236b; ii. 7a, 10a, 12b, 13b, 15b, 16b, 35b, 36a, 205a, 225b, 290a–b, 307b. The reference to Geoffrey de Sandiacre senior in *RH* ii. 307b raises the possibility that we are dealing with two men of the same name who cannot be easily distinguished from each other.

Many of the commissioners had a prior connection with the counties to which they were assigned, either in an official capacity or as local landholders. Earlier service as sheriff was the most common administrative link. Thus William de Boyvill, former sheriff of Northamptonshire, was appointed commissioner for Northamptonshire and Rutland, while both Richard de Coleshull and Thomas de St Vigor had spent periods as sheriff in Somerset and Dorset. Roger de Burghull, Sampson Foliot, William de Hevere, Fulk de Rycote, and William de St Clair had likewise served as sheriffs in the counties to which they were assigned. Among other connections, Fulk de Rycote had also served as coroner in Oxfordshire, as had Henry de Sheldon in Warwickshire, while William Bagod, commissioner for Staffordshire and Shropshire, had previously been entrusted with difficult diplomatic and judicial business in the Marches.[16]

A few commissioners belonged to the wider legal and administrative scene. As well as his involvement with the 1274–5 inquiry, Richard Creeping had been one of those charged with investigations into the export of wool to Flanders from Northumberland, Cumberland, and Westmorland in 1274 and was to be employed in June 1280 to hear complaints from the men of Jersey about the conduct of the bailiff of Otto of Grandison, lord of the Channel Islands.[17] He, Geoffrey Aguillon, fellow veteran of the 1274–5 inquiry, Geoffrey de Sandiacre, and Giles de Berkele later became assize justices, while Ralph Arnhall heard foreign pleas in the Lincolnshire eyre of 1281. William Gerberge's inglorious appointment as keeper of rolls for the northern circuit in 1292–4 has already been noted.[18] William Bagod and Fulk de Rycote also had experience as stewards to the earl of Cornwall.[19]

Many had local estates. Sampson Foliot held land in Oxfordshire, while Fulk de Rycote, his fellow commissioner, held

---

[16] *RH* ii. 33b; *Cal. Pat.* 1272–81, 47–8; P. Coss, *The Origins of the English Gentry* (Cambridge, 2003), 150.

[17] *Cal. Pat.* 1272–81, 69, 411.

[18] D. Crook, *Records of the General Eyre* (London, 1982), 148, 171; Moor, *Knights of Edward I*, iv. 209; see above, pp. 52–3. For Aguillon and Berkele I am indebted to Paul Brand.

[19] Moor, *Knights of Edward I*, i. 33; A. Polden, 'A Crisis of the Knightly Class? Inheritance and Office among the Gentry of Thirteenth-Century Buckinghamshire', in P. Fleming, A. Gross, and J. R. Lander (eds.), *Regionalism and Revision: The Crown and its Provinces in England 1200–1650* (London, 1998), 35.

land in both Oxfordshire and Berkshire.[20] John de Avenel, who replaced Geoffrey de Sandiacre in Cambridgeshire and Huntingdonshire in October 1279, held land in Cambridgeshire, as did William Muschet.[21] In 1277, John de Steingrave, member of a north Yorkshire knightly family, was leasing the manor of Stainton (Yorks.).[22] Oliver de Ingham and Richard Creeping were both well-known Norfolk knights. William de Middleton, commissioner for Northumberland, also appears to have been a local knight, although there are three contemporaries of the same name. His two namesakes were more distinguished, one being bishop of Norwich and the other keeper of the writs and rolls of the court of Common Pleas until August 1278, when he was made responsible for the vacant see of Canterbury.[23] Much of this information appears fortuitously on the patent rolls or in the returns of the hundred roll inquiries. It is impossible to ascertain the full holdings of most of the commissioners, but it is likely that many more of them held land locally. Giles de Berkele, Roger de Burghull, Hamo de Gatton, Thomas de St Vigor, and Paulinus of Cardiff demonstrably did so according to inquisitions *post mortem,* while others had been land-holders in neighbouring counties.[24] As Peter Coss has demonstrated, Henry de Sheldon and Henry of Nottingham, commissioners for Warwickshire and Leicestershire, and Nicholas of Cogenhoe, commissioner for Northamptonshire and Rutland, were members of a select group of knights frequently employed on royal business in their own localities, nor were they alone in this.[25]

[20] *RH* ii. 38b, 43a, 44b, 45a, 714a, 838a (Foliot), i. 18b; ii. 757a, 799a; *Cal. IPM* iv. no. 79 (Rycote). Foliot also held land in Wiltshire. *RH* ii. 233a, 260a, 269b, 276a and Rycote held half a knight's fee in Lavendon (Bucks.). Ibid. 349a.

[21] *RH* ii. 519b, 529b–31b, 533a, 534a–b, 556a, 566b (Avenel); 442b, 542b, 543b, 544a (Muschet). Geoffrey's land was in Norfolk, where his swans were being stolen. *Cal. Pat.* 1272–81, 178.

[22] G. E. C., *The Complete Peerage*, revised edn., 14 vols. (London, 1910–98), xii/1. 276; *Cal. Pat.* 1272–81, 203, 242.

[23] Greenway, 'Newly Discovered Fragment', 76; *Cal. Pat.* 1272–81, 146, 260–1, 276, 278–9, 316. Paul Brand kindly assisted with information on William de Middleton. Someone of that name was also commissioned to carry out Northumberland business in 1281. Ibid. 471.

[24] *Cal. IPM* iii, nos. 22, 229; iv. nos. 246, 458; v. no. 585. Roger de Bacheworth, commissioner for Middlesex and London, had held land in Hertfordshire and Master Adam de Crokedayk, commissioner for Northumberland, was a Cumberland man. Ibid. iv. nos. 48, 314; D. E. R. Watt, *A Biographical Dictionary of Scottish Graduates to AD 1410* (Oxford, 1977), 127–8.

[25] As well as serving as coroner, Sheldon had also been involved in gaol delivery

Information about the commissioners appointed as clerks to the proceedings tends to be more sparse. Indeed, although it can often be established, it is only an assumption that the third commissioner was invariably a clerk. All we know about Ralph le Botiler, the first clerk to the Yorkshire circuit, is that he was presented to the living at 'Adburton' in the southern province by the king's gift in June 1278.[26] Similarly Flurus is known only as having held the local living of Bletsoe in Bedfordshire. It is however evident that some clerks were more widely employed on government business. William de Plumpton and Master Adam de Botindon had been sent together as envoys to Aragon the year before their appointment to the hundred roll inquiry.[27] Stephen de Houedon and William of Luton had accompanied royal officials in Lancashire, Worcestershire, and Gloucestershire to buy grain for the army in July 1277.[28] In November 1275, Robert le Blund, clerk on the Kentish circuit, had been appointed along with the prior of St Katherine's without Lincoln to scrutinize the chirographers' chests at Lincoln and Stamford.[29] The most interesting of these career officials is Master Adam de Crokedayk, assigned as clerk to the Westmorland circuit, close to his home territory of Cumberland. His legal career in England was just taking off. He also prospered north of the border, serving Robert Bruce as attorney, steward, and finally as one of his auditors in the Great Cause, before dying in 1305. It is a measure of his worldly success that in later years he styled himself knight rather than master.[30] Roger de Drayton, clerk to the Nottinghamshire and Derby circuit, may also have gained advancement in the secular world, since a steward of the earl of Cornwall of that name met an untimely death in 1292.[31] In 1279, some of these clerks seem to have been bright men on the way up.

---

and commissions of *oyer and terminer*, while Nottingham had been an assessor for the fifteenth of 1275 in Warwickshire and Leicestershire. Both had estates in Leicestershire. Cogenhoe was similarly employed in Northamptonshire, where his estates lay. Coss, *Origins*, 141, 152–7. For other knights with this sort of profile, see Moor, *Knights of Edward I, passim.*

[26] *Cal. Pat. 1272–81,* 268.

[27] Ibid. 264–5. Plumpton had also been sent to Chester on a political mission associated with Llywelyn ap Gruffudd in 1274. Ibid. 42–3.

[28] Ibid. 219.

[29] Ibid. 127.

[30] Watt, *Biographical Dictionary,* 127–8.

[31] M. Prestwich, *Edward I,* 2nd edn. (New Haven and London, 1997), 281.

Before embarking on their duties, all the commissioners were required to take the oath appended to the commission on the patent roll. It is in French and couched in the second person plural as a mandate from the king:

You the inquisitors will swear to serve the king faithfully and well in the office to which you have been appointed and to attend to such office diligently and faithfully and to do faithfully everything within your power for the king and for all others. And you will not fail because of rich or poor, nor for reputation nor hatred, nor for favour nor power, nor for the estate of anyone, nor for benefit, gift, or promise that anyone offers or might offer you, nor will you fail through art or ingenuity to inquire faithfully into the rights of the king and to write them down faithfully and deliver them to the king as he has commanded you. And [you will swear] that you will not accept any benefice within Holy Church, nor pension, nor other benefit without the king's leave. So God and the saints help you.[32]

This oath is unusual for its enrolment rather than its existence; commissioners for the earlier inquiries would almost certainly have given similar undertakings, even though they have not been recorded. Oaths had been customary for members of the judiciary since the late twelfth century and a series of oaths required of those involved in the reforms of 1258 were included in the Provisions of Oxford.[33] This particular oath is very similar to that intended for justices in eyre, entered on the close roll for 1278. The penultimate sentence, with its promise not to accept benefices or pensions seems more appropriate to the clerical commissioners and indeed this part of the oath seems to have been borrowed from the oath taken by the justices' clerks, which was entered on the close roll following the justices' oath.[34]

There is little in the way of direct instructions for the conduct of the inquiry, but much can be inferred from the surviving returns and what is known from earlier inquiries. The first step as laid down in the commission was for the sheriffs to organize juries. The

[32] PRO, C66/98, m. 21[d]; *Cal. Pat.*, *1272–81*, 343. For the French text, see Appendix 2.

[33] P. Brand, *The Making of the Common Law* (London, 1992), 149; *Documents of the Baronial Movement of Reform and Rebellion, 1258–1267*, ed. R. F. Treharne and I. J. Sanders (Oxford, 1973), 100–3.

[34] Brand, *Making*, 150. The close roll entry is badly worn and was not therefore calendared. I am grateful to Paul Brand for his advice and especially for making his transcript of the MS entry available to me. PRO, C54/95, 1[d]; *Cal. Close, 1272–9*, 513.

order that 'We command our sheriff in the aforesaid counties that
on certain days and places etc. you summon before you a number
of knights and upright and lawful men from your bailiwick' is a
standard phrase.[35] The procedure is therefore assumed to have
been the same as for judicial eyres, where the bailiffs of each
hundred nominated four knights who, in turn, selected the jurors.[36]
The returns for Bampton and Ploughley hundreds in Oxfordshire
refer to the election rather than the appointment of jurors, but
since election in a thirteenth-century context was far removed from
modern practice, it amounted to the same thing.[37] The names of
these jurors, and ward jurors within towns, are sometimes listed at
the head of their verdicts. Normally there were twelve, but
numbers varied slightly.[38] They were sometimes referred to as
trustworthy and upright men or men representing the hundred.[39]
In many rolls, however, their names were either edited out subsequently or lost because the opening membrane of the roll has been
damaged. Such was the probable fate of jury lists on the worn
membranes for the town of Godmanchester and the hundreds of
Hurstingstone and Normancross in Huntingdonshire, since the
hundred rolls for this county are in a finished form and the other
two hundreds have full lists on the first membrane of their
returns.[40]

Although the juries theoretically comprised knights and 'upright
and lawful men', in practice, relatively few jurors were actually
described as knights or styled *dominus*. Most were known by

---

[35] For the Latin text, see Appendix 2.

[36] E. A. Kosminsky, *Studies in the Agrarian History of England in the Thirteenth
Century* (Oxford, 1956), 15–16; *Warwickshire*, ed. John, 3.

[37] *coram domino Sampsone Foliot et domino Fulcon' de Ruycote et sociis secum
electis* ... *RH* ii. 688a, 822a; Coss, *Origins*, 122–4.

[38] At Coventry and in the NW ward of Oxford thirteen were listed (although the
Coventry text claims twelve), for the vill of Stoneleigh (Warwicks.) ten, at
Cambridge fourteen, and in Queenhithe ward London eight. 'The Coventry
Hundred Rolls', ed. T. John in P. R. Coss (ed.), *The Early Records of Medieval
Coventry* (London, 1986), 370; *Warwickshire*, ed. John, 58–9; *RH* ii. 356a, 793b;
PRO, SC5/London/Tower/1, m. 1.

[39] As in Bread Street and Langbourn wards in London (*fidedigni* or *probi
homines*), or Thame hundred (Oxon.) (*viros legatos hundredi*). PRO,
SC5/London/Tower/9–10, mm. 15–16 (13–14); SC5/Oxon/Tower/14, m. 1; *RH* ii.
820a. The Rec. Comm. transcript is correct.

[40] *RH* ii. 591a, 598a, 607b, 633b, 665b. The list of jurors for Wootton hundred
(Oxon.) was recovered when the opening membrane of the roll was found in
unsorted Miscellanea. PRO, SC5/Oxon/Tower/16/1, m. 1.

patronyms, and sometimes identified with particular vills, as in the jury for Chesterton hundred in Cambridgeshire, where all the vills with one minor exception were represented in this way.[41] The predominance of substantial freemen in the juries of this county accords with the composition of the Cambridgeshire juries of 1274–5 analysed by Dr Scales. They were men of weight in their local communities, who had often acted before. At least half of the Wetherley jurors in 1279 had also served on the 1274–5 jury.[42] Oxfordshire and Huntingdonshire hundreds numbered rather more knights among their jurors, but none were major figures. In so far as it was possible to find the necessary evidence, Kosminsky analysed the holdings of 179 jurors from eighteen of the twenty panels named in the printed edition of the rolls. The richest of them was Robert Danvers, an Oxfordshire knight, whose four manors comprised just over three and a half knights' fees, but many more were freemen with modest landholdings.[43]

Under the terms of their royal mandate, the commissioners were enjoined to 'attend in person' at a set date 'in every place in the above counties'. They presided over the inquest at Witney (Oxon.), but elsewhere there is nothing to show that they travelled around their circuits.[44] Rather it seems that business was conducted in the county towns; the hearings for Wetherley and Northstow hundreds took place in Cambridge, for Leightonstone hundred in Huntingdon, for Lewknor hundred in Oxford.[45] Notwithstanding that, the opening passage associated with the Warwickshire returns asserts that inquisitions were made by the commissioners 'in all the vills and all the places throughout the counties of Warwickshire and Leicestershire', that for Guthlaxton hundred was held in Leicester.[46] In London, hearings for the three westernmost wards of Farringdon, Bread Street, and Castle Baynard, which resulted in a list of purprestures, were dealt with in the bishop of London's

---

[41] *RH* ii. 402a.

[42] L. Scales, 'The Cambridgeshire Ragman Rolls', EHR 113 (1998), 560–2.

[43] Kosminsky, *Studies*, 20–1, 258–69.

[44] *Oxfordshire Hundred Rolls of 1279*, ed. E. Stone and P. Hyde (Oxford, 1968), 91.

[45] *RH* ii. 446b, 554b, 607b, 782a.

[46] *facte sunt inquisitiones in singulis villis et singulis locis per comitatus Warr' et Leyc' per Henricum de Notyngham Henricum de Seldon et Johannem de Arundell clericum . . . Warwickshire*, ed. John, 25; Nichols, *History and Antiquities*, i/1, p. cx.

hall.[47] The appearance of the hundredal or ward jurors before the commissioners at these venues seems to have marked the final stage of the inquiry, since it is unlikely that the commissioners attended preliminary hearings.

The task of collecting answers to the questions posed by the articles was delegated. Scales thought that knights of the shire might have played a larger part at this stage of the 1274–5 inquiry than the evidence suggests.[48] The phrasing of the commission is also loose enough to permit such a possibility in 1279, although there is nothing else to support it. Whether or not these county figures were involved, there can be no doubt of the crucial role played by the hundredal jurors. In the Cambridgeshire hundreds of Wetherley and Staine and the Oxfordshire hundred of Bampton, they are formally associated with the commissioners, as indeed the commission envisaged: 'we commission you, and those with whom you associate yourselves'.[49] The commissioners gave them the articles and ordered them to return at a given date to present their findings under oath. This is spelt out in Wetherley hundred and also in some of the Oxfordshire and Huntingdonshire hundreds, where the jurors are recorded as bringing in verdicts on the articles given to them by the royal justices.[50]

The phrasing at the head of the returns for Bullingdon hundred and the half hundred of Ewelme in Oxfordshire, and for Queenhithe ward in London, implies that the jurors conducted the inquest alone.[51] This must usually have been the case in the early stages of information-gathering. In London and Oxford, the alderman for the ward was in charge. In the countryside, it is likely that this role fell to the first juror listed for the hundred. If a knight were among them, he presided. This is confirmed by the way in which the jurors were set out on the roll for Langtree hundred (Oxon.), with Lord John de Chausye's name inscribed across a two-column list of the remaining jurors.[52] Of village jurors, who provided much of the information at local level, there is almost no trace. At Long

---

[47] PRO, SC5/London/Tower/13, m. 21 (19). The hall was probably at St Paul's.
[48] Scales, 'Cambridgeshire Ragman Rolls', 565–6.
[49] *RH* ii. 483b, 554b, 688a; appendix 2: *assignavimus vos una cum hiis quos vobis associetis . . .*
[50] *commissis, deliberatis* or *traditis. RH* ii. 554b, 607b, 688a, 705a, 782a, 822a.
[51] *RH* ii. 710a, 751b; PRO, SC5/London/Tower/1, m. 1.
[52] *RH* ii. 774a; PRO, SC5/Oxon/Tower/4a, m. 1.

Stanton in Cambridgeshire the jury was said to be drawn from the neighbourhood (*de viceneto*). At Souldrop in Bedfordshire, Eversden in Cambridgeshire, Kirtlington in Oxfordshire, and several places in Stodfold hundred in Buckinghamshire, 'the vill' gave evidence, while at Lew and Clanfield in Bampton hundred (Oxon.) there is reference to hallmoots.[53] Separate jurors are named for the vills of Hanslope, Haversham, and Little Linford in Buckinghamshire, but as they are the same men in all but one instance, they cannot have been village jurors in any real sense.[54] In Warwickshire, however, the jurors for Stoneleigh vill were entirely different from those for Stoneleigh hundred.[55] Where they survive in the original, the verdicts from some of these local juries are not very sophisticated in their presentation. This is particularly true of those from the London wards. Three are in French, one of which is written in a distinctive spiked hand. Several are on scraps of parchment, the smallest of which is a mere 7.5 × 9 cm. Another return, small and misshapen, begins baldly 'Alanus de Castre ought to be a knight'.[56]

It is not clear whether local juries were summoned to a central venue or whether the hundredal jurors travelled around collecting information from each vill. In London, the hearings for Billingsgate ward were held in St Botolph's church in the ward, unlike a session for the wards of Faringdon, Bread Street, and Castle Baynard which had been conducted in the bishop of London's hall.[57] In the countryside, there are very occasionally hints of geographical progression in the structure of the returns, although there is no guarantee that the order in which the information has been recorded is the same as that in which it was collected. Such an underlying geographical pattern can be detected in parts of the Warwickshire returns, as demonstrated by the first eight entries for Kineton hundred.[58] The most striking instance however is the

---

[53] *RH* ii. 327b, 343b, 460a, 510a, 690b–1a, 822b.

[54] Ibid. 343b, 346a–b.   [55] *Warwickshire*, ed. John, 39, 58–9.

[56] *Alanus de Castre debet esse miles.* PRO, SC5/London/Tower/13, m. 19 (17); 15, m. 23 (21); 17, m. 25 (23); 19–20 mm. 27–8 (25–6); 23, m. 31 (30).

[57] PRO, SC5/London/Tower/23, m. 31 (30).

[58] *Warwickshire*, ed. John, 165–82. Compare the entries for Wellesbourne Mountford, Newbold Pacey, Ashorne, Charlecote, Barford, Wasperton, Packwood, and Moreton Morrell with the map, 20–1. All are located on the north-western side of the hundred, except for Packwood, belonging to the prior of Coventry, which was dealt with at the same time as his holding at Wasperton.

return for Normancross hundred in Huntingdonshire found on the unpublished Huntingdon roll.[59] The eleven membranes, which are sewn together end to end and which appear to be in part a fair copy, give no details of those before whom the evidence was sworn, but the vills which they describe follow a distinct geographical pattern beginning in the north of the hundred with Orton Longueville (see Map 2). The progression is not perfect. The two Peterborough Abbey manors of Alwalton and Fletton are dealt with together, although they are not contiguous. They nevertheless appear broadly in the correct geographical order. The one major divergence is caused by the remaining ecclesiastical estates which are gathered together at the end of the roll. In particular, the large group of Thorney Abbey holdings in the hundred were all entered at mm. 16–17.[60]

The existence of a single response for the whole hundred about liberties on the rolls for the Bedfordshire/Buckinghamshire circuit and separate membranes for the non-manorial articles on many of the Cambridgeshire/Huntingdonshire rolls could imply that this material was collected at a central venue in hearings separate from those held to gather the estate surveys.[61] Such an arrangement would be credible on purely practical grounds, given the different type of material required, but it is more likely that the information was extracted at the editing stage in order to create a separate record. Entries about suit of court, frankpledge, and other liberties were flagged on some of the Cambridgeshire rolls as if to aid the scribe in doing this.[62] However, the fact that similar flagging is to

[59] S. Raban, 'Fresh Light on the 1279 Hundred Rolls: Some Huntingdonshire Evidence', *Historical Research*, 61 (1988), 105, 112–14. I have become more certain that this roll belongs in some way to the corpus of 1279 returns since writing in 1988.

[60] They were Water Newton, Stibbington, Wansford, Haddon, Woodston, Stanground, Farcet, and Yaxley.

[61] Cambs.: Chilford, PRO, SC5/Cambs/Tower/4, m. 19 (damaged and unprinted); Flendish, *RH* ii. 430b–32b, PRO, SC5/Cambs/Tower/5, m. 1; Staine, *RH* ii. 483b–4b, PRO, SC5/Cambs/Tower/8, m. 1; Staploe, *RH* ii. 497a–8b, SC5/Cambs/Tower/9, m. 1; Whittlesford, *RH* ii. 570a–1a, SC5/Cambs/Tower/14, m. 1; Hunts.: Leightonstone, *RH* ii. 632b–33b, PRO, SC5/Hunts/Tower/3, m. 14; Toseland, *RH* ii. 665b–6b, PRO, SC5/Hunts/Tower/5, m. 1; Beds.: Willey and Bucklow, *RH* ii. 323a–b, PRO, SC5/Beds/Tower/2, m. 1; Bucks.: Mursley, *RH* ii. 338a–b, PRO, SC5/Bucks/Tower/1, m. 3; Stodfold, *RH* ii. 343b, PRO, SC5/Bucks/Tower/2, m. 4; Bunsty, *RH* ii. 350b, PRO, SC5/Bucks/Tower/3, m. 11; Lamua, *RH* ii. 353b, PRO, SC5/Bucks/Tower/4, m. 3.

[62] PRO, SC5/Cambs/Tower/6, 9, 10.

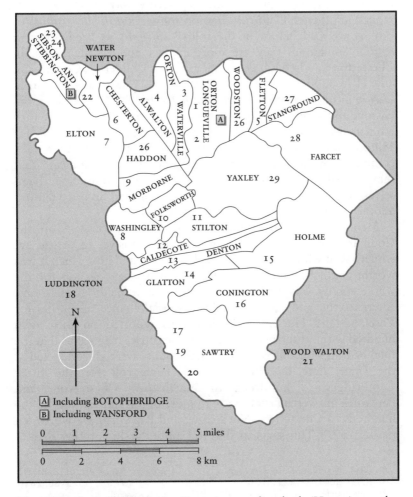

Map 2. Order of returns in Normancross hundred (Hunts.) on the Huntingdon roll

be found on the non-manorial membrane itself on the Whittlesford roll suggests that it is more likely that the information was being singled out for future action.[63] On some of the Cambridgeshire rolls, there is a good deal of ambiguous cross-referencing.[64] The hundredal jurors expressly and repeatedly 'say that they have replied in other rolls' (*dicunt quod responderunt in aliis rotulis*) or 'say as we said before in the roll(s)' (*dicimus ut prediximus in rotul'*). Sometimes they are more explicit about which rolls. In Chesterton hundred, on the membranes for Childerley, Cottenham, and Histon, 'they say as they said in the Chesterton [vill] roll' (*dicunt sicut predixerunt in rotulo de Cestreton*).[65] At Oakington, Girton, and Impington in Northstow hundred, they say that they have answered either on the rolls for Rampton or the rolls for Milton and Rampton.[66] It is more likely therefore that such comments by hundredal jurors here and elsewhere indicate that they wished to avoid repeating, and possibly contradicting, themselves, as the same evidence was required of them in one vill after another, rather than refer to separate hearings.

Mention of all four hundreds in Huntingdonshire on the Godmanchester and Leightonstone rolls in answer to article 22, which asked who administered each hundred and how much it was worth, could be taken as evidence that a single session for the whole county was held to deal with the non-manorial questions. Alternatively, and more probably, especially since the jurors for Toseland and Hurstingstone hundreds reported on their own hundred without further comment, these entries may tell us that the final hearings for this relatively small county were all conducted at the same time in Huntingdon.[67] Each roll for the three Cambridgeshire hundreds of Northstow, Chesterton, and Papworth answered article 22 with more or less full variants of 'the hundreds of Chesterton, Northstow, and Papworth are worth ten marks p.a.'.[68] This suggests that in Cambridgeshire, rather than at

---

[63] PRO, SC5/Cambs/Tower/14, m. 1.   [64] *inferius dictum est, ut supra*, etc.

[65] *RH* ii. 409a, 411a, 413b.   [66] *RH* ii. 451a, 458b, 464b.

[67] This article is not addressed in the PRO Normancross roll. *RH* ii. 598a, 605a, 633b, 666b.

[68] The fullest version, taken from *RH* ii. 407a, reads 'the hundreds of Chesterton, Northstow and Papworth are in the hand of the lord king in the custody of the sheriff through one bailiff and are worth ten marks p.a., but the bailiffs of these hundreds take more than the farm to the greatest injury of the whole community'. Variants can be found ibid. 451a, 452a, 454a, 458b, 469a.

a single hearing for the whole county, these three neighbouring hundreds were dealt with as a smaller unit. An answer to the same article in Wetherley hundred similarly implies a combination with Thriplow hundred, which was again contiguous.[69] Hearings for Northstow and Wetherley hundreds are known to have taken place at Cambridge, so such groupings suggest that villagers from several hundreds came before the jurors there at the same time.[70] Scales envisaged the collection of evidence on several smaller circuits for Cambridgeshire in 1274–5 when considering the role of the knights of the shire.[71] Similar arrangements, with or without the knights and probably at Cambridge, may have been adopted in the later inquiry. In a larger county than Huntingdonshire, it would have made sense to take hundreds in small groups rather than attempt to deal with them all on the same occasion.

The Cambridgeshire rolls show that, as one might have anticipated, hearings were structured around the articles. Much of the evidence was collected orally by means of questions put to villagers by the hundredal jurors. However, the commissioners had been ordered to 'make faithful inquiry of others in those counties about the tenures and fees'. Without the assistance of lords, it is doubtful whether detailed information about their tenants and their obligations or the nature of their demesnes could have been assembled. In most cases there is nothing to indicate whether seigneurial contributions were oral or in writing. Much no doubt depended on the size of the estate and the importance of its lord. Sometimes the proceedings may have been oral with title deeds or royal grants produced in support of claims. This appears to have been the case at Cambridge, where the chirograph between Barnwell Priory and John and Basilia le Kaleys was rehearsed at length.[72] Written submission was likely for larger estates. Once provided, it is probable that the details were checked by the hundredal jurors before being recorded alongside the oral testimony in the form of verdicts. This process of checking can be seen in action at Kenilworth in Stoneleigh hundred (War.), where villagers were cross-examined about suit to the prior of Kenilworth's court.[73]

---

[69] *RH* ii. 568a. Very few articles are cited in the Thriplow roll, so it offers no corroboration. Ibid. 542b–54b.

[70] Ibid. 446b, 554b.   [71] Scales, 'Cambridgeshire Ragman Rolls', 565–6.

[72] *RH* ii. 357a.   [73] *Warwickshire*, ed. John, 50.

Magnates, lay as well as ecclesiastical, probably made a single return for all their estates in a hundred. Those of Peterborough and Thorney Abbeys are entered together in both the surviving rolls for Normancross hundred (Hunts.).[74] Ramsey Abbey's estates at Old Weston, Ellington, Steeple Gidding, and the hamlets of Bythorn and Brington are grouped together in the same way at the end of the other manorial returns in Leightonstone hundred in the same county.[75] Similarly, returns for the estates of the bishop of Chester at Chadshunt and Gaydon in Kineton hundred (War.) are found alongside those for his third manor at Bishop's Tachbrook which lay further to the west.[76] The Lewknor roll (Oxon.) finishes with a consolidated entry for the earl of Cornwall's estates in the honour of Wallingford, opening with 'Here ends the hundred of Lewknor and here begins the honour of Wallingford in that hundred', while the last entry on the roll reads: 'Here ends the honour of Wallingford in the hundred of Lewknor'.[77] His estates belonging to the honour of St Valery in Bullingdon hundred in the same county were recorded in a comparable group, but without the headings.[78]

From time to time, membranes looking like the actual texts supplied by landlords can be found among the findings of the jurors. The entry for the demesne at Elton, a manor belonging to the abbot of Ramsey in Normancross hundred (Hunts.), on the Huntingdon roll is in a different hand in what is otherwise a fair copy, indicating that it had been incorporated as it stood into the roll.[79] The return for the earl of Gloucester's holdings in Bottisham (Cambs.), looks distinctively different from the other returns for Staine hundred. The membrane is narrower, its layout is different, and the parchment is much whiter. It cannot be a straightforward

---

[74] *RH* ii. 638b–49a; HR, mm. 9, 16–17.

[75] *RH* ii. 629a–32b. Since this roll is a finished copy, it is impossible to judge whether the return was submitted by the abbey. The estates of the prior of Huntingdon at Great Gidding, the abbot of Sawtry at Catworth, and the bishop of Lincoln at Spaldwick and its hamlets are not grouped at the end in this way. Ibid. 615b–16b, 625a–7a.

[76] *Warwickshire*, ed. John, 184–9. Bishops of Coventry often styled themselves informally as bishop of Chester, rather than bishop of Coventry and Lichfield.

[77] *Explicit hundr' de Leuekenor' et hic incipit honor Walingeford in eodem hundr'.* and *Explicit honor Walingeford in hundr' de Leuekenor'. RH* ii. 785a, 788b.

[78] *RH* ii. 715b–17b.

[79] HR, m. 10.

seigneurial submission, however, because it is clearly a jurors' verdict.[80] Much the same is true of part of the return for the hundred of Hugh de Plessis outside the north gate of Oxford; a jurors' verdict, but in an unusual hand.[81] Perhaps in both cases the lordship provided the scribe as well as the evidence put before the jurors. The return for the abbot of Eynsham's estate at Eynsham in Wootton hundred (Oxon.) is more evidently a product of the abbey *scriptorium*. As well as being written in a different hand, it contains quite a detailed history of the descent of the manor which is unlikely to have originated elsewhere.[82]

Internal evidence on its own sometimes offers a clue as to the seigneurial origin for a text. The way in which the entries on the return for the de Plessis hundred often begin with the name of a former tenant and then trace title to the current holder is suggestive of a seigneurial record, although it could be a way of supplying information about title—this is more characteristic of Cambridge than Oxford returns. The entry for Whitchurch in Langtree hundred (Oxon.), in which the estate is correctly assigned to Isabella de Forz at the beginning, but refers to a male lord when it comes to the tenancies, argues more conclusively for transcription from a seignorial source.[83] The Elton entry on the PRO roll for Normancross hundred also seems to be dependent on material supplied by the abbey. The description of the descent of the manor is virtually identical to that contained in an inquest held sometime after 1269 and preserved in the abbey cartulary:

[The PRO hundred roll text:]
The abbot of Ramsey holds the manor and vill of Elton with its appurtenances in chief from the lord king and this by grant of the bishop of Dorchester called Ethelric, which manor was confirmed by St Edward, William the Bastard, and other later kings of England, from king to king until the present king.[84]

[The cartulary text:]
'The abbot of Ramsey holds the manor and vill of Elton with its appurtenances in chief of the lord king, by grant of Ethelric, bishop of Dorchester.

---

[80] PRO, SC5/Cambs/Tower/8, m. 4.
[82] PRO, SC5/Oxon/Tower/16/1, m. 18.
[84] *RH* ii. 656a.

[81] SC5/Oxon/Tower/11.
[83] *RH* ii. 775b–6b.

Which manor was confirmed by St Edward, William the Bastard, and other later kings of England, from king to king until the present king.'[85]

This phrasing is also similar to that for the Ramsey manor of Lawshall in Babergh hundred in Suffolk: 'he has this by confirmation of all the kings of England from King Edgar to the present king', which in its turn differs from the phrasing characteristic of the manors belonging to Bury St Edmunds which comprise the bulk of the surviving text.[86] The opening passage of the return for Coventry also bears all the hallmarks of seigneurial influence. Although again expressed as the jurors' verdict, it is hard to see why they or the royal commissioners would have chosen to ascertain that Coventry Priory took precedence over the chapter of Lichfield Cathedral when it came to electing a bishop. Moreover, the number of unnamed heirs of previous tenants in the rest of the return incurs the suspicion that the verdict may have drawn on an out-of-date priory survey.[87]

Ecclesiastical estates were sometimes treated differently from those of lay lords. The first of the two membranes dealing with Thorney Abbey's estates on the Normancross portion of Huntingdon roll is worn as though it had once been stored separately. The grouping of all but the Peterborough Abbey estates together on the same roll implies that the ecclesiastical estates may have been dealt with together, landlord by landlord, perhaps on another occasion. Slight variations in terminology, common to these returns, but not found in the other membranes, strengthen this impression. The manorial buildings for example, described elsewhere as messuages, become 'the site of the manor' (*situs manerii*) in these entries.[88] The entry for Biddenham on the Bucklow roll (Beds.) has a similar grouping of ecclesiastical returns. A list of free tenants breaks off, leaving a gap on the dorse of the

---

[85] *Cartularium Monasterii de Rameseia*, ed. W. H. Hart and P. A. Lyons, 3 vols. (Rolls Series; London, 1884–93), i. 490. The inquest is dated 1218–19 in the cartulary, but this must be an error, since John de Balliol, who died in 1269, had seized the abbot's fishery and his widow was in possession when the inquiry was made. John of Elton, a free tenant recorded in the inquiry, was no longer in possession by the time of the hundred roll proceedings, which therefore must have been the later of the two texts. The descent given on the Huntingdon roll is markedly different from both. HR, m. 10.

[86] *The Pinchbeck Register*, ed. F. Hervey (Brighton, 1925), ii. 77.

[87] 'Coventry Hundred Rolls', ed. John, 370 and *passsim*.

[88] HR, mm. 10, 16, and schedule.

membrane. A description then follows of the holdings of the prior of Newnham, Lincoln Minster, the prior of Dunstable, and the abbot of Warden, one after the other.[89] The holdings of the abbot of Biddlesden and the prior of Luffield at Evershaw also appear to have been entered in a different hand on the roll for Stodfold hundred (Bucks.).[90] The Cambridge returns deal with holdings of the religious and the chancellor and masters of the university before proceeding to record tenancies, parish by parish.[91] The same is true on a smaller scale for the borough of Banbury (Oxon.).[92] Rather different entries among the Oxford returns are also suggestive. A fragment from the north-east ward consists entirely of rentals for ecclesiastical holdings, while the returns for the south-east ward and the Northgate suburb belonging to Hugh de Plessis provide totals for the rents of ecclesiastical tenements, including those of the university, in the margin or at the end, but not those of tenements belonging to lay landlords.[93]

The larger towns were also treated rather differently from the countryside because of the density and complexity of their settlement. London was incomparably the largest town in England with an estimated population ranging from 40,000 to 100,000.[94] This may explain why there is no sign that a tenurial survey was attempted or indeed required by the London articles; the task may have proved too intimidating even to contemplate. However, since we are reliant on the existing returns for knowledge of the articles and there is no tenurial return, there can be no guarantee that the information was never ordered. As with Domesday Book, the reasons why there is no survey for London can only be a matter of speculation. If it was attempted in either inquiry, it may simply have taken too long to compile or have been lost in the intervening centuries. The known articles of 1279 were much easier to answer, especially where information which had already been provided to

---

[89] PRO, SC5/Beds/Tower/2, m. 3^d; *RH* ii. 327b.
[90] PRO, SC5/Bucks/Tower/2, m. 3.   [91] *RH* ii. 356a–61a.
[92] PRO, SC5/Oxon/Tower/17, m. 1.
[93] PRO, SC5/Oxon/Tower/9c, m. 3, 10; *RH* ii. 801a–b, 803a–5a, 811a. In the SW ward there were totals for the burgesses and the Jews as well as the church. Ibid. 793a–b.
[94] Something between 80,000 and 100,000 is now thought likely. D. Keene, 'Medieval London and its Region', *London Journal*, 14 (1989), 107; G. A. Williams, *Medieval London, from Commune to Capital* (London, 1963), 20; R. H. Britnell, *The Commercialisation of English Society 1000–1500* (Cambridge, 1993), 115.

the London eyre of 1276 could be reiterated.[95] The ward jurors showed varying degrees of enthusiasm for the task. Extensive lists of purprestures and escheats were put forward by the Farringdon ward jury, but the jurors for Bridge and Bread Street wards made little effort to comply with the government's demands, either denying any relevant knowledge or referring the commissioners to the London eyre.[96]

Outside London, various approaches to collecting the information were adopted. In Oxford the hearings also took place ward by ward under the direction of the aldermen with their own juries. The work of Janet Cooper suggests that, in some wards, returns were made in rough topographical order by parishes.[97] In Cambridge, there was one jury of burgesses for the whole town and the wards were ignored in favour of the smaller scale offered by parishes, which were dealt with one by one. This at least seems to have been the theory. In practice, the struggle to combine a record of each individual's property with a topographical structure resulted in a confused compromise. All the holdings of a given individual were recorded at the same time as their first tenement, irrespective of parish, followed by any land held in the town fields. This meant that the underlying parochial format is often obscured.[98] The survey thought to be a copy of the King's Lynn return also proceeded topographically, but in smaller towns, inhabitants were simply listed, although they might be in a particular order.[99] In the Warwick return, one burgess followed another, starting with the mayor, but in Godmanchester and Marlow, no such social ranking is discernible.[100] A similar approach was taken at Coventry, although the customary division into the prior's portion of the town and that once belonging to the earl of Chester was observed.[101]

Returns for the larger towns generally survive as separate rolls. This was certainly true of those for Oxfordshire, the

[95] SC5/London/Tower/3, 5, 9, 11, mm. 8, 10, 15–16 (6, 8, 13–14).
[96] PRO, SC5/London/Tower/2, mm. 2–5 (2–3), 3, m. 8 (6), 9, m. 15 (13).
[97] RH ii. 788b, 793b, 796b; PRO, SC5/Oxon/Tower/8, 9a–b; 'The Hundred Rolls for the Parish of St Thomas, Oxford', ed. J. Cooper, Oxoniensia, 37 (1972), 166.
[98] RH ii. 356a–93a; PRO, SC5/Cambs/Tower, 1 (pt 3 unprinted).
[99] The Making of King's Lynn, ed. D. M. Owen (Oxford, 1984), 157; E. and P. Rutledge, 'King's Lynn and Great Yarmouth: Two Thirteenth-Century Surveys', Norfolk Archaeology, 37 (1978), 92–4.
[100] Warwickshire, ed. John, 26–38; RH ii. 353b–5b, 591a–7b.
[101] 'Coventry Hundred Rolls', ed. John, 372, 382.

Cambridgeshire/Huntingdonshire circuit, and Marlow, the only town recorded on the Bedfordshire/Buckinghamshire circuit. It cannot be verified for Warwickshire because the exchequer text containing the returns for Warwick and the borough of Bretford are in book form and the returns for Coventry survive only as a seigneurial copy.[102] Smaller market towns tended to be embedded in the hundredal returns. The twenty-two burgesses on Elena la Zouche's manor at Swavesey (Cambs.) were recorded on the roll for Papworth hundred, while forty-nine shops and their burgage tenants at Linton in the same county appear on the Chilford roll.[103] Burgesses appear among other tenants at Kimbolton and Holme in Huntingdonshire and at Middleton Stoney in Oxfordshire.[104] Why these places should have been included on the hundred rolls when the return for Witney (Oxon.), an equally modest town, exists as a separate roll is unclear, but since the return seems to be an original verdict and does not belong to the main corpus of rolls in the National Archives, perhaps it was missing when the other verdicts were transcribed. The presence of a hamlet on the Bampton roll, appurtenant to the bishop of Winchester's Witney estate, would strengthen this possibility.[105]

Despite the physical separation and non-manorial structure of the returns for larger towns, the hearings they record appear to have been closely integrated into the rest of the inquiry. Making due allowance for their urban features, they follow broadly the same format as manorial returns. The fee farm and any burghal privileges tend to be dealt with first, followed where appropriate by details of lords and their liberties and then lists of tenants.

Although the commission had enjoined cooperation on everyone, irrespective of rank, this was not always achieved. In Willey and Bucklow hundred (Beds.), there was a wholesale refusal to provide information by the tenants of William de Munchesney in Stagsden, the earl of Gloucester in Turvey, and the Hospitallers in Souldrop.[106] Similarly, in Mursley hundred (Bucks.) there is a list of those from Mursley and its hamlet of Salden who would not tell

---

[102] Ibid.; *Warwickshire*, ed. John, 25–38, 54–5.
[103] *RH* ii. 417a–b, 469b.
[104] Ibid. 621b–2a, 652b, 833b.
[105] Burgesses are mentioned under liberties, but do not otherwise appear. PRO, SC11/13; *Oxfordshire Hundred Rolls*, ed. Stone and Hyde, 91–105; *RH* ii. 703b.
[106] *RH* ii. 323a–b; PRO, SC5/Beds/Tower/2, m. 1ᵈ.

the jurors about their holdings. All were tenants of the honour of Berkhamsted and were said to be acting on the instructions of the bailiffs.[107] This looks like seigneurial resistance, either to any obligation to participate in the inquiry or to the questioning of tenants about information which their lords had supplied. This evidence comes from a single circuit in the form of notes appended to membranes dealing with liberties. The absence of similar reports from other circuits does not necessarily imply greater cooperation elsewhere. It may simply reflect the different way in which information has been preserved. It was not only in London that a level of ignorance approaching obstruction was professed by jurors. On the manor of Roger de St Martin at Waterden in Gallow hundred (Norfolk), 'it is not known' (*ignoratur*) appeared frequently enough to warrant marginal headings drawing attention to the problem, but was infrequent in most of the other returns for the hundred.[108] The expression 'they were not able to inquire' also appears fairly frequently throughout the rolls, but probably means that the information was unavailable rather than deliberately withheld.[109] Whatever local resistance may have taken place, there are no signs of the sort of intimidation of jurors or even commissioners found in the 1274–5 returns.[110] Unsurprisingly, the very different nature of the two inquiries produced different reactions. Whereas in 1274–5 corrupt officials were keen to cover their tracks, in 1279 it is more likely that lords, fearing the encroachment of royal jurisdiction or suspecting that the information might be used for fiscal purposes, were sometimes reluctant to have their submissions examined too closely.[111]

There is not much information about the timescale within which the inquiry was carried out, since only a few rolls are dated and the hearings they record belonged to different stages of the proceedings. The earliest precisely dated inquisition is that for Lewknor

---

[107] *RH* ii. 338b; PRO, SC5/Bucks/Tower/1, m. 3[d].

[108] ULL, Fuller Coll., 7/5, m. 8.

[109] *inquirere non possunt, nec possunt inquirere, inquiri non potest*; e.g. *RH* ii. 679a (Toseland hundred, Hunts.), 783a (Lewknor hundred, Oxon.); *Pinchbeck Register*, ed. Hervey, ii. 96 (Thedwastre hundred, Suff.).

[110] Cam, *The Hundred*, 43–4.

[111] Kosminsky thought that, where it is possible to make comparisons with landlords' own records, there was a tendency to under-value rents. E. A. Kosminsky, 'The Hundred Rolls of 1279–80 as a Source for English Agrarian History', *Ec. HR* 3 (1931–2), 33.

hundred (Oxon.) held on 10 April 1279, within a month of the issue of the commission. It was conducted before the commissioners, suggesting that the inquiry there was nearly complete.[112] Suffolk hearings may also have begun promptly if they were held in tandem with the inquiry into those who should have become knights. An original verdict survives from Hartismere hundred, dated 25 April 1279, delivered before two of the three commissioners.[113] The return for Pimhill hundred in Shropshire is dated 24 August 1279 and, in London, hearings are known to have taken place in Queenhithe ward on 5 September 1279 and in Billingsgate ward a few days later on 11 September.[114] Some rolls note only the regnal year 7 or 8 Edward I. Thus proceedings at Shrewsbury, in Leightonstone and Toseland hundreds (Hunts.), Bullingdon hundred and the royal demesne manor at Woodstock (Oxon.) cannot be dated more closely than before 20 November 1279.[115] Hearings at Bampton hundred (Oxon.) can be narrowed down a little further because they record Richard Chastilon as a landholder and he was dead by 12 November.[116] Internal evidence of this sort is likely to permit the closer dating of other hearings in due course. At least four of the inquisitions held before the end of Edward's seventh year were again heard before the commissioners, implying that the work was almost finished. A note at the head of the copy of the two surviving Warwickshire rolls claims that inquests were also held in Warwickshire and Leicestershire in the seventh year. This is supported by the late copies for the Leicestershire hundreds of Guthlaxton and Gartree. However, hearings before the commissioners for Stoneleigh hundred in Warwickshire are dated 14 December 1279 and those for Coventry on 31 January 1280, both in the following regnal year.[117] Some of the Oxfordshire hearings may also have extended into 1280. Although the rolls for the borough and hundred of Banbury (Oxon.) are undated, the jurors were at work after the death of Richard Gravesend, bishop of

---

[112] *RH* ii. 782a.
[113] Oliver de Ingham and John de la More. PRO, E198/1/7.
[114] Shropshire Archives, 6001/28, 53; SC5/London/Tower/1, m. 1; 23, m. 31 (30).
[115] Shropshire Archives, 6001/28, 21; *RH* ii. 607b, 665b, 710a, 839b.
[116] *Oxfordshire Hundred Rolls*, ed. Stone and Hyde, 8 n. 2.
[117] The inquisition for Stoneleigh vill was also held after 20 Nov. 1279, but the exact date is not given. *Warwickshire*, ed. John, 25, 39, 58–9; 'Coventry Hundred Rolls', ed. John, 370; Nichols, *History and Antiquities*, i/1, pp. cx, cxix.

Lincoln, on 18 December 1279.[118] In contrast to Huntingdonshire, it appears that proceedings in Cambridgeshire, part of the same circuit, were also held in Edward's eighth rather than his seventh regnal year. This is stated on the rolls for Wetherley and Chesterton hundreds and can be inferred from internal evidence for Chilford hundred. The date on the opening paragraph of the Northstow roll is damaged, but it is evident from the manuscript, if not the printed edition, that the hearings were held on 7 April 1280.[119] Returns for the borough of Marlow (Bucks.) are also dated 8 Edward I.[120]

It is clear that there was considerable variation in the timing of the different inquiries, but there is no reason why they should all have happened at once. The difficulty of getting all three commissioners together and the competing claims on their time have already been observed. Indeed, it seems likely that in some hundreds business proceeded in the presence of two only.[121] Clearly, hearings could take place very fast when conditions were favourable, just as they had in 1274–5. Then the verdicts of the Shropshire juries had been collected in six days and all the surviving returns were made within five months.[122] However, signs that in some areas the 1279 inquiry was drifting towards its second year must reinforce the likelihood that in many places it simply petered out.

The wording of the commission suggests that a second inquiry was envisaged if the first proved inadequate: commissioners were ordered to carry out their task 'in such a manner that your faithfulness, industry and circumspection may be perpetually commended and so that you may not be confuted by a fresh inquisition or attaint on account of negligence or insufficiency on your part'. The most compelling evidence that some of the work may have been repeated is the unpublished return for Normancross

---

[118] *RH* ii. 705a; PRO, SC5/Oxon/Tower/17, m. 1.

[119] *RH* ii. 402a, 446b, 554b. The heirs of John de Burgh, who died *c.*3 Mar. 1280, were cited as tenants at Little Abington in Chilford hundred. Ibid. 423b; Greenway, 'Newly Discovered Fragment', 75; *Oxfordshire Hundred Rolls*, ed. Stone and Hyde, 8 n. 1.

[120] *RH* ii. 353b.

[121] Pimhill hundred (Salop.), Lewknor hundred (Oxon.) and Gartree hundred (Leics.). Shropshire Archives, 6001/28, 53; *RH* ii. 782a; Nichols, *History and Antiquities*, i/1, p. cxix. See above, Ch. 2.

[122] Prestwich, *Edward I*, 93–4.

hundred on the Huntingdon roll.[123] Parallel to the text in the National Archives, very close in date but significantly different in content, it could be just such an earlier and unsatisfactory effort. If this part of the roll were not associated in some way with the inquiry, it is very difficult to see why else it might have been drawn up. Even though Thorney Abbey enjoyed the right to administer the hundred, the returns make no sense as a seigneurial document. Moreover, the first six membranes, which relate to Leightonstone hundred, are unambiguously part of the 1279 inquiry. The membranes relating to Normancross hundred also contain references to *Quo waranto* which are characteristic of it.[124] Another possibility is that the Huntingdon roll text represents preliminary evidence, subsumed into the final roll, rather than the product of a self-standing inquiry.

Neither of these two possibilities is precluded by its date, which was certainly earlier than that of the roll in the National Archives. Tenants who were alive when the Huntingdon roll returns for Normancross hundred were compiled were referred to in the past tense by the time of the printed roll, although the fact that the new tenant was seldom mentioned by name suggests that the interval between the two records was not great.[125] Edward I is several times mentioned as king at the time when the earlier information was collected, so it must post-date his accession in 1272.[126] It must also have been after 10 June 1278 when the writ for an inquisition *post mortem* for the estates of Baldwin de Drayton in Orton Longueville and Botolphbridge was issued, since John, his son and heir, appears as the tenant.[127] Further support for a date close to the PRO roll comes from the entry for Stilton, where it is claimed that Richard earl of Gloucester had withdrawn his suit from the county and hundred courts twenty or more years previously. An undated entry for the same vill associated with Kirkby's Quest, probably drawn up *c*.10 September 1285 when inquiry was made in neighbouring Leightonstone hundred, asserted that the suit had been withdrawn twenty-seven years ago or more. This

[123] HR, mm. 7–16; Raban, 'Fresh Light', 109–16.
[124] HR, mm. 1–6.
[125] e.g. in the entry for Glatton. HR m. 13; *RH* ii. 650a–1a; Raban, 'Fresh Light', 109–10.
[126] HR, mm. 16–17 in the entries for Woodston and Whittlesey Mere.
[127] *Cal. IPM* ii. no. 260; PRO, C133/19/3; HR, m. 7.

implies that the earlier information was put forward in the autumn of 1278.[128] Of course, this sort of statement should not be taken too literally. Nevertheless, when combined with the rest of the evidence, returns in the Normancross section of the Huntingdon roll seem to belong to a date no earlier than mid-1278 and before the hearings of the PRO roll, which took place sometime between the March commission and the end of the regnal year in November 1279.[129]

Since the PRO roll is an edited, possibly finished text, while the Huntingdon roll text is closer to the proceedings it records, the argument that both belonged to the same inquiry might seem attractive, especially as there are instances where the two sets of returns are virtually the same. Free tenants are often recorded in the same order.[130] There is also a striking identity in the two rolls between the accounts for the descent of the Vescy manor in Chesterton. The PRO return reads:

Lord William de Vescy holds a manor in the vill of Chesterton which was once held in chief of the lord king in chief [*sic*], which manor the same Lord William holds of Lady Agnes de Vescy, his mother and the said Angnes [*sic*] had it in exchange from Lord Gilbert de Clare, earl of Gloucester. And the same Lord Gilbert had it by gift of Nigel de Amoundevile. And the same Nigel had it by gift of Lord Giles de Merk. And the same Giles held it from the king in chief for half a knight's fee. And it belongs to the fee of Boulogne.[131]

While according to the Huntingdon roll:

Lord William de Wescy holds a manor in the vill of Chesterton which was once held in chief of the lord king. Which manor the same Lord William holds of Lady Agnes de Wescy, his mother. And the said Angnes [*sic*] had it in exchange from Lord Gilbert de Clare, earl of Gloucester. And the same Lord Gilbert had it by gift of Nigel de Amoundevile. And the same Nigel had it by gift of Lord Giles de Merk. And the same Giles held it in chief from the lord king. And it belongs to the fee of Boulogne.[132]

---

[128] HR, m. 13; PRO, SC5/Hunts/6, m. 2; Raban, 'Fresh Light', 110.

[129] Although the damaged head of the PRO roll for Normancross means that it cannot be dated, it is likely that the inquisitions were held at the same time as those for the other hundreds in the county. *RH* ii. 607b, 633b, 665b.

[130] e.g. at Orton Waterville. HR, m. 8; *RH* ii. 637a–b. For the status of the PRO text, see below, Ch. 4.

[131] *RH* ii. 654a–b.

[132] HR, m. 9.

Even the precise spelling of Agnes de Vescy's name is replicated in both documents. However, neither the order of free tenants nor that of manorial descents is consistently the same throughout both sets of returns. This is illustrated by the descent of the abbot of Ramsey's manor of Elton which, on the Huntingdon roll, differs considerably from that of the printed roll which, as we saw earlier, had been drawn from a text found in the abbey cartulary.[133] The Huntingdon roll text reads:

They say that the abbot of Ramsey holds the manor of Elton in free, pure and perpetual alms in chief of the lord king, whence a certain ancient king called Cnut gave the said manor to a certain Dane whose name is unknown, and at the same time there was a certain bishop of Dorchester called Aylryth who bought the said manor from the said Dane and endowed and enfeoffed abbot Aylsi of Ramsey and the convent of that place with that manor in free, pure and perpetual alms. And thus it was held in chief from king to king and it is not known by what warrant.[134]

More seriously, the nature of the information on the printed roll differs fundamentally from that of the Huntingdon roll text. Once again an entry for Caldecote provides a convenient example for the purpose of comparison. Here is the Huntingdon roll text:

Caldecote [marginated]
Lord William de Brws hold the manor of Caldecote from Lord Robert de Brus for a third part of a knight's fee. And it belongs to the honour of Huntingdon. And the messuage of that manor including the gardens and other revenues is worth 13s. 4d. p.a. Item he has there one and a half carucates of land worth £3. 15s. p.a. Item he has two acres of meadow worth 8s. p.a. Item he has a certain mill worth 20s. p.a.
villeins [marginated]
Item he has fifteen villeins there, who between them hold ten and a half virgates of land rendering annually in common for all services £10. 10s.
cottars [marginated]
Item he has five cottars who hold cottages rendering annually in common 12s. 6d. Item Lord William de Brws is patron of the church of Caldecote. And he has the right as of the honour of Huntingdon.
Free tenants [marginated]
Item Iuo Cartarius holds one virgate of land for life rendering to the said Lord William 10s p.a. Item Alicia Cosin, Thomas Faber, and Marjeria

---

[133] *RH* ii. 656a; *Cart Rames*, i. 490. See above, p. 77.
[134] HR, m. 10.

daughter of Nicholas hold one virgate of land by charter rendering one pound of pepper p.a. Item John Faber holds a toft and croft rendering 6d. p.a. And the marsh for the whole vill, turbaries, and pasture, is worth 30s. p.a.
Sum total £18. 19s. 4d.[135]

The Huntingdon roll returns are far briefer than the text of the PRO roll (above, pp. 39–40) and consist almost entirely of cash valuations. The different categories of tenant are also recorded in a different order. On the Huntingdon roll, villeins and cottars are dealt with before free tenants, while on the PRO roll the free tenants come first. Although the number of villeins at Caldecote is the same in both texts, the rent they pay is considerably higher on the PRO roll. The number of cottars and their rent are also greater. Neither the rector, his tenants, nor the two frankalmoin tenants are mentioned on the Huntingdon roll. Moreover, the brevity of the entry for the free tenants conceals the fact that Thomas Faber and Margery daughter of Nicholas were subtenants of Alice Cosin. Caldecote is not untypical in these discrepancies. Subtenants who, according to the PRO roll, formed a sizeable proportion of the community on the Thorney Abbey manors of Yaxley and Woodston are often omitted altogether or else their relationship with others is distorted, as happened at Caldecote.[136] Although parish priests were recorded in other vills, their tenants were usually omitted.[137] Detailed descriptions of labour services which feature on many of the larger manors in the PRO roll, are one of the most notable omissions from the Huntingdon roll. With the latter's emphasis on valuation, they were superfluous. The PRO roll thus contains so much information that is absent from the Huntingdon roll and what they have in common is for the most part expressed so differently that, although it is chronologically possible that the latter was one of the sources for the final return, on balance it seems more likely that they were part of two separate, albeit linked, investigations.

The contents of some of the hundred rolls for other counties have more in common with the Huntingdon roll returns for

---

[135] HR, m. 13.
[136] *RH* ii. 640a–4a; HR, mm. 16–17.
[137] Not invariably however. At Chesterton, it is the Huntingdon roll return rather than the PRO roll which records the rector's tenants. *RH* ii. 656a; HR, m. 9.

Normancross than those on the PRO roll, strengthening the case
for some sort of relationship between the Huntingdon roll and the
inquiry, even if its exact nature is unclear. The emphasis on financial information finds an echo in other counties, particularly
Oxfordshire. The valuations in Oxford itself have already been
noted. Nor was it just a question of recording rents. In all but one
ward and in the suburban hundred belonging to Hugh de Plessis,
figures were often checked and annotations made: 'and the aforesaid land is hardly worth the said rent' or 'and it is not worth
more'. Revised valuations were also included in the return for the
borough and liberty of Shrewsbury—'and it is now worth . . . .'.[138]
The roll for Chadlington hundred (Oxon.) has a summary valuation at the end of each section of the manorial surveys, although in
other respects its contents are similar to rolls without valuations.[139] Also in Oxfordshire, in the returns for Woodstock and the
vill of Banbury annual rents are totalled at the end of the roll, while
at Witney they are noted on the dorse, possibly in a different
hand.[140] A similar valuation for assized rents and for toll income
appears at the beginning of the return for Marlow (Bucks.).[141] The
rolls for the Bedfordshire/Buckinghamshire circuit, Toseland
hundred in Huntingdonshire, the East Anglian and Warwickshire/
Leicestershire circuits and most of Oxfordshire hundreds also
follow the same order as the Normancross returns on the
Huntingdon roll in recording villeins before free tenants.

What is one to make of these varied returns? Those which have
summary valuations bear a close resemblance to extents drawn up
for inquisitions *post mortem*. The comments on valuations in
Shrewsbury and some of the Oxford rolls might have tax implications. Several of the membranes in the Gallow hundred roll lay
great stress on scutage payments, both in the findings themselves
and the marginal notation.[142] They were also carefully recorded in

---

[138] See above, p. 79. *RH* ii. 788b–96b, 798a–803a, 805b–11b; 'Hundred Rolls',
ed. Cooper, 168–73; PRO, SC5/Oxon/Tower/8, 9a, 9c, 18; SC5/Oxon/Tower/11,
m. 2; Shropshire Archives, 6001/28, 21–48, partly printed in 'A Late-Thirteenth
Century Rental of Tenements in Shrewsbury', ed. U. Rees, *Transactions of the
Shropshire Archaeological and Historical Society*, 66 (1989), 82–4.
[139] *RH* ii. 726a–47b; PRO, SC5/Oxon/Tower/5.
[140] PRO, SC5/Oxon/Tower/15; Oxon/Tower/17, m.2; SC11/13, m. 3^d; *RH* ii.
842a; *Oxfordshire Hundred Rolls*, ed. Stone and Hyde, 98, 105.
[141] *RH* ii. 353b.
[142] ULL, Fuller Coll., 7/5, mm. 1–2, 12–13.

some, but not all, of the returns for hundreds such as Ploughley (Oxon.) and Northstow (Cambs.).[143] The detailed manorial descent found at Elton on the Huntingdon roll or evidence provided for the Ramsey estate at Graveley, in Cambridgeshire, appears to come straight from the abbey's archives.[144]

The uneven appearance of valuations may be explained by unrecorded articles similar to that found in the Shrewsbury return.[145] More generally, it is possible that jurors faced with the demands of the inquiry, but with very little guidance as to how to proceed, either used their initiative and adopted the sort of format most familiar to them or simply received and adapted material which was already to hand. If this were the case, then it might explain why initial returns were sometimes found wanting and a second set of hearings undertaken. A second bite at the cherry is the more credible when one recalls the sort of non-cooperation experienced by jurors in Bedfordshire and Buckinghamshire.[146]

On balance, the Normancross returns on the Huntingdon roll probably represent the findings of an earlier inquiry which was superseded by the much fuller evidence embodied in the later, PRO roll. Elsewhere earlier findings of this sort may have been used alongside material collected later. This would explain the rather hybrid rolls for the Cambridgeshire hundreds of Chesterton and Northstow, where many of the valuations of villein labour services are given in the manner of the Huntingdon roll return for Normancross hundred, even though the order in which tenants are described follows that of the later PRO roll.[147] Not all early returns were summary, however. The earliest known roll, that for Lewknor hundred (Oxon.), drawn up shortly after the start of the inquiry, has the longer type of labour service entry.[148] Conversely, the relatively late set of returns for Wetherley hundred (Cambs.), compiled after 20 November 1279, has the briefer valuations.[149] Perhaps the answer lies in the presence of the commissioners. The Lewknor roll is unique in referring to them in the first person; the commissioners speak of 'our court'. They may have imposed their more informed notion of what was required on the proceedings. Yet, this

[143] *RH* ii. 446b–66b, 822a–39b.
[144] *RH* ii. 472a–b.
[145] Shropshire Archives, 6001/28, 51.
[146] See above, pp. 81–2.
[147] *RH* ii. 407a–13a, 448b–66b.
[148] *RH* ii. 782a–8b.
[149] *RH* ii. 554b–67a.

cannot be the complete answer, since they were present at the Bampton inquisition (Oxon.), where valuations were also employed.[150] Perhaps they were forced to accept that in some hundreds the fragmentation of holdings and extensive commutation of labour services meant that valuations were the only practical way to describe tenant obligations or maybe they felt that they had no time for further investigation.

With regard to the ordering of peasant holdings, as opposed to the content of the entries, it is worth noting that, whereas the commission required information in the order of villeins, cottars, and free tenants, the articles, as recorded on the Cambridgeshire rolls, placed free tenants ahead of villeins and cottars.[151] The ordering of the Huntingdon roll return for Normancross hundred suggests that jurors may have begun work from the commission rather than the articles. If this was the case, the large number of other rolls which share the same ordering may imply that the commissioners were sometimes content to accept tenurial information in whatever order it was presented, providing that it contained sufficient detail.

The surviving rolls are such a complex assortment that a full explanation of how they came to be drawn up based largely on deductions from their contents can never be adequate. Collecting the information required by the articles was only the first stage in a Herculean task. Much of the detail, painstakingly ascertained and written down in the verdicts of the juries, was later removed by editors. The picture one forms of the inquiry can thus vary considerably from circuit to circuit due to the subsequent shaping of its findings. Understanding the precise nature of the surviving manuscripts and where they fitted into the processing of the vast quantity of information which had been gathered is therefore another facet of understanding the inquiry itself and will be the subject of the following chapter.

[150] *RH* ii. 688a–705a.
[151] See below, Appendix 2 and Appendix 3A, art. 7.

4

Ordering the Information

Rolls survive in one form or another, in whole or in part, for some fifty-six hundreds together with thirteen towns and suburbs.[1] Even a cursory examination reveals that they comprise different stages in the process of collecting information and then ordering it. This offers both a challenge and an opportunity to historians. The availability of texts from every stage in the inquiry provides a much better insight into how it was carried out than if it had been brought to completion and all the earlier drafts destroyed. Disentangling the relationship between them is however a formidable task, which no doubt explains why it has taken so long for anyone to undertake a study of the rolls in their entirety in spite of their obvious importance as a source.

Within the parameters of the commission and articles of inquiry, the commissioners were left with considerable freedom to direct proceedings as they thought fit. As with Domesday Book, therefore, the phrasing and content of the returns differed somewhat from one circuit to another. For the most part, these circuit identities, while identifiable, are not particularly strong. There are certain idiosyncrasies of terminology: it was on the Warwickshire and Leicestershire circuit for example that commissioners were known as inquisitors, whereas elsewhere they were more commonly described as 'justices of the lord king'.[2] The returns

---

[1] The hundred of Hugh de Plessis, a suburb of Oxford, has been counted among the urban rolls, but Kenilworth in Warwickshire, which may have been a borough although this is not evident from the hundred rolls, has been omitted. M. W. Beresford and H. P. R. Finberg, *English Medieval Boroughs: A Handlist* (Newton Abbot, 1973), 174. A number of communities in the hundred rolls themselves record burgesses or have other urban features. See above, Ch. 3 and below, Ch. 5.

[2] *The Warwickshire Hundred Rolls of 1279–80*, ed. T. John (Oxford, 1992), 39, 58; 'The Coventry Hundred Rolls', ed. T. John in P. R. Coss (ed.), *The Early Records of Medieval Coventry* (London, 1986), 370; J. Nichols, *The History and Antiquities of the County of Leicester* (Wakefield, 1971), i/1, pp. cx, cxix.

from the Bedfordshire/Buckinghamshire circuit were exceptionally concise. These rolls also paid unusual attention to mortmain tenure and, with the exception of Stodden hundred, for which only one membrane survives, liberties were always dealt with on a separate membrane.[3] Although a similar policy regarding all non-manorial questions was also adopted for some of the Cambridgeshire and Huntingdonshire rolls, the way in which information was recorded differed between the two circuits. In Bedfordshire and Buckinghamshire, bare details were recorded vill by vill, usually under the heading of liberties. In Cambridgeshire and Huntingdonshire, by contrast, the articles were spelt out, albeit often in an abbreviated form, and then the answers were given. This practice was observed whether the answers appeared on a separate membrane or alongside the manorial information for each vill. Since some of the rolls on this circuit belong to the final stage in the proceedings, the retention of the questions must have been a matter of choice and not merely a feature of unedited returns.

The shire often seems as important a unit as the circuit. In Huntingdonshire, as in Warwickshire and Leicestershire, commissioners were referred to as 'inquisitors', whereas the Cambridgeshire rolls use the more common 'justices of the lord king'.[4] It is only in Bedfordshire that we find the phrase 'with their smallholder tenants' (*cum suis tenentibus de parvis tenuris*) alongside free tenant entries, while marginal headings indicating those who held land at farm or had chirograph deeds were peculiar to Buckinghamshire.[5] More striking, although not perhaps surprising, is the uneven pace at which the work was carried out between counties. The finished appearance of all but one of the Huntingdonshire rolls contrasts sharply with the partially processed state of some of those for Cambridgeshire.[6] Similarly, while the surviving Oxfordshire rolls are late or finished texts, there is nothing to show that the inquiry had even begun in Berkshire, although this might simply be an accident of survival. On these circuits, it appears likely that the work was undertaken

[3] S. Raban, 'The Church in the 1279 Hundred Rolls', in M. J. Franklin and C. Harper-Bill (eds.), *Medieval Ecclesiastical Studies in Honour of Dorothy M. Owen* (Woodbridge, 1995), 187 and below, Chs. 5 and 6.

[4] *RH* ii. 402a, 542b, 554b, 607b, 665b.

[5] e.g. *RH* ii. 328a, 332a, 336a, 346a.

[6] See below, pp. 101–6 and Ch. 6.

on a county-by-county basis rather than proceeding simultaneously throughout the circuit. This may not have been invariable however. On the Bedfordshire/Buckinghamshire circuit, the hundreds with surviving rolls are clustered in the north-west of both counties in relatively close proximity, possibly indicating concerted action overriding the county boundary.

Sometimes no consistency is apparent even at county level. Whereas villeins are always given ahead of free tenants in Bedfordshire and Buckinghamshire and in what survives from the East Anglian and Warwickshire/Leicestershire circuits, practice differed from hundred to hundred on the Cambridgeshire/Huntingdonshire circuit and in Oxfordshire. As we have seen, cash totals for rents and valuations appear in some rolls only, particularly in Oxfordshire hundred rolls and one of the texts for Normancross hundred in Huntingdonshire.[7] Similarly, summary totals of land are a unique feature of some vills on the roll for Whittlesford (Cambs.), while alienations were valued solely in Leightonstone hundred (Hunts.).[8] Only the PRO text of the Normancross roll records in the opening description of the demesne for each vill, how many acres there were to the virgate and how many virgates to the hide, although there are a good many references to the size of the virgate scattered among details of tenancies on other rolls belonging to the circuit.[9]

The one circuit with a really distinctive and systematic style of its own was that for East Anglia. It may be relevant that one of its commissioners, Richard Creeping, was an experienced investigator who had already served in the 1274–5 inquiry.[10] His awareness of the problems encountered in the earlier undertaking may have encouraged him to assert a tight control over the inquiry from an early stage. Unlike other returns, those for this circuit do not spell out the holdings of villeins and cottars in detail. Typically an entry reads 'x villeins hold x messuages and x acres of land', with no details of rent obligations, even in the form of summary valuations. By contrast, free tenants and their tenants, the nature of their holdings and rents, appear to be meticulously recorded. Given the

---

[7] See above, Ch.3.

[8] *RH* ii. 571a, 575b, 578a–80a, 584b–5b, 610b, 614a–b.

[9] *RH* ii. 635a–65b. Such references are listed in J. Kanzaka, 'Villein Rents in Thirteenth-Century England', 55 (2002), 595 n. 13.

[10] See above, p. 62 n. 7.

complexity of tenure in this region, the skill with which this has been reduced to order is impressive, even if there were omissions in the interest of clarity.[11] The format of the returns is remarkably uniform, with much use of standard terminology. Lords are stated to be 'chief lords of the vill', subtenants are heralded by 'his tenants recorded below' and scutage payments are often noted with more or less abbreviated versions of the standard phrase 'x when scutage is assessed at twenty shillings, if more, more, and if less, less'. Where original returns exist, the rolls are also fairly uniform in layout. Those for Gallow hundred and the vill of Hevingham all have marginal headings for different categories of tenant. Such marginalia have been largely edited out of the Suffolk returns preserved in the Bury St Edmunds registers and the various texts for Holkham, but all the returns for this circuit dealt with villeins and cottars ahead of free tenants. Information about liberties, which was usually recorded directly after the size of the manor, often included the typically East Anglian rights of 'bull and boar, fold rights and stray animals'.[12] It is the very strength of the circuit style which has enabled scholars to identify many of these texts as part of the 1279 inquiry.[13]

Of course, some of the differences between and within circuits may be more apparent than real. The varying degree of editing to which the information was subjected makes it hard to be sure how far one is making valid comparisons. Greater individuality is to be expected in jurors' verdicts than in fully edited returns. While the commissioners were responsible for the inquiry as a whole, many of the detailed decisions as to layout and terminology must have fallen to lesser officials and scribes. Moreover, where they drew on seigneurial documents, they must often have echoed the usage of their various exemplars. Cicely Howell cites some of the different

---

[11] See below, Ch. 5.

[12] ULL, Fuller Coll., 7/5; B. M. S. Campbell, 'The Complexity of Manorial Structure in Medieval Norfolk', *Norfolk Archaeology*, 39/3 (1986), 256–61; Norfolk Rec. Off., NRS 14761; *Lordship and Landscape in Norfolk 1250–1350*, ed. W. Hassall and J. Beauroy (Oxford, 1993), 215–30, no. 253; CUL, Ee, iii, 60, fos. 234ʳ–319ᵛ, printed in *The Pinchbeck Register*, ed. F. Hervey (Brighton, 1925), ii. 30–282; BL, Harl. MS 743, fos. 149–257ᵛ, printed in E. Powell, *A Suffolk Hundred in the Year 1283* (Cambridge, 1910), 5–65; CUL, Add MS 3395.

[13] Campbell, 'Complexity', 233; D. E. Greenway, 'A Newly Discovered Fragment of the Hundred Rolls of 1279–80', *Journal of the Society of Archivists*, 7 (1982), 76–7. See below, Ch. 6.

terms used to describe villeins and cottars in East Cambridgeshire in illustration of this.[14] Similarly, in the Oxfordshire rolls, peasants were recorded under more than a dozen different labels, some reflecting the size of their holdings, some the terms on which they held them and the remainder, their legal status. The superlative skill of the editor of Exchequer Domesday has cast a long shadow over his successors, leading to an unconscious expectation of an equally systematic rendering of later findings. Already an amazing achievement at the end of the eleventh century, the intricate web of tenures two centuries later meant that such ruthless consistency was scarcely a realistic option. One should not expect the multitude of scribes recording local verdicts on different circuits to conform to a pattern in any but the broadest sense. Even on the East Anglian circuit, it is noticeable that on the Gallow roll there is a good deal of variation in the features singled out for marginal annotation in the different vills. Scutage obligations loomed large in the mind of the scribe at Burnham Thorpe, while at Waterden it was the ignorance of the jurors.[15]

Starting in the 1960s, historians began to disentangle the different stages in processing the information which the surviving rolls represent. Eric Stone, in his introduction to the edition of the Bampton roll (Oxon.), first drew attention to the fact that, while Bampton hundred had a finished roll, other rolls belonged to an earlier stage in the proceedings. The two stages that he envisaged were further elaborated into a threefold process by Trevor John. He suggested that the first stage involved the collection of information by local jurors. This was then reduced to some sort of order before a final stage, in which fully edited texts were drawn up having been pruned of all extraneous matter. In this analysis the Bampton roll was assigned to the penultimate stage.[16] Even this fails to do justice to the variety and inconsistency of the ways in which the original returns were assembled and subsequently treated. In practice, the boundaries between the three stages were often blurred. Editors might work on the actual verdicts without first making fair copies. Likewise, what appeared to be finished

---

[14] C. Howell, *Land, Family and Inheritance in Transition: Kibworth Harcourt 1280–1700* (Cambridge, 1983), 27.

[15] ULL, Fuller Coll., 7/5, mm. 1–2, 8.

[16] *Oxfordshire Hundred Rolls of 1279*, ed. E. Stone and P. Hyde (Oxford, 1968), 8–9; *Warwickshire*, ed. John, 5–7.

texts could still be the subject of revision. What passed for a finished roll on one circuit, might seem more analogous to a partially edited roll on another. Completed rolls may also have existed in more than one copy. It was the norm for multiple copies of plea rolls to be drawn up for the keeper of rolls and writs and individual justices. There is limited evidence that the same practice could have obtained for the hundred roll commissioners, although only one copy was returned to official custody.[17]

The earliest stage of the inquiry saw the recording of the jurors' verdicts for each vill, often succeeded by a neater fair copy, inscribed on one or more membranes, according to need. Some returns were entered on both sides of the parchment, others on one side only. There was little standardization either of size or layout, although even first drafts were sometimes neatly written with marginal headings. These verdicts, together with an occasional seigneurial return, were then collected together for the whole hundred. At this point, they were sewn together, usually at the head, although in some hundreds chancery style was preferred. In the form in which we now have them, many of the resultant rolls are incomplete, but there is little to indicate whether this is because missing returns never existed, were never handed in, or were lost during the intervening centuries.

In order to establish what is missing, the first step is to know what should be present and this is not always easy. The composition of many hundreds altered during the nineteenth century. Sometimes boundaries were simply realigned, but changes could also be more radical, involving the assignment of detached portions to the hundreds in which they lay geographically. Good examples of these anomalous portions, which had often arisen because they belonged to great estates based outside the hundred, can be found in the Oxfordshire hundreds belonging to the bishop of Lincoln and the earl of Cornwall.[18] In cases like these, later boundaries offer no clue as to why returns crop up in a hundred some distance away from the estate's location.

The parishes of Everton and Thurning illustrate how complicated it can be to assess whether or not a return exists, even when

---

[17] The one exception is a single membrane for Girton in Northstow hundred (Cambs.) which is to be found in the National Archives in addition to the return on the hundred roll itself. SC5/8/5/5, m. 6.

[18] See below, Ch. 6.

the later change was a simple matter of reuniting what had been divided by county boundaries. Everton lay partly in Biggleswade hundred in Bedfordshire and partly in Toseland hundred in Huntingdonshire, while in Thurning the boundary between Northamptonshire and Huntingdonshire ran down the main street, leaving part of the parish in Leightonstone hundred and part in Polebrook hundred.[19] In theory part of each parish should have figured in the surviving Huntingdonshire rolls, and up to a point this is true. However, the entry for Everton is confined to a brief mention of the Earl Marshall's view of frankpledge among the non-manorial responses on the Toseland roll and there is no mention of the abbot of Crowland's manor at Thurning on the Leightonstone roll, although it had been recorded under Huntingdonshire in Domesday Book.[20] A good deal of local knowledge is often required to evaluate the comprehensiveness of the surviving returns with any confidence.

Internal evidence occasionally permits loss of returns to be proved, even if it does not explain why they have disappeared. In Lamua hundred (Bucks.) and Toseland hundred (Hunts.), Everton was not the only settlement to be mentioned under liberties or broader non-manorial issues without any corresponding entry among the returns for the vills.[21] Assuming that this information was probably extracted from the verdicts for each vill and not collected on a separate occasion, the presumption must be that returns once existed for these vills. The recovery of scattered fragments elsewhere among the national archives shows how easily membranes, especially damaged ones, could become detached over the course of time and are only slowly being reassembled.

Although the absence of returns can rarely be explained, some probably reflect genuine contemporary gaps in the record. About these, one might occasionally make an educated guess. The banlieu of the abbot of Ramsey receives only a brief mention on the Hurstingstone roll (Hunts.), with the implication that it had been withdrawn from the hundred at an unknown date. Its manors could be missing from the roll because the abbey claimed exemp-

---

[19] *VCH, Beds.*, ii. 226; *VCH, Northants.*, iii. 109.
[20] *RH* ii. 628b–29a, 666b; *Domesday Book* ed. J. Morris *et al.* (Chichester, 1975), *Huntingdonshire*, 5: 2.
[21] See below, Ch. 6.

tion from the survey.[22] A similar claim by the bishop of Ely on behalf of his soke might also lie behind the absence of returns from the Isle of Ely, for which there is only a single membrane representing lay estates at Witcham.[23] Unwillingness on the part of the crown to accept this situation could explain the commission addressed to Geoffrey de Sandiacre, one of the 1279 commissioners, and Andrew of Ely, the bishop's steward, in January 1280, ordering them to make inquiry into the knights' fees and feodalities in the Isle.[24] Although precedent may have been on the side of the monks, since none of the precincts of the great fenland abbeys had been included in Domesday Book, it would have been wholly in character for the king to challenge their right. We know too that lack of cooperation on the part of those giving evidence, perhaps for similar reasons, accounts for some of the missing evidence in Bedfordshire and Buckinghamshire.[25] Sheer undocumented dilatoriness on the part of those charged with completing and forwarding the verdicts may well lie behind other missing returns.

Distinguishing original verdicts from fair copies made during the earlier stages of editing is not easy, but certain criteria for assigning them to one stage or the other can be suggested. Where returns are very varied in size and shape, as in some of the London verdicts, one can be confident that one is dealing with originals.[26] A variety of hands may indicate originals rather than copies, but not invariably, since apparently finished rolls such as that for Ploughley hundred (Oxon.) are sometimes written in more than one hand.[27] Single membranes with no sign of stitching are probably originals, especially where, as in the case of the roll for Hevingham (Norfolk), the spacing is uneven and there are a number of deletions.[28] Conversely, where entries run from one vill to another on the same membrane, as on the Wetherley roll (Cambs.), this is prima-facie evidence for a scribal copy from the verdicts before

---

[22] *RH* ii. 605a. The banlieu consisted of Bury, parts of Great Raveley and Wistow, Upwood, and Ramsey itself. *VCH, Hunts.*, ii. 188.

[23] *RH* ii. 568a–9b.

[24] *Cal. Pat.* 1272–81, 407. For the career of Andrew of Ely, see *The Earliest English Law Reports*, ed. P. A. Brand, 2 vols. (Selden Society; London, 1996), ii, pp. xxxiv–xxxv.

[25] See above, Ch. 3.

[26] PRO, SC5/London/Tower/1–26. See below, Ch. 6.

[27] PRO, SC5/Oxon/Tower/13.

[28] Campbell, 'Complexity', 234–6; Norfolk Rec. Off., NRS, 14761 29 D4.

him.[29] Even here the line is not clear cut, however. The Normancross portion of the Huntingdon roll appears to be a fair copy which nevertheless incorporates the conspicuously original return relating to the demesne at Elton among its membranes.[30] Another apparently useful criterion has to be rejected. Although it might seem that where jurors' verdicts were cast in the first person plural, returns could reasonably be deemed to be originals, this is not always the case. Some scribes preferred to record verdicts more formally in the third person, while later copyists quite often retained the first person of their exemplar or used a mixture of the two. Thus, while 'we do not know' (*nescimus*) occurs frequently on some of liberties' membranes of the finished Buckinghamshire rolls, some of the returns for Gallow hundred (Norfolk), belonging to an earlier stage of the inquiry, report that 'it is not known' (*ingnoratur*).[31] On the Bampton roll (Oxon.), both 'they do not know' and 'we do not know' linger like archaeological remains in returns which, apart from the list of names at the head of the roll and a couple of references to hallmoots, have little to show that jurors or articles played any part in the inquiry.[32]

The Gallow hundred roll is a good example of original returns or fair copies which were then worked on at the editing stage. They are written in several hands, one of which is clear but distinctively ornate.[33] Each vill begins on a separate membrane and covers two or three membranes. The roll is therefore likely to be an assemblage of early returns. In this composite form, it was then revised by a single scribe. Details of rents and tenements were erased and corrected figures substituted as at m. 6. Several membranes end with details of advowsons entered in a darker ink, although elsewhere this information was entered at the appropriate point in the original hand. The most extensive of these additions concerns the three churches at Burnham Thorpe. The first two are recorded in the same hand as the rest of the membrane but the third, inscribed in darker ink, adds 'The prior of Peterstone holds a quarter part of

[29] PRO, SC5/Cambs/Tower/12.
[30] HR, m. 10; Raban, 'Fresh Light', 112.
[31] *RH* ii. 343b, 350b, 353b; ULL, Fuller Coll., 7/5, mm. 5–6, 8.
[32] e.g. *RH* ii. 688a, 689b. For the hallmoots, ibid., 690b, 691a.
[33] ULL, Fuller Coll., 7/5, mm. 10–13. Diana Greenway identifies at least five different hands. Greenway, 'Newly Discovered Fragment', 76.

the advowson of the church of Saint Andrew and the prior of Walsingham three parts, through whom and by what means is unknown'.[34] That additional material was sought at this stage of the proceedings can be seen from the Hevingham return. When it was first drawn up, the jurors did not know the nature of the prior of Broomholm's tenure, but the entry to that effect was later cancelled and 'the barony of Ry' inserted in its place.[35]

These Norfolk returns were working documents, intermediate between the Norfolk hearings and finished rolls which are now lost, if indeed they were ever drawn up. That they remained in the locality, rather than being returned to the exchequer, thus makes sense. Illuminating as they are about the earlier stages of the inquiry, however, it is the returns for the Huntingdonshire/Cambridgeshire circuit which provide the best insight into the way in which the findings were handled. This circuit furnishes us with the largest collection of material in absolute terms (332 out of the 556 pages of the Record Commission edition) as well as the largest number of unpublished rolls and fragments.[36] It represents every stage in the inquiry, from original verdicts to fair, final copies. It is, moreover, the only circuit where more than one contemporary text for a hundred or vill has survived. These are the returns for Leightonstone and Nomancross hundreds on the Huntingdon roll and the single membrane for Girton in Northstow hundred in Cambridgeshire.[37] There is also a later copy of the Bourn verdict in Longstow hundred, again in Cambridgeshire.[38]

Both Stone and John chose the Northstow hundred roll from this circuit to exemplify an earlier stage in the processing of verdicts.[39] The membranes, of varying width, are neatly written in several hands without much correction, and each vill begins on a new membrane. They look like fair copies of original verdicts, stitched together at the head and then subjected to checking and

---

[34] 'Prior de Peterston tenet quartam partem advocationis ecclesie sancti Andree et prior de Walsingham tres partes per quem vel quomodo nescitur', with a marginal note 'Advocatio eccleise nescitur per quos', ULL, Fuller Coll., 7/5, m. 2.

[35] Norfolk Rec. Off., NRS, 14761 29 D4; Campbell, 'Complexity', 235, 259.

[36] See below, Appendix 1.

[37] HR; PRO, SC5/8/5/5, m. 6.

[38] Christ's College, Cambridge. I am grateful to Stephen and David Baxter for sharing their discovery of the Bourn copy with me.

[39] *Oxfordshire Hundred Rolls*, ed. Stone and Hyde, 8–9; *Warwickshire*, ed. John, 5.

editing.[40] Several membranes are annotated *exam'* at the foot. This is expanded at the end of the first part of m. 6 to 'examined, except it is not recorded to which person or persons the rent ought to be paid'.[41] On m. 8, a sentence in a different hand about frankpledge and assise of bread and ale is cancelled with an interlined note 'vacated because it is elsewhere'. This entry, which is omitted from the Record Commission edition, is one of several annotations in other hands on this membrane.[42] As already noted, on several membranes symbols direct attention chiefly to entries about suit of court, frankpledge, and other liberties.[43]

The return for Ramsey Abbey's manor at Girton, which survives as a single membrane in the National Archives, must belong to the inquiry in some way, but it is not clear how it fits in. It is more concise than the text of the Northstow roll itself, so cannot be the original verdict. The most striking difference is the omission of all but one of the articles found on the Northstow roll. The information is also presented in a different order. Liberties are dealt with immediately after the demesne entry and the rector's fee appears among the free tenants rather than standing alone after the crofters. Thus far, the membrane could be an edited version of the fair copy on the roll, especially as the latter has marginal symbols beside the reordered entries. Such a simple explanation will not suffice, however, because each text contains material that is missing from the other. The roll does not mention that the rector's fee is held in free alms of the abbey by ancient enfeoffment, nor that a villein virgate comprises 30 acres. There are also some factual discrepancies. According to the roll, the rector held 28 acres in demesne and had a subtenant called Peter Capellanus, whereas according to the membrane, his demesne comprised 29 acres and one rod and his tenant was called Peter Swetlove. Only the membrane, in a separate entry at the end, noted that 'all the aforementioned villeins hold at

---

[40] PRO, SC5/Cambs/Tower/6. As Stone observed, the membranes are not now in their original order. *Oxfordshire Hundred Rolls*, ed. Stone and Hyde, 8 n. 5.

[41] *Exam' preterquam non nominatur in rotulo isto cui vel quibus redditus debet reddi.*

[42] *Et est visum franci plegii et capit emendacionem panis et cervisie sed nesciunt quo waranto.* [Interlined] *vacat quare alibi.* A second insertion on the same membrane relating to scutage owed to Gilbert Peche, with a further addition in another hand *sed nesciunt quo waranto*, is included in the Rec. Comm. edn. *RH* ii. 457a.

[43] See above, Ch. 3.

the lord's will with their works'.[44] This suggests an alternative possibility whereby the membrane was submitted by the abbey and the roll records the variants offered by the jurors. None of these explanations quite fit all the evidence however.

Although the roll for Northstow hundred has been chosen to illustrate the initial stages of editing, others could have served equally well. The twenty-two-membrane roll for nearby Longstow hundred has similar characteristics, apart from the fact that its membranes have been sewn together end to end.[45] Written in a variety of hands, it also seems to comprise a fair copy of the original verdicts.[46] There are a number of scribal additions and interlineations, not all of which are printed in the Record Commission edition, or where they are printed, identifiable as such. For example, parts of the head and dorse of m. 22 are omitted altogether from the printed text and there is nothing to show that the entry relating to the tenement of Thomas Passavant on m. 8 has been added in darker ink.[47] As in the Northstow roll, answers to the non-manorial articles are found alongside the description of holdings and, once more, marginal symbols draw attention to entries relating to liberties.[48] Similar marginal flags can be found on the Papworth roll, but are so sparing that it confirms that they are unlikely to have functioned as an aid to the compilation of a separate membrane for the non-manorial responses. Here also the hand of a checker or reviser can be seen at work, asking about the succession of John Freisel's holding in Over and adding 'at the will of the abbot' to the description of the abbot of Ramsey's villein tenancies at Knapwell.[49]

Despite almost invariably sharing the checking and flagging found on these rolls, some of the other rolls for the county seem rather more finished. The grouping of all the responses to the

[44] *ad voluntatem domini ad operibus eorundem.* PRO, SC5/Cambs/Tower/6, m. 9; SC5/8/5/6.

[45] PRO, SC5/Cambs/Tower/10 (1–2); *RH* ii. 507a–42b.

[46] Most vills have one or more membranes to themselves, but m. 21^r has the end of the Longstow return and that for Hardwick, while the dorse has the return for Hatley St George. Longstow and Hatley St George are almost contiguous, but Hardwick is well away to the north-east of the hundred, so there is no obvious reason why they might have been dealt with as a unit.

[47] *RH* ii. 523a.

[48] As on mm. 3^r, 20^d–21^r; *RH* ii. 514a–17a, 537b–9a.

[49] SC5/Cambs/Tower/7, m. 7, 9.

non-manorial articles on a single membrane for the whole hundred and the consistent positioning of information about the parish church in each vill at the head of the returns in Staploe, Whittlesford, Chilford, and Flendish hundreds bears witness to the sorting and reordering required for a final draft.[50] The Thriplow and Wetherley rolls also seem to belong to a slightly later stage in the editorial process. On both rolls, the articles were largely edited out and the relevant material incorporated alongside the manorial surveys. The parchment of the Thriplow roll was also ruled in the same way as some of the finished rolls elsewhere. Perhaps these hundreds were among the first in Cambridgeshire to be dealt with and further progress had been made with their returns before the inquiry was abandoned and the rolls called in regardless of the state they had reached.[51]

As these rolls show, the line between a fair copy of original returns and a final text is not always an easy one to draw. Once more, it has to be a matter of inference. Rolls written on evenly sized membranes, with parchment which has been ruled, sewn end to end, and containing few or no amendments, have a good claim to be regarded as final drafts. The presence of a seal turns out not to be a useful criterion in identifying such rolls because there are so few of them. Unlike the Ragman rolls, they are largely conspicuous by their absence. The sole survivors are to be found on the Mursley roll (Bucks.) and the return for the royal manor of Woodstock (Oxon.).[52] The latter has slits indicating the former existence of multiple seals, as do most of the rolls from the Bedfordshire/Buckinghamshire circuit and the Dorchester, Thame, and Ewelme rolls (Oxon.). There are also seal tags on the Langtree and Wootton rolls (Oxon.), but this still leaves many apparently finished rolls without any surviving hint of a seal.[53]

---

[50] SC5/Cambs/Tower/4, 5, 9, 14.

[51] PRO, SC5/Cambs/Tower/11, 12, 14. For what little is known about the timing of hearings on the Cambridgeshire/Huntingdonshire circuit, see above, pp. 83–4. For evidence that Wetherley and Thriplow may have been dealt with together, see above, p. 75.

[52] PRO, SC5/Bucks/Tower/1, m. 1; SC5/Oxon/Tower/15.

[53] PRO, SC5/Oxon/Tower/4a, m. 14; SC5/Oxon/Tower/4b, m. 8; SC5/Oxon/Tower/6; SC5/Oxon/Tower/14, m. 3; SC5/Oxon/Tower/16, pt 2, m. 3; SC5/Bucks/Tower/1, *passim*; SC5/Bucks/Tower/2, mm. 1, 3–4; SC5/Bucks/Tower/3, *passim*; SC5/Bucks/Tower/4, *passim*.

The rolls for Leightonstone, Hurstingstone, and perhaps Toseland hundreds are finished texts, probably because Huntingdonshire hearings were held earlier than those for Cambridgeshire. All are neatly written, with entries mostly running from vill to vill across membranes.[54] The texts have been heavily edited. Virtually all references to the articles have been excised from the returns for each vill, although answers to some of them have been incorporated alongside the manorial surveys. The Leightonstone and Toseland rolls also have the articles gathered together on one membrane and either answered or cross-referenced with the rest of the roll.[55] The same procedure may have been followed on the Hurstingstone and Normancross rolls, but since the heads have been badly damaged, it is impossible to say. In other respects, the Normancross roll seems more analogous to the Wetherley and Thriplow rolls and therefore closer to an intermediate draft.[56]

The almost equally finished, parallel text for part of Leightonstone hundred on the Huntingdon roll throws further light on the final stages of the inquiry.[57] While nearly identical, each version contains material absent from the other. This means that there must once have been three very similar texts, each differing from the other in minor ways. One of the most interesting of these discrepancies reveals that revisions and additions were made until a very late stage in the proceedings. In all but the last three full entries on the roll preserved in the National Archives, some details about advowsons were recorded in the form of interpolations. This information was part of the original text in the remainder, as if the decision to include it was taken while copying was in progress. The Huntingdon roll version by contrast rarely mentions advowsons at all. Where an entry does occur, as in the return for Brampton, the jurors pleaded ignorance as to when and how the crown had given the living to the canons of Lincoln. By

---

[54] PRO, SC5/Hunts/Tower/2–3, 5. Such Huntingdonshire hearings as can be dated were held before the end of Edward I's seventh year, while some of those for Cambridgeshire definitely belonged to the eighth year.

[55] PRO, SC5/Hunts/Tower/3, m. 14; SC5/Hunts/Tower/5, m. 1; *RH* ii. 632b–3b, 665b–6b.

[56] *RH* ii. 598a–b, 633b; PRO, SC5/Hunts/Tower/4. Although membranes are sewn end to end, the Normancross roll is written in a variety of hands with corrections, cancellations, and additions.

[57] HR, mm. 1–6.

the time an entry was interlined on the PRO manuscript, however, the scribe was able to note that it belonged to them 'by gift of the old King Henry'.[58] This echoes the way that advowsons were treated on the Gallow roll (Norfolk).[59] At West Barsham the information appears at the end of the Waterden membrane on m. 9, as well as in the return itself on m. 13. In the return for Cambridge itself, the membrane recording advowsons is stitched at the end of the second roll and is smaller than others.[60] The implication of these and other corrections and additions on the Norfolk and Cambridgeshire rolls is that further information was incorporated at all stages of the editing in response to the work of checkers.

The text for Normancross hundred found on the Huntingdon roll suggests a less straightforward scenario. Obscurity surrounding the origins and purpose of this roll makes it hard to know how much weight to attach to its evidence but, if as seems likely, it was part of the inquiry, its earlier date shows that information about advowsons was already available to the scribe when he began compiling the final roll. This implies that, in Normancross hundred at least, the interlineations may have resulted from a change in editorial policy rather than the insertion of information searched out at the last minute. Some of the information about liberties found on the earlier roll is also absent from the PRO manuscript, although it is conceivable that it could have been included in a return covering the non-manorial articles for the whole hundred which is now missing. At Alwalton, for example, it is recorded that the abbot of Peterborough has view of frankpledge and used to attend the sheriff's tourn twice a year. In neither case was his warrant for this known, nor how long ago he had withdrawn from the tourn.[61] With all its ambiguities, the evidence nevertheless suggests that considerable importance was attached to the inclusion of information about advowsons at a late stage in the proceedings. This is reinforced by its uneven appearance in the Oxfordshire rolls, which were probably the earliest to be completed. Only

[58] *ex dono Regis Henrici veteris.* SC5/Hunts/Tower/3, m. 14; HR, m. 2[d]; Raban, 'Fresh Light', 108.

[59] e.g. ULL, Fuller Coll., 7/5, mm. 2, 4.

[60] PRO, SC5/Cambs/Tower/1, pt 2, m. 35. Although now the second of three rolls, it could originally have been the final membrane of the return.

[61] HR, m. 9.

rarely, as in the return for Mongwell in Langtree hundred, was the missing information interlined.[62]

The Oxfordshire returns comprise the most sizeable group of completed rolls. They exist for every hundred except those of Binfield and Bloxham and all were written on one side of parchment, often carefully repaired, and sewn end to end. Unlike those from earlier stages in the inquiry, returns for individual vills usually run from membrane to membrane. The rolls vary in the extent to which they bear signs of checking and amendment and also in the neatness of their appearance, but despite these superficial differences, they were all subjected to a broadly similar editorial policy. Virtually all reference to the articles has been removed. The roll for Wootton hundred is unusual in retaining a lingering vestige whereby a number of returns end with the phrase 'And concerning the other articles with which they have been charged, they know nothing as they say under oath'.[63] Although jurors were sometimes listed at the head of rolls, further traces of their presence in the form of 'they say' or 'they do not know' are rare. Information culled from the non-manorial articles was generally summarized in the opening or concluding section for each vill. Unlike the haphazard treatment of advowsons, accounts of the descent of manors and obligations feature largely in these summaries, sometimes with a surprisingly large amount of detail. Such for example was the account of Henry III's alienation of his demesne manor at Piddington in Bullingdon hundred in part exchange for Lyndhurst in the New Forest or the service owed by Brian de Bampton' during the war in north Wales for his manor at Idbury in Chadlington hundred.[64] The early start made on the inquiry in Oxfordshire probably accounts for the commissioners' success in bringing it almost to completion. It may also explain why the contents of the Lewknor roll, the earliest for which we have a date, lack the neat coherence of vill-by-vill structure found in most other hundreds. It appears that the sorting of seigneurial returns which took place elsewhere did not happen in this hundred.[65] A note on the

---

[62] PRO, SC5/Oxon/Tower/4a, m. 2.

[63] *Et de aliis articulis de quibus onerati sunt nichil sciunt ut dicunt per sacramentum.* RH ii. 861a, 863b, 867b, 875b.

[64] *RH* ii. 717b, 733b.

[65] Ibid. 782a–8b.

Bullingdon roll, however, suggests that it could reflect arrangements dictated by honorial jurisdiction.[66]

The returns from the Bedfordshire/Buckinghamshire circuit are not only finished, but also the most fiercely edited of all the surviving rolls. All reference to the articles has disappeared and the editor of the Stodfold roll in particular almost rivals his Domesday predecessor in the ruthlessness of his compression.[67] Posterity has therefore fallen heir to concise but comparatively uninformative returns. There is nothing to indicate when the hearings were held or why work which it had been possible to complete in a handful of hundreds was apparently not carried out elsewhere. Unless returns have been lost, this is especially surprising in Buckinghamshire, because it was around this date that Stodfold and Lamua became associated with Rowley as the three hundreds of Buckingham, and Bunsty with Seckloe and Moulsoe as the three hundreds of Newton.[68] One might have expected that all three hundreds in each group would have been treated in the same way. When so much has been expunged, it is interesting to observe what the editors chose to retain. Many of the parishes in Willey and Bucklow hundred bordered on the Great Ouse, so it is not surprising that fisheries were recorded in unusual detail.[69] For the most part, however, it is details of mortmain tenure and estates with a complicated tenurial history which were singled out for relatively generous treatment.

A considerable body of returns from Shropshire, the East Anglian circuit and all but possibly one of those from the Warwickshire/Leicestershire circuit survive only in the form of transcripts. These inevitably reveal less about the way in which the verdicts were edited. Before one can assess how far they represent finished rolls, it is necessary to understand what they are and how they came into being.

Returns exist for Suffolk solely because they were copied into various compilations belonging to the abbey of Bury St Edmunds.

---

[66] *Dicunt juratores quod Drapcote* (Draycot) *est infra hundred' de Bolendon' et est de honore de Walingford'quarum non sequitur cum hundredo de Bolendon'.* PRO, SC5/Oxon/Tower/3, m. 21. As a result, its return was included on the roll for the earl of Cornwall's hundred of Ewelme. *RH* ii. 757a–b.

[67] *RH* ii. 338b–43b.

[68] *Feudal Aids* (London, 1899–1920), i. 89.

[69] *RH* ii. 323b–33b.

In so far as one can judge, the original verdicts had reached at least the stage of editing, although annotations and corrections which would confirm that the exemplar belonged to this part of the process can no longer be identified. The monks themselves engaged in further editing. They selected only what affected their interests in the eight most westerly hundreds of the county. This meant that in Blackbourn hundred, for example, there are no returns for Euston, Little Fakenham, Hepworth, Norton, Thelnetham, or Wattisfield.[70] The first copyist also omitted what he thought to be superfluous. As well as marginal headings, this included details of minor tenancies. He made this plain at Little Livermere, where he wrote 'other freemen whose names I omit are tenants'.[71] In the state in which it has been transmitted, the text could either be an intermediate draft left in the locality like the Gallow roll, or a finished return to which the monks for some reason had access. There is some evidence to support the latter possibility. In the Bury manuscripts, the text is mistakenly attributed to the eyre of Solomon Rochester in 1286–7.[72] The confusion may have arisen because Rochester had the 1279 rolls with him when he came to Suffolk. He is known to have borrowed previous justices' rolls for his earlier eyres in Surrey and Hampshire, so it is possible that he brought the hundred roll returns to assist him with *Quo waranto* hearings.[73] There is nothing to explain how the monks of Bury St Edmunds were able to copy them, but the Bury Chronicle tells us that two clerks engaged in the eyre were at Bury in 1287, shortly after the last known Suffolk hearings.[74] Perhaps the 1279 returns were in their possession at the time and perhaps the abbey took advantage of the opportunity to extract details of places where they held land. Craven Ord, the nineteenth-century owner of the Bury transcript CUL Add 3395, also possessed some of Rochester's plea

---

[70] Powell, *Suffolk Hundred*, 3.

[71] *ceteri liberi quorum nomina omitto sunt tenentes.* It must have been the scribe who made the initial transcript because the same phrase occurs in both 14th-cent. copies which are independent of each other. Powell, *Suffolk Hundred*, 3, 41; *Pinchbeck Register*, ed. Hervey, ii. 227.

[72] *Pinchbeck Register*, ed. Hervey, ii. 30; Powell, *Suffolk Hundred*, 1, 5; CUL, Ee, iii, 60, fo. 234ʳ; CUL, Add MS 3395, fo. 1ʳ; BL, Harl, MS 743, fo. 149ʳ. For the dating, see below, Ch. 6.

[73] D. Crook, *Records of the General Eyre* (London, 1982) 22.

[74] *The Chronicle of Bury St Edmunds*, ed. A. Gransden (London, 1964), 88.

roll, another link between the returns and the eyre, albeit tenuous and possibly coincidental.[75]

The much later Leicestershire transcripts produced by William Burton in 1615 were made for antiquarian reasons and bear no signs of seigneurial pruning. It is not easy to establish what sort of exemplar he used. The commonly cited text for the two surviving returns for Guthlaxton and Gartree hundreds is that of John Nichols's edition of 1795, taken from Burton's transcripts. It is, however, somewhat misleading in that it conceals the fact that Burton copied two versions of the returns for each hundred.[76] For Guthlaxton hundred, these consisted of a first, highly compressed version of the returns, followed by the fuller text used by Nichols.[77] The extent to which they differ is illustrated by a comparison between the two returns for Enderby.

From the first Burton transcript:

Enderby [marginated] Who [the jurors] say that it belongs to the Leicester fee and Robert de Nevile is its lord and he holds the said vill from the earl of Leicester for a quarter part of a knight's fee; there are twenty virgates of land there, of which the abbot of Leicester holds one virgate and the abbot of Garendon holds one and a half virgates.[78]

From the second Burton transcript, printed by Nichols:

Enderby [marginated] Enderby belongs to the Leicester fee and Robert de Nevile, its lord, holds eight virgates of land in demesne there with his step-mother's dower, and a windmill and a watermill. Item seventeen virgates of land in villeinage held by thirty one serfs (*servi*). Item he has three cottars (*cotaria*). Item the abbot of Croxton has one and a half virgates of land there in pure alms which a certain freeman holds of the abbot. Item the abbot of Leicester has one virgate of land there in pure alms which two free tenants hold from him. The said Robert has a wood which is called *Tlwe . . .* there and it is in the forest of Leicester. And he holds the said vill from the earl of Leicester for a quarter part of a knight's fee for scutage and service, and the said earl from the king. And the said earl has view of frankpledge and regalian rights there. There is no warren there, nor chace, etc.[79]

---

[75] By an irony, Craven Ord may have obtained his copy of the hundred roll text from Thomas Astle, Keeper of the Public Records. J. H. Baker and J. S. Ringrose, *A Catalogue of English Legal Manuscripts in Cambridge University Library* (Woodbridge, 1996), 577–8, 654–5.

[76] Bodl. MS Rawlinson B, 350, fos. 2–31, 34–7, 42–51; Nichols, *History and Antiquities*, i/1, pp. cx–xxi.

[77] Bodl. MS Rawlinson, B, 350, fos. 2–31, 34.   [78] Ibid., fo. 3.

[79] Ibid., fos. 14–15; Nichols, *History and Antiquities*, i/1, p. cxi.

Although briefer in its entries, the first text included a number of vills missing from the fuller version. Nichols therefore created a composite text by adding them to a few returns for Guthlaxton hundred which were already present at the end of his preferred text for Gartree hundred.[80] For this latter hundred, he used the first of Burton's two transcripts, having apparently overlooked the second transcript between fos. 42 and 51. This included returns for many more vills as well as a more accurate text. It was easily enough done because Burton's two Gartree transcripts did not run consecutively. Unlike the two versions of the Guthlaxton returns, those for Gartree, where both returns exist, are almost identical.

Unfortunately little is known about the provenance of Burton's texts, nor why there should be two of them for each hundred. Hilton believed that he drew on a Cotton manuscript.[81] Burton himself merely stated that the first transcript for Guthlaxton hundred came from 'an old parchment roll', an attribution carried over by Nichols to the second transcript, although it does not feature in Burton's second heading.[82] One can only speculate as to whether Burton's exemplars were original returns, seigneurial copies, or, as Hilton suggests, an exchequer digest.[83] A seigneurial copy would seem the least likely if one or more of the exemplars was in roll form. The first Guthlaxton transcript could have been based on some sort of official extract roll, while the second has many of the features of the finished returns found elsewhere. Estate information has been stripped to its bare bones of the number of tenants and the quantity of land held in demesne and by the tenantry. Mention of the articles has been reduced to 'concerning other articles, nothing' at the end of some entries. Textual variants and discrepancies on matters of fact, such as whether it was Garendon or Croxton Abbey which held one and a half virgates in

---

[80] Nichols added returns for North and South Kilworth, Shenton, Twycross, Bruntingsthorpe, Peatling Magna and Parva, Kirkby Mallory and Polesworth in Hemlingford hundred (War.) to those for Desford, Barlestone in Market Bosworth and 'Horton' already in Burton's second transcript. Bodl. MS Rawlinson, B, 350, fos. 9–11, 37.

[81] R. H. Hilton, *The Economic Development of Some Leicestershire Estates in the Fourteenth and Fifteenth Centuries* (Oxford, 1947), 7 and n.

[82] *ex originali rotula membranea veteri.* Bodl., MS Rawlinson, B, 350, fos. 2, 11; Nichols, *History and Antiquities,* i/1, p. cx. In Nichols's text the note reads 'ex originali rotulo membranaceo veteri'.

[83] Hilton, *Economic Development,* 7.

Enderby, make it questionable whether Burton's first transcript is a summary of the second. It appears to have more in common with an inquisition of 1296 cited by Nichols later in his *History*.[84] However, Burton's headings are categorical that both the returns belong to an inquisition conducted in Edward I's seventh year by named hundred roll commissioners.[85]

Burton notes that the first of his Gartree hundred texts was in a later hand.[86] A post-medieval copy could explain the otherwise puzzling inclusion of some Guthlaxton returns and why the second transcript, possibly from an earlier exemplar, was the better text. The text of the first transcript ends with 'finis Lapworth', so perhaps it may have belonged to Edward Lapworth of Sowe, who owned a fifteenth-century tax assessment for Warwickshire transcribed by Dugdale and who perhaps belonged to the Warwickshire family of Lapworths.[87] Sowe, now Walsgrave-on-Sowe, lies to the north-east of Coventry, while Lapworth, from which the family took its name, is part of a detached portion of Kineton hundred, ironically missing from the hundred roll returns.[88] It is plausible that a man with local antiquarian interests might have acquired Leicestershire material incidentally if he owned either some of the original returns from the Leicestershire/Warwickshire circuit or a copy. The Gartree returns are less heavily edited than those for Guthlaxton hundred, listing both names and tenements of the free tenants, but they too are consistent with the general corpus of late or finished rolls to which John ascribes them.[89]

The surviving returns for Stoneleigh and Kineton hundreds in Warwickshire are similar in content to those for Gartree hundred

---

[84] Nichols, *History and Antiquities*, iv/1, 157.

[85] Bodl., MS Rawlinson, B, 350, fos. 2, 11. All three commissioners for the inquiry are named in both transcripts. There are minor differences between the names of the jurors on the two folios, but nothing which could not be attributable to faulty transmission.

[86] *recentiore charactere scripta*. Ibid., fo. 34; Nichols, *History and Antiquities*, i/1, p. cxix.

[87] MS Dugdale 12; F. Madan, H. H. E. Craster, and N. Denholm Young, *A Summary Catalogue of Western Manuscripts in the Bodleian Library at Oxford*, new edn., vol. ii/2 (Oxford, 1937), 1075–6, no. 6502. I am indebted to Paul Brand for this reference.

[88] *Warwickshire*, ed. John, 20–1.

[89] Ibid. 7.

apart from the inclusion of named servile tenants and their rents. John argued that they belonged to the penultimate stage of editing because they still incorporated so much detail of doubtful value to the crown. This cannot be taken for granted, however, since the finished rolls for Huntingdonshire also retained such information. It is the sort of point which can sometimes be resolved by reference to the manuscript returns, but the only text remotely likely to fall into this category is the one found among the miscellaneous books of the Exchequer King's Remembrancer.[90] It is interesting in that, if it is indeed an original return, it is uniquely in the book format laid down in the commission. John thought that it was not beyond the bounds of possibility that it was associated with the original return and it is tentatively classified as a return in the catalogue of the National Archives. The balance of probability is against this however. The text is certainly a copy, but this would of course be true whether it was an edited return or one that had been subsequently transcribed. It does not appear to be polished enough for a final draft, but nor does it contain the emendations and additions to be expected of an intermediate draft. The general consensus is that it is most probably either a contemporary or early fourteenth-century copy made within the exchequer, the case for the later date resting on palaeographical evidence.[91] Aside from the information it contains, therefore, the value of this manuscript lies more in the clues it offers as to the subsequent use of the hundred rolls than the process of the inquiry itself.

Two other medieval texts of the Warwickshire returns survive, both unequivocally later transcripts. One, a late fifteenth-century text, which is also in book form, is a copy of the exchequer text.[92] More important in the present context is the late fourteenth-century copy of a rather fuller, independent text which almost certainly belonged to Coventry Priory. This contains an otherwise unrecorded return for Coventry itself and only includes vills where the priory had estates. Although it differs in many minor spellings and some details, it is not sufficiently different to suggest that it

---

[90] PRO, E164/15.

[91] *Warwickshire*, ed. John, 6–8; Greenway, 'Newly Discovered Fragment', 74. I am grateful to both Diana Greenway and Paul Brand for their opinion on the date of the script.

[92] Univ. Nottingham Lib., MiO 14; *Warwickshire*, ed. John, 8–12, 14.

was drawn from an earlier stage in the inquiry.[93] The most significant variations tend to relate to the priory itself. Such was the entry about the prior's appropriated chapel at Pinley or the variant wording of the opening section of the Willenhall return where the prior's military obligations to the crown are described.[94] The exemplar for this text might have been something comparable to the variant version of the final text for Leightonstone hundred in Huntingdonshire found on the Huntingdon roll, perhaps with the priory copyist using his preferred spelling and even making additions.[95] Copies of returns for a handful of estates where the bishop of Coventry had an interest also survive in a Coventry Priory cartulary. There has been speculation that these might have been taken from original verdicts, but they are in too poor a condition for any real conclusion to be drawn.[96]

Understanding the text of the Shropshire returns is particularly important because it constitutes the sole evidence that the inquiry took place outside its generally acknowledged confines and that the articles might have varied from circuit to circuit. Apart from a fifteenth-century copy of a rental belonging to Lilleshall Abbey which appears to be derived from part of the Shrewsbury verdict, the Shropshire returns survive only in a transcript made by Joseph Morris in the nineteenth century.[97] Joseph, who died in 1860, and his brother George were genealogists. This narrow focus caused him to be selective in what he copied. At the beginning of the return for Pimhill hundred, he explains that he is transcribing extracts only and later notes the existence of peasant tenants whom he has omitted. Moreover, since the latter part of the return was 'imperfect from damp and misadventure', he substituted material from other Edwardian inquisitions.[98] The Shrewsbury return, which he

---

[93] Shakespeare Birthplace Trust, Stoneleigh MSS, DR 18/31/3; *Warwickshire*, ed. John, 12–14.

[94] *Warwickshire*, ed. John, 120, 146.

[95] See above, p. 105.

[96] There is also a post-medieval copy of the returns for two vills, but this has nothing to add. *Warwickshire*, ed. John, 15.

[97] Shropshire Archives, 6001/28, 21–62; 'A Late-Thirteenth Century Rental, of Tenements in Shrewsbury', ed. U. Rees, *Transactions of the Shropshire Archaeological and Historical Society*, 66 (1989), 79–84.

[98] R. A. Preston, 'George and Joseph Morris: Genealogists of Shropshire', *Shropshire Family History Journal*, 10, (1989), 102–3. Shropshire Archives, 6001/28, 53, 57.

copied first, is fuller, but there he soon adopted the practice of recording details of peasant tenements in tabular form.[99] He has very little to say about his exemplars. The state of the Pimhill return implies that he may have been working from a medieval text, but a marginal note on the Shrewsbury return mentions an 'original transcript', so the matter is unresolved.[100] For a source on which so much depends, it is unfortunate that the integrity of the transcript is questionable in so many ways, but since its exemplar survived into the nineteenth century, there is always the hope that it may resurface.

Like the hundredal returns, the separate urban rolls range in a similar way from original verdicts to final drafts and, because towns were well integrated into the inquiry as a whole, often show the same characteristics as those for the hundreds in the same circuit. Thus, the Cambridge and Godmanchester rolls rehearse the articles alongside the responses and were also fully edited.[101] The rolls for the borough and hundred of Banbury open with very similar wording about royal custody owing to the death of the bishop of Lincoln to whom both belonged and the format of the borough return is similar to that of vills elsewhere in the hundred. They differ in layout, suggesting that they were not the work of the same scribe, but both were annotated at the end in a different hand to record that they were held in chief by the bishop of Lincoln.[102] Because they have been preserved in book form, one can only judge the returns for Warwick and Coventry by their contents, but *mutatis mutandis* they too fit well into the general pattern for the county.[103] This is less true of Oxford. The returns for the borough are neat, final copies just like those of the county.[104] However, the distinctive preoccupation with the value of holdings, especially those of churchmen, and to a lesser extent Jews, which characterizes the Oxford rolls was far less marked in the returns for

---

[99] See e.g. 'Late-Thirteenth Century Rental', ed. Rees, 82–3, where it is reproduced.

[100] Shropshire Archives, 6001/28, 42.

[101] PRO, SC5/Cambs/Tower/1 (3 pts); SC5/Hunts/Tower/1; *RH* ii. 356a–93a, 591a–8a.

[102] PRO, SC5/Oxon/Tower/2, Oxon/Tower/17; *RH* ii. 705a.

[103] *Warwickshire*, ed. John, 25–38; 'The Coventry Hundred Rolls', ed. T. John in P. R. Coss (ed.), *The Early Records of Medieval Coventry*, (London, 1986), 370–94.

[104] PRO, SC5/Oxon/Tower/8 (SW ward), 9a and 18 (NW ward), 9b and 10 (NE ward), 9c (SE ward), 11 (Northgate suburb).

Oxfordshire as a whole. Apart from the returns for the smaller boroughs of Banbury, Witney, and Woodstock, only Chadlington hundred has rent totals, and they are nothing like as elaborate.[105] As with the advowson entries on the Huntingdonshire rolls, the assessments as to how far rents represented the full value of holdings on the Oxford rolls may have resulted from a change of policy part way through the proceedings. None are found in the north-east ward, while in the remaining wards and Hugh de Plessis's Northgate suburb, some of the information was added as the rolls were compiled but more was added later. The sum total of rents for certain landholders which are found in all the returns except those for the north-west ward also look like an afterthought. For the north-east ward, they are on a separate roll as if they might not have been part of the original return. On the roll for the south-west ward, they form a supplement on the final membrane in the same larger hand as the comments on rents. Only on the return for the south-east ward does it look as if all the information was available to the scribe who drew it up. Not only is it in a single hand, but the ecclesiastical and university tenements are sorted by landholder and their rents totalled at the end of each list of holdings.[106]

Taking the surviving rolls as a whole, it is clear that a great deal of individual initiative went into marshalling the material which had been collected. This makes it impossible to reduce the process to neat, well-defined stages, but there can be no doubt about the immensity of the task. The production of a finished roll was as onerous as the conduct of the inquiry itself. It involved drafting the initial verdicts and gathering seigneurial submissions, possibly amalgamating them into a fair copy, followed by checking, supplementing, and reorganizing the information, before drawing up the final version, perhaps in triplicate.

Allowing for variations between the practices of different circuits, a high proportion of the rolls returned to central keeping are either finished or very nearly so. Whether the remainder were

---

[105] See above, Ch. 3.
[106] All types of landholder were included in the SW ward, but only ecclesiastics and the university in the two eastern wards. PRO, SC5/Oxon/Tower/8, m. 7, Oxon/Tower/9c, m. 3, Oxon/Tower/10, m. 2; *RH* ii. 793a–b, 800b–01b, 803a–5a. The different approaches are most easily compared in Graham's reorganized edn. 'Description of Oxford from the Hundred Rolls AD 1279', ed. R. Graham, in *Collectanea*, 4th ser. (Oxford Historical Society, 47, Oxford, 1905), 3–7.

regarded as adequate for their intended use in their rough state or whether their scribes simply ran out of time and sent as much as they had managed to achieve is unknown. Nevertheless, along with their limited geographical distribution, the fact that some rolls were submitted in an unfinished state must strengthen the case for believing that the inquiry was aborted.

5

Uses of the Rolls

It is generally agreed that the findings of the 1279–80 inquiry were not put to observable use during the Middle Ages either as the basis for judicial proceedings or as an authoritative record to which reference could be made.[1] Their utility was inevitably prejudiced by the likely absence of returns from many parts of the country and the varied contents of those which did exist. The estate surveys which formed the greater part of the returns did not readily lend themselves to action. They were best suited to being a repository of information like Domesday Book, but there is no sign that they were used in this way, despite the suggestion in the commission that the king intended the findings to be available to others as well as himself.[2] Unlike the 1274–5 verdicts, those of 1279–80 created no deluge of complaints calling for prosecutions and legislation. Articles focusing on liberties certainly revealed ample evidence of franchises and property held without known warrant, but arrangements for *Quo waranto* hearings had already been substantially modified in 1278 and, if anything, seem to have lost momentum after 1280.[3] Could it really have been the case that, after such high ambition and prodigious effort (albeit regionalized), the findings went wholly to waste?

Although hindsight suggests that no further action was taken, this does not appear to have been a foregone conclusion. The way in which the rolls were checked and annotated, with missing information added until a late stage in the proceedings, implies that

---

[1] e.g. M. Prestwich, *Edward I*, 2nd edn. (New Haven and London, 1997), 236; E. A. Kosminsky, *Studies in the Agrarian History of England in the Thirteenth Century* (Oxford, 1956), 23.

[2] *quod nobis et aliis constare possit ad plenum de premissis.* See Appendix 2 and above, p. 37.

[3] D. W. Sutherland, *Quo Warranto Proceedings in the Reign of Edward I* (Oxford, 1963), 42–3.

those responsible believed that their work still mattered, even if they were somewhat confused as to its purpose. The separation of liberties, or the answers to the non-manorial articles, on some rolls were perhaps intended to make it easier to challenge the alienation of regalian rights, although they could have been nothing more than a way of reducing the mass of material to order. That officials regarded this information as more important than the estate surveys may be inferred from an annotation to the return for Hilton and Fen Stanton in Toseland hundred (Hunts.) to the effect that 'the abbess [of Tarrant] has entry through Joan queen of Scotland as appears in the principal roll'.[4] Logically this principal roll must be the membrane dealing with the non-manorial articles, although there is no trace of such an entry there.

The strongest suggestion that action was planned once the inquiry was over comes from the Warwickshire/Leicestershire circuit. The copy of the Warwickshire returns made at the exchequer and the shorter version of the return for Guthlaxton hundred (Leics.) transcribed by Burton, could each have been working documents prepared by royal officials after the returns were submitted. Neither can be accepted as such unequivocally, however, since as we have seen, the former could conceivably be the return itself and the latter might belong to a different inquiry.[5]

In the absence of hard evidence, annotations offer the best guide as to the possible use of the returns, even though it is unclear precisely who the annotators were, when they marked the rolls, or what they had in mind when doing so. We have already observed that the copious flagging of liberties and reports of tenure without known warrant on the Cambridgeshire rolls were likely to have been later additions.[6] Several vills in Willey and Bucklow hundred (Beds.) have annotated instructions to investigate further but no answering insertion. This may also mean that they were made after the roll was complete, especially as the Bedfordshire returns were fair, final copies with few signs of editorial work in progress.[7] If so,

---

[4] *Abbat[issa] habet ingressum per Johannam Reginam Scocie ut patet in principio rotulo.* PRO, SC5, Hunts/Tower/5, m. 5[d]; *RH* ii. 679a. The non-manorial articles appear on the first membrane of the roll. *RH* ii. 665b–6b.

[5] See above, Ch. 4.   [6] See above, Ch. 3.

[7] Against the returns for Sharnbrook, Souldrop, Poddington, Wymington, and Turvey. PRO, SC5/Beds/Tower/2, mm. 2[r], 3[d], 4[r–d], 5[d]; *RH* ii. 324a, 327b, 329a, 330b, 333a.

it indicates that the returns were regarded as a possible springboard for further investigation. We know that in 1275 Walter of Wimborne, justice and royal attorney, went through all the plea rolls and inquiries then in the treasury and marked matters touching the king's interest. Perhaps the annotations on the 1279–80 returns represent a similar process.[8]

If the Warwickshire text was indeed an exchequer copy and not the original return, its annotations are of particular interest because they must post-date the inquiry. Written in a variety of hands, most of them take the form of a pointing hand or the word *nota* singling out matters of tenure or liberties. Questions of woodland or warren seem to have attracted special attention.[9] The claim of Richard de Loges that 'he has no warrant other than by ancient tenure without charter' is both underlined and marked *nota*.[10] In a few cases it is hard to see why entries were singled out. The names of apparently obscure tenants are sometimes underlined.[11] Still more inexplicable, unless they relate to unknown cases or queries, are the occasional instances where the obligations of servile tenants were noted. At Charlecote, work owed on the mill pool was marked and at Walton Mauduit the liability to pay aid and the requirement to purchase licences for the sale of cockerels or the marriage of their sons and daughters was underlined.[12] Whether it is the exchequer text for Warwickshire or the hundred rolls for other counties, however, there can be little doubt that matters of warrant were the principal focus of interest to annotators.

How this interest was then expressed is hard to tell. Use continued to be made of the Ragman rolls as the courts struggled to work their way through the findings of the 1274–5 inquiry. Such pleas merited their own heading on the Bedfordshire eyre roll for 1287, while it was the commissioners of 1274–5, not those of 1279–80, who were mentioned in the Huntingdonshire proceedings of

---

[8] *Select Cases in the Court of King's Bench under Edward I*, ed. G. O. Sayles (London, 1936–9), i, pp. cx–cxi.

[9] e.g. PRO, E164/15, fos. 7ᵛ, 12ʳ, 45ʳ.

[10] *dicit se non habere warentam aliquam nisi per antiquam tenuram sine carta.* PRO, E164/15, fo. 43ᵛ; *The Warwickshire Hundred Rolls of 1279–80*, ed. T. John (Oxford, 1992), 143.

[11] As on PRO, E164/15, fos. 76ʳ and 91ʳ; *Warwickshire*, ed. John, 208, 251.

[12] PRO, E164/15, fos. 61ᵛ, 85ʳ; *Warwickshire*, ed. John, 173 (where the annotation is not given), 231.

1286.[13] Sutherland estimated that a high proportion, although by no means all, of writs *Quo waranto* in the eyres of the 1280s had their origins in the Ragman findings, but there is no comparable evidence for hearings which might have originated in its successor.[14] Following the arrangements instituted by the Gloucester parliament of 1278, all those holding franchises were now expected to make their claim to them at the beginning of an eyre. It was then left to justices to decide how many of these should be tried. Rather than make a selection, Gilbert de Thornton, king's serjeant on the Huntingdonshire eyre of 1286 and the Bedfordshire eyre of 1287, obtained writs *Quo waranto* against all claimants for all their liberties.[15] It is therefore likely that the only use for the returns from 1279–80 was to provide background information. To that end, they were probably looked over fairly soon after they were submitted, their contents noted and highlighted for ease of reference, but they were never acted on in any systematic way.

Although it is not altogether clear why questions of warrant were so often singled out for attention, there can be no doubt about the position regarding scutage. The information contained in the returns was not thought to be important. This is surprising given the change in royal policy towards its levy earlier in 1279. Comprehensive information about the obligations of both lords and their tenants would have been useful to exchequer officials who were newly intent on siphoning off the difference between the sums currently paid to the crown by tenants-in-chief and the amount, based on older liabilities, which these lords collected from their tenants.[16] Arguably just such a record had been intended when the commission asked 'from what fees and other tenures scutage was customarily given and is owed and how much from the fees of every honour' and the order was carried forward unaltered into the articles.[17] In the event, attention paid to the subject in the returns was uneven. Scutage obligations were generally recorded on the East Anglian circuit. At Burnham Thorpe and West Barsham in Gallow hundred (Norfolk), the scribe even thought it important

---

[13] *Placita de Quo Warranto* (London, 1818), 13a, 293a; D. Crook, *Records of the General Eyre* (London, 1982), 155–6.

[14] Sutherland, *Quo Warranto*, 60–5.   [15] Ibid. 26–7, 66–7.

[16] See above, Ch. 2.

[17] See below, Appendix 1 and Appendix 3A, art. 6.

enough to single them out for regular margination.[18] On the Cambridgeshire/Huntingdonshire circuit, particular care was sometimes taken to see that obligations were properly recorded. On the roll for Leightonstone hundred (Hunts.), the checker demanded to know how much scutage was owed and the answer was duly inserted.[19] The article about knights' fees and their scutage obligation also received an unusually full answer covering the whole of this hundred on the final membrane.[20] At Lolworth in Northstow hundred (Cambs.), the obligation of Philip de Colevile was inserted in a different hand.[21] Elsewhere its inclusion was much more erratic. On the roll for Lewknor hundred (Oxon.) for example, scutage was recorded under marginated headings for some vills, but omitted altogether in others.[22] This inconsistency meant that the record of scutage liability was of no administrative value. The absence of annotation against scutage obligations on the exchequer text of the Warwickshire returns confirms this. Even if it was a copy made some years after 1279, one might have expected scutage to remain a matter of note since the exchequer was actively, if intermittently, chasing scutage debts well into the fourteenth century.[23] There were, however, alternative and more satisfactory sources of information about knights' fees available.

Although unforeseen at the time of the commission, it is possible that the findings of the inquiry had their biggest impact on the church. Information about ecclesiastical property became increasingly prominent as the royal commission was translated into articles and the jurors responded to them. It is equally evident that ecclesiastical holdings were considered unusually important by the scribes who drew up and edited the verdicts and the subsequent checkers. The incorporation of valuations of the holdings of religious institutions in the final drafts of the Oxford rolls and the

---

[18] ULL. Fuller Coll., 7/5, mm. 1–2, 12–13.

[19] PRO, SC5/Hunts/Tower, 3, m. 10.

[20] *RH* ii. 632b–3a.

[21] PRO, SC5/Cambs/Tower/6, m. 8. A further hand then noted that the jurors did not know the warrant for this. The nature of the entry is not evident in *RH* ii. 457a.

[22] PRO, SC5/Oxon/Tower/7; *RH* ii. 782a–8b. The inclusion of scutage begins halfway through the roll and largely, but not completely, coincides with returns for the honour of Wallingford.

[23] H. M. Chew, 'Scutage under Edward I', *EHR* 37 (1922), 333–6; M. Jurkowski, C. L. Smith, and D. Crook, *Lay Taxes in England and Wales 1188–1688* (London, 1998), p. xxi.

inclusion of information about advowsons at the last minute in those on several circuits make this plain.[24] So too does the way in which the donor and approximate date of acquisition were generally given for ecclesiastical, but not lay, lords in Willey and Bucklow hundreds (Beds.) and to a lesser extent in Stodfold hundred (Bucks.).[25] Once the inquiry was complete, the church continued to be the subject of attention. The instructions to make further inquiry in Bedfordshire all concerned ecclesiastical holdings where information about title had been unobtainable and where, in the case of the 100 acre holding of the prior of St Neots, the jurors had reported that they could see no warrant for it 'other than by intrusion'.[26] The same roll has 'church' written alongside the prioress of Harrold's appropriated church at Steventon and 'religious' against the Hospitallers' tenement at Odell. Similar annotations can occasionally be found on the Cambridgeshire rolls.[27] Church estates and privileges loomed large among those flagged as being held without known warrant. This may be less significant than it appears, however, since many had been acquired in the distant past, making it hard to produce written evidence of title. This was strikingly evident in burgage tenements held in mortmain in Cambridge.[28] The sheer number of times throughout the rolls that juries reported that the church had been unable to show warrant could well have given rise to a distorted impression of ecclesiastical aggrandizement.

In the light of all this special attention, the question arises as to what, if any, part the inquiry played in provoking the enactment of the Statute of Mortmain on 14 November 1279. Apart from the statute itself, there is no contemporary explanation as to why this measure forbidding further acquisition of any sort by the church was enacted. The text claimed that it was due to concern for the loss of feudal incidents suffered by lords and the threat to the defence of the realm resulting from the decline in the number of

---

[24] See above, Ch. 4.

[25] e.g. *RH* ii. 325b (Felmersham), 327a–b (Biddenham), 341a–b (Lamport); S. Raban, 'The Church in the 1279 Hundred Rolls', in M. J. Franklin and C. Harper-Bill (eds.), *Medieval Ecclesiastical Studies in Honour of Dorothy M. Owen* (Woodbridge, 1995), 187.

[26] *nisi per intrusionem*. PRO, SC5/Beds/Tower/2, m. 5[d]; *RH* ii. 333a.

[27] PRO, SC5/Beds/Tower/2, mm. 4[r], 5[r]; SC5/Cambs/Tower/7, m. 2; SC5/Cambs/Tower/12, m. 7; *RH* ii. 328a (where the annotation is not given), 331b, 470b, 564a.

[28] PRO, SC5/Cambs/Tower/1, *passim*.

knights.[29] This can be taken at face value, although it was not the whole story. Anxiety on both scores had been expressed intermittently by lay lords in the preceding decades and modern calculations suggest that it was justified as the nature of knighthood changed and became more exclusive.[30] It has been suggested that Edward I's concern for the economic plight of fighting knights was one factor behind his Jewish legislation.[31] A similar sentiment may also have informed the move against mortmain tenure, since many knightly tenants had sought an answer to their financial problems by selling their estates to religious houses.[32] The enactment of mortmain legislation was not in itself remarkable; it was widespread in continental Europe by the later thirteenth century. It is the timing rather than the fact of the legislation which requires explanation and makes it especially interesting in this context.

There has been a good deal of speculation on the subject.[33] Edward I's stormy relations with his new archbishop, culminating in Pecham ordering the posting of copies of Magna Carta at the entrance to churches, may have contributed to the decision to legislate, although it has been pointed out that the archbishop had retracted most of his more challenging acts in parliament by 11 November at the latest, three days before the enactment of the statute.[34] Paul Brand has drawn attention to the confused state of the law whereby clause 14 of the Provisions of Westminster continued to be invoked in court cases, although it had been dropped from the reissues of 1263 and 1264 and omitted from the Statute of Marlborough in 1267. This inconsistency was highlighted in a case heard on the Yorkshire eyre in the Trinity Term 1279, in which the Master of the Templars claimed that there was no statutory basis for a challenge to an acquisition in mortmain and asked

---

[29] *Statutes of the Realm* (London, 1810–28), i. 51.

[30] P. Coss, *The Origins of the English Gentry* (Cambridge, 2003), 90–3, 108. For what follows, see S. Raban, *Mortmain Legislation and the English Church 1279–1500* (Cambridge, 1982), Ch. 1, and P. Brand, *The Making of the Common Law* (London, 1992), Ch. 11.

[31] R. R. Mundill, *England's Jewish Solution: Experiment and Expulsion, 1262–1290* (Cambridge, 1998), 266–7.

[32] e.g. Raban, *Mortmain Legislation*, 143–4.

[33] Brand, *Making*, 242–4.

[34] Raban, *Mortmain Legislation*, 25–6; Prestwich, *Edward I*, 251–2; Brand, *Making*, 243.

that judgment be reserved until the king's will was known.[35] This could explain why the question of mortmain tenure came before the king and his council at this particular date. Few of the hundred rolls had been completed by the time the statute was enacted, but many of the hearings must already have taken place and those advising the king about the possibility of legislation would have been aware of the proceedings in their capacity as landlords. Although one cannot claim that the inquiry was instrumental in promoting the statute, the scale of the church's tenure of land and franchises, many held without satisfactory warrant, may have come as a revelation. This would explain why the attitude of the government hardened into a swingeing prohibition on all further ecclesiastical acquisition, instead of requiring churchmen to obtain seigneurial licences, as precedent would have suggested.

There may have been other, equally unintended, consequences of the inquiry arising from its impact on those involved at a local level. The 'charter of liberties' granted by Thomas de Akeny to his men in Holkham *c*.1275–80 had been a direct result of evidence put before the jury for North Greenhoe hundred (Norfolk) in the 1274–5 inquiry.[36] It is conceivable that the act of committing customary services to writing, especially on small lay estates where literate practices were not deeply entrenched, generated a similar desire for confirmation of the *status quo* on the part of tenants elsewhere. Because of the nature of medieval records, however, grants of this sort have rarely survived. It is equally possible that those lords who did not have surveys of their own to put before the jurors found the information collected for the crown useful for their own administrative purposes. Such is the implication of copies found among seigneurial records.

Had exchequer officials regarded the rolls as completely useless, they might well have been discarded within a few years of the inquiry. This was certainly the fate of the Gascon archive once Aquitaine was lost to the crown in the mid-fifteenth century. As it was, the rolls were retained and included in the grand sorting and calendaring of exchequer records under Walter Stapeldon in the 1320s. It may however reflect contemporary assessment of their

---

[35] P. Brand, *Kings, Barons and Justices* (Cambridge, 2003), 277–80.
[36] *Lordship and Landscape in Norfolk 1250–1350*, ed. W. Hassall and J. Beauroy (Oxford, 1993), 30, 165–6, no. 150.

respective value that, while the 1274–5 rolls were returned to Westminster, those of the 1279–80 inquiry remained at the Tower, the treasury's secondary repository.[37] This relegation may go some way to explain the damage and possible loss which befell the rolls, since many of the muniments stored in the Tower are now in poor condition.[38]

In sum, it was impossible for the 1279–80 hundred rolls to fulfil the original expectations of the crown in commissioning the inquiry. However, there is no necessary correspondence between the king's motives at the outset and the use to which the verdicts were actually put. Although too little was achieved to provide an authoritative source of information comparable to Domesday Book, this did not mean that the findings were regarded as completely useless. They were examined and annotated as if for future reference. They probably contributed to the climate of opinion which gave birth to the Statute of Mortmain, and perhaps account for the harshness of its terms. They may well have generated local reactions which are now beyond our reach or been copied for private use more often than we appreciate. They were certainly deemed worthy of keeping in the great sorting and cataloguing projects of Edward II's reign. However, it is in modern times that they have really come into their own.

The importance of the 1279–80 hundred rolls for historians has been understood since the late nineteenth century.[39] There is no thirteenth-century source to compare with them for a detailed picture of land tenure in parts of the Midlands and East Anglia, as well as for a great deal of information about franchises, colonization, and more incidental material included when lords were justifying their title. They have accordingly proved a mine of information for scholars with widely differing interests. All too often, however, their contents have had to be used uncritically because the nature of the rolls has been imperfectly understood.

---

[37] The present PRO class SC5 was created artificially in the 19th cent. M. S. Giuseppi, *Guide to the Records of the Public Record Office*, 3 vols. (HMSO, London, 1963–8), i. 190; M. Buck, *Politics, Finance and the Church in the Reign of Edward II: Walter Stapeldon Treasurer of England* (Cambridge, 1983), 167–8; V. H. Galbraith, 'The Tower as an Exchequer Record Office in the Reign of Edward II', in A. G. Little and F. M. Powicke (eds.), *Essays in Medieval History Presented to Thomas Frederick Tout* (Manchester, 1925), 231.

[38] Information kindly supplied by Paul Brand.

[39] Kosminsky, *Studies*, p. v.

The very comprehensiveness which makes them so valuable is deceptive. In order to feel confident in drawing conclusions, users need to be able to appreciate their limitations.

In reducing complicated tenures to succinct descriptions, compromises had to be made. One can see this by setting the hundred roll return for the Montchesny fee in Holkham alongside a roll of its rents and customs dating from 1272–3. Although the two documents are almost contemporary, the estate is scarcely recognizable as the same holding.[40] There is no doubt whatsoever that many small subtenancies on manors throughout the rolls were oversimplified or omitted altogether. This can be proved by comparing them with other contemporary surveys. Discrepancies between such tenants listed in the returns for Caldecote, Yaxley, and Woodston in the PRO and Huntingdon rolls for Normancross hundred in Huntingdonshire have already been noted.[41] A rental for Islip (Oxon.) drawn up soon after 1279 contains ninety-one customary tenants, whereas there are only sixty-nine in the hundred roll return.[42] As Eric Stone observed in the context of Bampton hundred (Oxon.), unfree tenants on very small holdings were particularly likely to suffer under-enumeration, but the Ely surveys of 1277 show that freeholders were not consistently recorded either.[43] This makes it highly questionable how far the hundred rolls can be taken as a register of tenants. They are, of course, just as inadequate as Domesday Book as a census of population, but their confinement to the Midlands and East Anglia has protected them from the unsatisfactory calculations to which the latter has been subjected.[44]

How far the hundred rolls can be regarded as territorially comprehensive, even within their restricted geographical bounds, is also suspect. It is evident that most places within a hundred are

---

[40] *Lordship and Landscape*, ed. Hassell and Beauroy, 217–20, 233–46, no. 255.

[41] See above, Ch. 3.

[42] B. Harvey, *Westminster Abbey and its Estates in the Middle Ages* (Oxford, 1977), 208 n. 2.

[43] *Oxfordshire Hundred Rolls of 1279*, ed. E. Stone and P. Hyde (Oxford, 1968), 10; B. Dodwell, 'The Free Tenantry of the Hundred Rolls', *Ec. HR* 14 (1944), 166–7.

[44] For a summary of these see E. Miller and J. Hatcher, *Medieval England: Rural Society and Economic Change, 1086–1348* (London, 1978), 28–9; B. M. S. Campbell, *English Seigniorial Agriculture 1250–1450* (Cambridge, 2000), 403, table 8.06.

usually mentioned unless there is a good reason to the contrary, but this does not guarantee that every manor or hamlet within a parish has been included.[45] There are also gaps in the surveys themselves. These are obvious where rolls are damaged, but less so in other instances. Kosminsky drew attention to freeholders missing from Bourn, Comberton, and Madingley (Cambs.) and the omission of property belonging to Eynsham Abbey at Weald and Filkins (Oxon.), only revealed when he compared the hundred rolls with seigneurial records.[46] When the differences between the contents of rolls arising from local decisions about what to record, as well as varying degrees of subsequent editorial pruning, are also taken into account, it would be a very rash historian who took the inclusiveness of the hundred rolls for granted.

There is the separate and more general question of reliability, both of the information collected at the time of the inquiry and in the later transmission of its findings. There is ample evidence from other proceedings that royal officials were open to bribery. The *Liber Memorandorum* of Barnwell Priory in Cambridge preserves an account of payments of 40 shillings made to each of the serjeants during the 1286 eyre, as well as the less questionable gifts of fodder and provisions for the justices and their entourage.[47] The chapter accounts of Lincoln minster show a gift of 100 shillings to the escheator and a mark to his chief clerk when they came to inquire into acquisitions in mortmain in 1313.[48] Despite their oaths, the commissioners of 1279 may have been equally prepared to turn a blind eye in return for offerings, while jurors in their turn may have been vulnerable to pressure as well as corruption. The fact that some lords refused to cooperate with the inquiry shows that it was regarded with suspicion.[49] If it was widely perceived as having tax implications, the temptation to understate revenues may have proved irresistible. Kosminsky cites Ballard's observation that hundred roll rents were lower than those to be found on the contemporary pipe rolls of the bishop of Winchester.[50] Coss similarly

---

[45] See above, Ch. 4.

[46] Kosminsky, *Studies*, 32–3. Weld in Kosminsky's text.

[47] *Liber Memorandorum Ecclesie de Bernewelle*, ed. J. W. Clark (Cambridge, 1907), pp. xv, 171.

[48] Raban, *Mortmain Legislation*, 88.   [49] See above, Ch. 3.

[50] E. A. Kosminsky, 'The Hundred Rolls of 1279–80 as a Source for English Agrarian History', *Ec. HR* 3 (1931–2), 30.

pointed out that the rents for Richard de Loges's estate at Sowe in the Warwickshire returns were considerably lower than those recorded in his inquisition *post mortem* of 1293, although the interval between the two surveys means that this may not be a fair comparison.[51] Jurors described demesnes in different ways. In Normancross hundred (Hunts.), they gave precisely defined land measurements.[52] Elsewhere they sometimes used fiscal measures unchanged since Domesday, providing a poor guide as to the actual amount of land involved.[53] Persuasively detailed descriptions of villein obligations characteristic of some hundreds are open to misinterpretation.[54] Enumeration of labour services did not mean that they were performed. Commutation, wholesale on a year-to-year basis, or by the sale of individual works, was common. Moreover, payments such as aid and tallage were rarely given cash values. These are the sorts of problem which can best be resolved by reference to contemporary manorial accounts, but this can only be done where they are available. The estates of minor lords are usually undocumented. Inquisitions *post mortem,* heavily exploited as a substitute, sometimes capture manors belonging to these elusive individuals but, as official records, are open to many of the same disadvantages as the hundred roll verdicts. Moreover, few are exactly contemporary.

Making due allowance for observable omissions, both Kosminsky and Barbara Dodwell remained cautiously optimistic that accurate information had been put before the jurors, while Rodney Hilton argued that the Warwickshire hundred rolls might include subtenants who were ignored in landlords' own surveys.[55] Even supposing that this was generally true, some data was corrupted as the returns were copied and edited. This can be seen by comparing the parallel rolls for Leightonstone (Hunts.). At Keyston, for example, Geoffrey de Keyston and Julian' Burel were said to hold half a virgate for 12 shillings per annum in the PRO

[51] P. Coss, *Lordship, Knighthood and Locality* (Cambridge, 1991) 136–7.

[52] e.g. *RH* ii., 638b, 648a.

[53] Kosminsky, *Studies*, 29, 36.

[54] For the different ways in which labour obligations were recorded, see J. Kanzaka, 'Villein Rents in Thirteenth-Century England', *Ec. HR* 55 (2002), 596–7, esp. n. 17.

[55] Kosminsky, *Studies*, 28–35; B. Dodwell, 'The Free Tenantry of the Hundred Rolls', *Ec. HR* 14 (1944), 167; *The Stoneleigh Leger Book*, ed. R. H. Hilton (Dugdale Society; Oxford, 1960), p. xxxviii.

roll and 12 pence in the Huntingdon roll.[56] Similar errors affecting names and especially numbers were noted by Kosminsky.[57] Many of these slips were trivial, but they have the power to mislead. The enormous rent of 100 shillings paid by a subtenant of William de Waldesef for a two virgate freeholding at Woodston in Normancross hundred (Hunts.), for which the abbot of Thorney received only 7 shillings per annum, could be interpreted as a convincing demonstration of the loss suffered by overlords from fixed rents. It could equally well be a contemporary mistake which had crept in during editing. Indeed the latter may be supposed, partly because of the sheer size of the rent, but chiefly because the Huntingdon roll records a 7 shilling rent from the subtenant.[58] Nevertheless, to suspect error is one thing, to prove it is often another. Later copyists introduced further errors as John demonstrates with regard to the Warwickshire hundred rolls, quite apart from deliberate omission or selection arising from the cavalier attitude of Nichols to Burton's transcripts for Leicestershire or Morris to his unknown Shropshire exemplar.[59] Moreover, as we have already observed, while the Record Commission edition is generally faithful in its readings, minor errors are not hard to find and its shortcomings with regard to annotations and interpolations are a handicap to scholars.[60]

Like Domesday Book, the 1279–80 hundred rolls are the equivalent of a snapshot, taken at a fixed point in time. This too imposes limitations on their use, particularly when compared with the more dynamic court and account rolls, running from year to year, which were becoming common by the later thirteenth century. However, no historical source is without problems of transmission and interpretation and the richness of the 1279–80 returns more than compensates for the caution required in their use. The unique insight they offer into otherwise undocumented estates ensures them a special place among the treasure house of material available

---

[56] PRO, SC5/Hunts/Tower/3, m. 4; *RH* ii. 614b; HR, m. 2; S. Raban, 'Fresh Light on the 1279 Hundred Rolls', *Historical Research*, 61 (1988), 107. The rent has been correctly transcribed in the Rec. Comm. text.

[57] Kosminsky, *Studies*, 26 n. 5; 27 nn. 1–2.

[58] The original has been correctly transcribed in the Rec. Comm. text. PRO, SC5/Hunts/Tower/4 m. 8; *RH* ii. 643a; HR, m. 16.

[59] *Warwickshire*, ed. John 9–11, and above, Ch. 4.

[60] See above, pp. 6–7.

for thirteenth-century England. No other source since Domesday Book had described small estates and set them in the context of better documented lordships in the county community. Its value to historians is borne out by the range of studies it has generated.

One of the most exciting aspects of the Domesday survey has been its amenability to statistical analysis. The 1279–80 hundred rolls have also proved tempting in this respect even though, without the spare consistency of Exchequer Domesday, they pose more of a challenge. The assorted nature of the returns means that one cannot rely on comparing like with like. The extent to which land measures were not standardized is made plain by the variations in those set out among the PRO roll for Normancross hundred.[61] Even the size of the acre varied from place to place. Assumptions have to be made at every turn for the purpose of calculation. Should tenants for life or terms of years, for example, be classified as villeins or freeholders? How should cash values be assigned to labour services? Moreover, use can only be made of information which is provided. It is unfortunate that the banlieu of Ramsey Abbey is missing from the roll for Hurstingstone hundred (Hunts.), in view of the importance attached to evidence from this area, even though its inclusion would probably have strengthened the arguments put forward.[62] A good deal of material which does exist necessarily has to be discarded as unsuitable for classification.[63] Results based on statistics should never be made to bear more weight than their shaky foundations can sustain but, as Kosminsky pointed out, their goal is to make 'possible results which are unattainable by other methods of investigation'.[64] Rather like an impressionist painting, while the detail is a poor guide to reality, the overall effect nonetheless conveys a sense of truth.

Among those who have taken up the statistical challenge of the hundred rolls, Kosminsky remains pre-eminent, even though his great analysis of estate structure, part of *Studies in the Agrarian History of England in the Thirteenth Century,* was first published in the 1930s. Dividing estates into small, medium, and large, he painstakingly calculated percentages of land held in demesne and

---

[61] *RH* ii. 635a–65b.
[62] e.g. Kosminsky, *Studies*, 118–19; Kanzaka, 'Villein Rents', 601.
[63] Kosminsky, *Studies*, 88; Kanzaka, 'Villein Rents' 595.
[64] *Studies*, 40.

by different categories of peasant. This revealed that large estates often coincided with those held by the church and that these tended to approximate most closely to the classical manor described by Seebohm and Vinogradoff: large demesnes apparently serviced by customary labour. Inevitably, given the date at which he wrote, and his career as a Moscow academic and member of the Academy of Sciences of the USSR, Kosminsky was much preoccupied with issues then fashionable in Marxist historiography.[65] The debate has since moved on, although the question as to how far servile labour was exploited by landlords has been given a new lease of life by John Hatcher's contention that custom ensured that villeins often enjoyed some protection from the high land values prevailing in late thirteenth-century England.[66] The advent of computers has transformed this type of investigation. Once more, historians of Domesday have led the way, but John Palmer, one of the pioneers in this field, regarded the 1279–80 hundred rolls as another obvious candidate.[67] It is for these reasons, rather than any inadequacy in Kosminsky's careful assessment of the evidence, that the hundred rolls have been crying out for further analysis.

Junichi Kanzaka has been the first to exploit the potential of 'the new technology'. The initial fruit of his meticulously constructed database of tenements recorded in the Record Commission edition and in the Warwickshire hundred rolls has been to test Hatcher's hypotheses through an analysis of the factors governing the level of peasant rents. Drawing on records for nearly 30,000 peasant holdings, he concluded that custom, rather than market forces or seigneurial coercion, did indeed play a determining role in fixing the level of rents paid by servile tenants in parts of the Midlands, although the high level of labour obligations to be found in Huntingdonshire could be attributed to the power of ecclesiastical landlords.[68] The beauty of computer analysis is that, while it does not abolish the need for careful assessment of the raw evidence, once this has been done and a database established, it is an infinitely

---

[65] For his career, see Hilton's introduction to the 1956 English tr. of *Studies*, p. xv.

[66] J. Hatcher, 'English Serfdom and Villeinage: Towards a Reassessment', *Past and Present*, 90 (1981), 24.

[67] J. Palmer, 'Domesday Book and the Computer', in P. Sawyer (ed.), *Domesday Book* (London, 1985), 172.

[68] Kanzaka, 'Villein Rents', 598, 617.

flexible tool for further investigation. Now that such a database exists, a rich future harvest can be anticipated.

Kanzaka found cash sums assigned to villein services on the Normancross portion of the Huntingdon roll a useful means of verifying the accuracy of the values he had calculated in place of labour services for the purposes of analysis.[69] His work in turn provides welcome reassurance about the figures from the roll which I used for my own contribution to the debate. This is set out in detail elsewhere, but an account of the main findings follows.[70] Unlike Hatcher and Kanzaka, I focused on rents from the point of view of landlords rather than peasants, since the exceptionally rich data for Normancross hundred, dominated by great monastic estates, lends itself to an assessment of the policies of ecclesiastical lords. Altogether religious houses held fifty-one manors in twenty-eight villages and hamlets. Of the remainder, most estates belonged to minor knightly families whose activities could not be otherwise monitored and without which no comparative judgement could be made.

The distinction in the Huntingdon roll between cash and labour rents owed by villeins and the cash values assigned to each component reveals that, rather than exploiting their servile tenants, as historians have often supposed, ecclesiastical lords often received a lower return from villein land than lay lords because they retained the right to a higher proportion of rent in the form of labour.[71] While Kanzaka's work shows custom as a moderating influence on the level of villein rents in the Midlands as a whole, in north Huntingdonshire the best protection for servile tenants apparently lay in the preservation of their labour obligations. Even where works were sold annually, evidence from Ramsey Abbey suggests that the rates for these had probably become fixed at a low level over time.[72]

One can infer that the advantage of labour rents was well understood by peasants from an accusation brought in 1278 that the

[69] Ibid. 597–8.

[70] S. Raban, 'Landlord Return on Villein Rents in North Huntingdonshire in the Thirteenth Century', *Historical Research*, 66 (1993), 21–34.

[71] See Table 4. Rents in kind were too small to be significant and tended in any case to be commuted alongside labour services.

[72] J. A. Raftis, *The Estates of Ramsey Abbey: A Study in Economic Growth and Organisation* (Toronto, 1957), 225.

TABLE 4 *Villein rents in Normancross hundred (Hunts.) according to the Huntingdon roll*[a]

	In cash	In labour	Per virgate	Acres per virgate	Pence per acre
Lay estates					
Botolphbridge (Boyeby)	£6 8s. 8d.	—	32s. 2d.		
Botolphbridge and Orton Longueville (Drayton)	£1 2s. 0d.		22s. 0d.		
Orton Longueville (Longueville)	£13 4s. 0d.	£3 3s. 2½d.	29s. 9d.		
Chesterton (Vescy)	£1 0s. 0d.	3s. 6¾d.	23s. 6¾d.	30	9.4
Chesterton (Cantilupe)	£5 0s. 0d.	£1 0s. 2½d.	24s. 0½d.	30	9.6
Chesterton (Waldesef)	£1 10s 0d.	7s. 3¾d.	24s. 11d.		
Washingley (Lovetot/Washingley)	£1 17s. 0d.	6d.	15s. 0d.	25	7.2
Washingley (Serjeanty)	£1 18s. 0d.	8d.	15s. 5d.		
Folksworth (Huse)	5s. 0d.	5s. 0d.	10s. 0d.		
Folksworth (Russel)	8s. 0d.	10s. 0d.	9s. 0d.		
Caldecote (Brus)	£10 10s. 0d.		20s. 0d.	25	9.6
Denton (Ingoldeby)	£1 0s. 0d.		20s. 0d.	25	9.6
Denton (Gobaud)	£2 10s. 0d.		20s. 0d.	25	9.6
Sawtry (Moyne)	£17 0s. 0d.	£1 17s. 1d.	22s. 2d.	25	10.6
Sawtry (Beaumeys)	£1 4s. 0d.	£1 17s. 3d.	10s. 2½d.	25	4.9
Luddington (Moyne)	£4 10s. 0d.		20s. 0d.	30	8.0
Wood Walton (Beynvile)	£6 8s. 0d.	1s. 1d.	17s. 10d.	20	10.7
Glatton and Holme (Cornwall)	£28 16s. 0d.	£2 2s. 8d.	15s. 1d.	24	7.5
Conington (Brus)	£12 0s. 0d.	—	20s. 0d.	30	8.0
Average					8.7
Ecclesiastical estates					
Alwalton (Peterborough)	£1 7s. 4¾d.	£12 15s. 7¼d.	~22s 0d.[b]	25	~10.6

Fletton (Peterborough)	£1 14s. 8d.	£3 18s. 8d.	~22s 0d.[c]	25	~10.6
Chesterton (Royston)	£2 0s. 0d.	5s. 3d.	22s 7½d.		5.0
Elton (Ramsey)	£2 0s. 0d.	£8 0s. 0d.	10s. 0d.	24	
Morborne (Crowland)	£10 0s. 0d.	£2 10s. 0d.	16s. 8d.		
Water Newton (Thorney)		£15 10s. 0d.[d]	20s. 0d.	26	9.2
Sibson (Thorney)		£1 0s. 0d.	13s. 4d.	30	5.3
Sibson (Templars)		£1 17s. 6d.	12s. 6d.	30	5.0
Stibbington (Thorney)		£1 0s. 0d.	10s. 0d.	30	4.0
Haddon (Thorney)		£16 12s. 0d.	15s. 10d.[e]	24	7.9
Woodston (Thorney)		£13 12s. 0d.	16s. 0d.	25	7.7
Stanground (Thorney)		£8 0s. 0d.	18s. 10d.[f]	30	7.5
Farcet (Thorney)		£15 0s. 0d.	20s. 0d.	30	8.0
Yaxley (Thorney)		£40 0s. 0d.	20s. 0d.	30	8.0
Average					7.4
Average for hundred					8.1

[a] The following estates in the hundred had no villein rents recorded. Lay estates: Orton Waterville (both Waterville manors), Stilton (Hemington, Beynvile, and a third manor in wardship), Denton (Hurianus and Griffin). Ecclesiastical estates: Orton Waterville (Lincoln), Stilton (Bushmead), Conington (Sawtry, Chicksand, Huntingdon, and St Margaret's hospital), Washingley (Templars), Sawtry (the abbey), Wansford (Thorney). The printed hundred roll suggests that there were villeins on the Denton estate, despite their absence from the Huntingdon roll, and that they paid much the same rent as villeins on other manors in the vill (*RH* ii. 658b). Where villein rents are recorded, the cash sums are often confirmed by the hundred roll.

[b] This includes tallage and other dues owed by villeins and cottars amounting to £7 19s. 5d. p.a., thereby adding 7–8s. p.a. to the value of a villein virgate, assuming that payments were proportionate to the size of holding. Rent excluding these payments was 14s. 1½d. per virgate and 6.8d. per acre.

[c] As at Alwalton, customary tenants together paid a substantial further sum—£6 3s. 4d., worth perhaps one mark extra per virgate. Rent excluding this would be 8s. 9d. per virgate and 4 2d. per acre.

[d] This column combines labour and cash.

[e] The text values each virgate at 16s. or 8d. per acre

[f] The text values each virgate at 20s. or 8d. per acre.

reeve at Elton had been bribed by the richer tenants to avoid a change to cash payments.[73] Significantly, the highest return on villein land in the hundred was enjoyed by Hugh de Boyeby, all of whose rent on his manor at Botolphbridge was taken in the form of money.[74] So, while the unusually heavy labour rents characteristic of ecclesiastical lords in this hundred may well have been the result of their coercive power in times past, the hundred rolls suggest that by the later thirteenth century they were reluctant to exercise their economic muscle.

They also reveal that ecclesiastical lords showed a more proactive attitude towards their freehold rents. By 1279, the return on some freeholdings in Normancross hundred had become derisory. The one virgate and half virgate tenements each rendering 2 pence p.a. on the Drayton manor at Orton Longueville and Botolphbridge were extreme, but most freehold rents fell far short of the return on a villein virgate.[75] Both Peterborough and Thorney Abbeys can be seen buying out free tenants on their demesne manors over a long period of time.[76] By the time of the inquiry, of the three major free tenants on Thorney Abbey's manor at Woodston, one had already sold most of his land to the abbey and to his fellow tenants and the other two were to dispose of theirs over the coming decades.[77] At Water Newton, only 9 acres remained in the hands of freeholders. One holding had certainly been purchased; another given to the abbey in return for a corrody.[78] Further purchase had taken place at Stibbington.[79] It is also likely that Ramsey Abbey recovered a large holding in Elton from John de Aylingtone.[80] Leases for life or fixed terms were also making their appearance on ecclesiastical manors at this time and became a firm policy under Abbot Odo of Thorney at the turn of the century.[81]

---

[73] *Select Pleas in Manorial and Other Seignorial Courts*, ed. F. W. Maitland (Selden Society, 2; London, 1889), 95.

[74] HR, m. 7.   [75] Ibid.

[76] E. King, *Peterborough Abbey* (Cambridge, 1973), 53–4, 66–9; S. Raban, *The Estates of Thorney and Crowland* (University of Cambridge, Department of Land Economy, Occasional Paper, 7; Cambridge, 1977), 62–3.

[77] *RH* ii. 643a; Raban, *Estates*, 63, 72.

[78] *RH* ii. 646b.   [79] Ibid. 648b.

[80] Ibid. 656a–b. No mention is made of recovery, but John's tenure is recorded in the past tense and most of the cottars on the holding are paying rent to the abbot.

[81] Ibid. 640a–1b; CUL, Add MS 3021, fo. 451; Raban, 'Landlord Return', 30.

While churchmen were often prepared to accept returns below the market rate on their land, or remedy the matter legitimately through purchase, the Normancross rolls further suggest that this was not necessarily true of smaller lay lords. By means of life leases, Wydo de Waterville enjoyed rents averaging *c*.20 shillings per virgate p.a. on the manor he held from Peterborough Abbey at Orton Waterville.[82] The same approach can be discerned on Ralph de Wassingle's manors at Washingley, but with more variable results.[83] Add these measures to the higher return on villein land enjoyed by these lords and it is evident that they were proportionately more successful than their infinitely richer and more powerful ecclesiastical neighbours. There is no indication as to how they achieved this, but if coercion took place they seem to have been the more likely perpetrators. Often resident on their manors and with fewer tenants to deal with, they were in a better position to enforce their will. The lone villein on the Vescy manor at Chesterton, who paid one of the highest rents in the hundred, was far more exposed to pressure than the twenty obstructive villeins managed by a corrupt reeve on the Ramsey Abbey manor at Elton.[84] It is worth noting that the earl of Cornwall, the only substantial lay landlord in the hundred, was scarcely more successful than the church in achieving a realistic return on his rented land at Glatton.[85]

The factors governing peasant rents were extremely complex and regionally specific. Nevertheless, the Normancross hundred rolls make it plain that older notions of harshly exploitative ecclesiastical landlords can no longer be sustained. If such rapacious lords existed, they were more likely to have been knights, many of whom had relatively modest resources and were therefore driven to take action.

There is broad support for this interpretation from work done on other Midland counties, where knightly society has been scrutinized in order to establish whether or not it was in crisis.[86] David Carpenter has established that knights in Oxfordshire were also acting assertively in the face of uneconomic rents, increasing their return from villein land and either buying out freeholders or raising

---

[82] HR, m. 8; *RH* ii. 637b–8a.   [83] HR, m. 11; *RH* ii. 635a–b.
[84] See Table 4; HR, m. 9; *RH* ii. 655a.   [85] See Table 4; *RH* ii. 650a–2a.
[86] See Coss, *Origins*, ch. 4, for a summary of this debate.

rents among the remainder.[87] With regard to Warwickshire, Peter Coss argued that the truly rapacious, while of knightly stock, were more likely to be *curiales* such as Walter de Merton, Adam de Stratton, or Geoffrey de Langley.[88] Thus, while the estates of the church appeared 'custom bound', Langley was able to raise rents through a combination of 'capital and coercion'.[89] As in Huntingdonshire, such conclusions would have been impossible without the hundred rolls. Although a successful family like the Langleys might leave a cartulary, the estates of failing families, such as that of the Nerbones at Stivichall, would otherwise have disappeared without trace.[90]

Historians seeking to discover more about the free peasantry on whom these lords set their sights have also found the hundred rolls well suited to the task, not least because they permit a fuller picture of the numerous freeholders who held land in more than one place. Barbara Dodwell drew attention to the markedly higher proportion of free tenants in Cambridgeshire and Bedfordshire, which she attributed in part to a legacy of Scandinavian settlement.[91] More recently, M. Barg showed that more than half of the freeholders in Oxfordshire, Huntingdonshire, and Buckinghamshire were not in fact peasants. They were better represented among the Cambridgeshire and Bedfordshire freeholders, as Dodwell's findings might lead one to expect, but even there about 30 per cent of free tenancies were in the hands of craftsmen, tradesmen, gentry, and, above all, ecclesiastics.[92] While the boundary between petty traders, artisans, and peasants was far from clear cut, and the remaining tenements would have been largely occupied by peasant subtenants, the sizeable presence of more powerful people in the tenurial ladder illustrates how serious a problem lords faced if they wanted to regain control of their freehold land.

Two surveys as broadly similar in structure as Domesday Book

---

[87] D. A. Carpenter, 'Was there a Crisis of the Knightly Class in the Thirteenth Century? The Oxfordshire Evidence', *EHR* 95 (1980), 742–5.

[88] P. Coss, 'Sir Geoffrey de Langley and the Crisis of the Knightly Class in Thirteenth-Century England', in T. H. Aston (ed.), *Landlords, Peasants and Politics in Medieval England* (Cambridge, 1987), 186–7.

[89] Coss, *Lordship*, 116–19, 124–5.

[90] Coss, 'Sir Geoffrey de Langley', 177, 198–9.

[91] Dodwell, 'Free Tenantry', 164–8.

[92] M. A. Barg, 'The Social Structure of Manorial Freeholders: An Analysis of the Hundred Rolls of 1279', *Ag. HR* 39 (1991), 111.

and the 1279–80 hundred rolls invite comparison as a means of assessing change over the intervening centuries. The most important study of this sort to date was initiated by J. B. Harley working on Warwickshire.[93] Undertaken at the height of the debate over M. M. Postan's model of demographic growth to *c.*1300 followed by a Malthusian crisis, Harley argued that, by the later thirteenth century, there had been a dramatic increase in population in the wooded Arden district of Stoneleigh hundred, but that in the anciently settled Feldon district of Kineton hundred some communities had barely grown at all or even declined slightly. From this he concluded that the population had already reached saturation point in the Feldon area by 1086, whereas opportunities for colonization remained in the Arden area to the north. This differential development carried with it social consequences. Whereas in the colonizing hundred of Stoneleigh 50 per cent of landholders were free, freeholders constituted only 30 per cent of the tenant population in Kineton hundred.[94] There were also differences in the manorial structure of the two hundreds. While Kineton was characterized by classic seigneurial estates with large demesnes and substantial numbers of villeins, Stoneleigh experienced a high population density, with peasants existing precariously on small-scale agriculture. These findings have been somewhat modified by Trevor John, partly because he was able to bring to bear a greater familiarity gained through editing the hundred rolls.[95] He concluded that population growth in the Feldon area was greater than Harley had allowed and that the commercial vitality of Coventry was responsible for some of the high-density settlement in Stoneleigh hundred.

Surprisingly perhaps, the urban returns have never been studied as an entity. Even attempts to exploit the most substantial returns, those for Oxford and Cambridge, have an air of frustration about them. Helen Cam described the Cambridge rolls as 'an almost embarrassingly detailed picture of the town', while Rose Graham

---

[93] J. B. Harley, 'Population Trends and Agricultural Developments from the Warwickshire Hundred Rolls of 1279', *Ec. HR*, 2nd ser., 11 (1958), 8–18. Idem, 'The Settlement Geography of Early Medieval Warwickshire', *Institute of British Geographers: Transactions and Papers*, 34 (1964), 115–30.

[94] Idem, 'Population Trends', 14.

[95] T. John, 'Population Change in Medieval Warwickshire: Domesday Book to the Hundred Rolls of 1279–80', *Local Population Studies*, 59 (1997), 41–53.

felt it necessary to reorganize the Oxford rolls into parishes rather than wards in order to make them easier to use.[96] Consisting largely of lists of tenants and their holdings, these rolls have mostly attracted topographers. They were drawn on heavily by those compiling the *Victoria County Histories*, but the most thorough attempt so far to reconstruct street frontages used the putative King's Lynn return.[97] Valuable though the returns have been for this purpose, given the paucity of information about urban conditions in the late thirteenth century, it might seem curious that they have not been exploited more widely. Economic historians are increasingly convinced that commercialization had penetrated English society far more deeply at this period than was once appreciated, even though it is estimated that only 10 to 15 per cent of the population lived in towns.[98] The hundred rolls, so informative on rural matters, might have been expected to make some contribution to this debate. That they have not done so must be attributed to their limitations.

Most disappointing of all are the returns for London. They add little to an evaluation of the largest and most sophisticated town in the realm, although the fact that it was the subject of special articles reinforces its primacy. Unlike King's Lynn, the returns are not conveniently topographical. Painstaking attempts to reconstruct the layout of each parish have necessarily had to draw on other sources.[99] Investigation into the property of those evading knightly status throughout the realm demonstrates the supra-regional catchment of its population, but much of the information contained in the verdicts echoes that already available on the 1276 eyre roll.[100]

Superficially the remaining urban returns look more promising, but it quickly becomes evident that the towns depicted in the rolls are to some extent an illusion created by different approaches to collecting and editing the data. This is illustrated by the much more

[96] *VCH, Cambs.*, iii. 7; 'Description of Oxford from the Hundred Rolls', ed. R. Graham, in *Collectanea* (Oxford, 1905), 1.

[97] E. and P. Rutledge, 'King's Lynn and Great Yarmouth', *Norfolk Archaeology*, 37 (1978), 94–101.

[98] R. H. Britnell, *The Commercialisation of English Society 1000–1500* (Cambridge, 1993), 115; E. Miller and J. Hatcher, *Medieval England: Towns, Commerce and Crafts, 1086–1348* (Harlow, 1995), 278.

[99] For the project based on the Museum of London, see D. Keene, 'A New Study of London before the Great Fire', *Urban History Yearbook* (1984), 12–13.

[100] See above, Ch. 3.

active land market revealed in Cambridge and its suburb of Barnwell than in Oxford.[101] Greater attention was paid to title in the Cambridge returns, where ownership over several generations was recorded. This multiplied the incidence of purchases in comparison with the number revealed by the more restricted tenurial histories provided for Oxford, where the emphasis was on rent yields. That the distinction was a matter of record rather than reality is confirmed by the return for the Oxford suburb of Northgate. Administratively a separate hundred in the hands of Hugh de Plessis, its return broadly conformed to those for the rest of Oxford. However, it was more like Cambridge in recording previous tenancies and hence registering a higher proportion of sales.[102]

Outside the larger towns, frequent reference to markets and fairs bears witness to the commercial infrastructure existing in the Midlands and East Anglia, but here the hundred rolls add little to information already preserved on the charter rolls. Moreover, the fact that a lord possessed (or had usurped) the right to hold a market or fair was no guarantee that much trading took place. The region was not richly endowed with settlements with borough status.[103] This explains the small number of separate urban returns. However, as we have seen, settlements with urban characteristics are sometimes to be found among the manorial returns.[104]

While not enormously informative, the hundred rolls bear witness to the fact that much thirteenth-century trade still took place in surroundings which were essentially rural. At Linton the marginal heading for the list of shopkeepers described them as 'free tenants, burgesses in name'.[105] At Kimbolton (Hunts.) the tenants of a string of messuages appear under the heading of 'burgesses and cottars'.[106] On the earl of Cornwall's manor at Holme (Hunts.), eight burgesses holding cottages with yards were entered after a long list of smallholders.[107] St Ives, home to one of the great annual fairs of thirteenth-century England, nevertheless retained its identity as one of the abbot of Ramsey's manors for the rest of the

---

[101] PRO, SC5/Cambs/Tower/1, 3 pts., SC5/Oxon/Tower/8–10, 18; *RH* ii. 356a–93a, 788b–805a; 'The Hundred Rolls for the Parish of St Thomas, Oxford', ed. J. Cooper, *Oxoniensia*, 37 (1972), 168–73; 'Description', ed. Graham, 3–63.
[102] SC5/Oxon/Tower/11; *RH* ii. 805a–11b; 'Description', ed. Graham, 75–98.
[103] M. W. Beresford and H. P. R. Finberg, *English Medieval Boroughs* (Newton Abbot, 1973) *passim*.
[104] See above, Ch. 3.   [105] *Liberi tenentes nomine burgag*', *RH* ii. 417a.
[106] *RH* ii. 621b.   [107] *RH* ii. 652b.

year. The hundred roll mentions frontages reserved for the abbot at the time of the fair, but otherwise gives the impression of an agricultural community. There is no indication among villein labour services of the obligation to make hurdles and keep watch at the fair as recorded in the abbey's own surveys for St Ives, Wistow, and Needingworth.[108] Evidently the hundred rolls cannot be relied upon for the whole picture. Mention of the tollbooth and stall in a long and detailed return for the abbot of Thorney's principal manor at Yaxley (Hunts.) is unusual.[109] Many other such features must have passed unremarked in briefer returns.

The foregoing account shows that the hundred rolls have been an important source in almost all the major controversies surrounding the English medieval economy and society during the past half century. In addition, countless historians have drawn on them for local or regional studies. Coss's work on lordship in Warwickshire and Hilton's on society in the West Midlands come to mind, but anyone researching in the counties for which they survive has made use of them to a greater or lesser degree.[110] Principally valued by social and economic historians for the systematic use to which they can be put, they also contain nuggets of information of interest to other historians. Such might be the accounts of the confiscation of a knight's fee at Chinnor and Sydenham in Lewknor hundred (Oxon.) suffered by Walter de Vernon for refusing to render military service to King John during the war with France or the background to the disputed title to the hamlet of Westbury in Mursley hundred (Bucks.).[111] To some extent the distinctive value of the rolls as a source of information for all the estates within a given county may be overtaken by new approaches to records which on their own are more limited. Bruce Campbell has gleaned exciting results by aggregating data from huge numbers of inquisitions *post mortem* and manorial accounts, culminating in *English Seigniorial Agriculture 1250–1450*.[112]

---

[108] The villein obligations are recorded under Slepe, the name of the manor. *RH* ii. 603b–4a, 605a; *Cart. Rames*, i. 290, 301, 358–9.

[109] *RH* ii. 641a.

[110] Coss, *Lordship*; R. H. Hilton, *A Medieval Society: The West Midlands at the End of the Thirteenth Century* (London, 1966).

[111] *RH* ii. 334a, 783a.

[112] For the number and geographical distribution of documents used in his databases, see Campbell, *English Seigniorial Agriculture*, 34–5, table 2.01, 38, fig. 2.02, 46–54.

Thus, inquisitions *post mortem,* used by Kosminsky as a check on the veracity of the hundred rolls, have now assumed a higher profile in their own right. The superiority of Campbell's data over the 1279–80 hundred rolls lies in its ability to capture additional types of information and its coverage of the whole country, even if the north-west and south-west of England are thinly represented. Moreover, the application of this method, along with Geographical Information Systems, has permitted the production of maps which 'invite comparison with the Domesday Survey'.[113] Notwithstanding these innovative applications of modern technology, it is inconceivable that the hundred rolls will be wholly superseded. Campbell, for example, continued to draw on Kosminsky's conclusions in order to create a structural context for his analysis, albeit with reservations.[114] Furthermore, inquisitions *post mortem* and account rolls are biased against just those minor lay lords for which the hundred rolls are so important. What remains to be seen is what the ingenuity of the next generation of scholars can wring from them.

---

[113] Quoted from advance publicity for B. Campbell and K. Bartley, *Lay Lordship, Land and Wealth: A Socio-Economic Atlas of England 1300–49* (Manchester, 2003).
[114] Campbell, *English Seigniorial Agriculture*, 26, 36, 57–9.

6

The Surviving Rolls

The surviving rolls are such a varied body of documents that a general survey is of limited practical help to users. This chapter is designed to assist those who wish either to study one particular area or need information about the manuscript rolls which is not evident from older printed editions. The following pages describe the rolls and attempt some assessment of the completeness of the coverage for each hundred. The presence of a return for an individual parish is fairly easy to check. However, only detailed topographical knowledge can establish whether or not it contains a full record of all the holdings associated with the vill and any outlying hamlets. That must await further local study.

BEDFORDSHIRE AND BUCKINGHAMSHIRE CIRCUIT

Some returns survive for all the north-western hundreds in both counties, with the exception of Rowley hundred in Buckinghamshire. The rolls are finished in appearance and the information they contain is highly compressed. All the rolls have separate membranes dealing with liberties, except for Stodden hundred in Bedfordshire, where the roll is too fragmentary to be certain. The rolls are now sewn at the head, but stitch marks suggest that they were originally sewn end to end. Although there are only four hundred rolls for Buckinghamshire, they include a handful of returns for vills associated with other hundreds. In addition to those mentioned below under the entry for their modern hundred, there are returns for Tyrthrop in Ashendon hundred and Stokenchurch in Desborough hundred, both on the roll for Lewknor hundred in Oxfordshire.[1]

---

[1] *RH* ii. 784b–6a. Stokenchurch was transferred to Buckinghamshire in 1895.

BEDFORDSHIRE

Stodden hundred[2]

The roll consists of a single membrane of approximately 23 × 60 cm, written on both sides of the parchment. It provides details of landholdings in Riseley in the main part of the hundred, and for the three detached vills of Clapham, Oakley, and Milton Ernest. It is a fully edited text with no annotations, but there appear to be gaps into which information was later inserted by the original scribe. No mention is made of regalian rights. This implies that there was once at least one further membrane containing this information, as there is for other rolls on the circuit.[3] The heading 'Stodden hundred: concerning liberties and tenures' is similar to those found on some of the membranes of the Willey and Bucklow roll. Swineshead, which lies geographically within the hundred, was then attached to Leightonstone hundred (Hunts.), where its return appears alongside other holdings associated with the earl of Hereford. It was transferred to Bedfordshire in 1896.[4]

Willey and Bucklow hundreds[5]

The roll consists of six membranes, approximately 24.5 cm wide and varying markedly in length. The membranes, written in several hands, are sewn at the head. All but the liberties membrane are ruled and four are written on both sides of the parchment, with returns running from vill to vill across membranes. The roll is a finished text with few corrections. There are a small number of interesting annotations. As with the Stodden roll, gaps appear to have been left in places for the insertion of missing information. Membranes dealing with estates have slits for seals. There are manorial surveys for every vill in the hundred, but some vills are not mentioned on the liberties membrane. The latter has a note about non-cooperation on its dorse.

F. A. Youngs, *Guide to the Local Administrative Units of England*, 2 vols. (Royal Historical Society; London, 1980–91), i. 40.

² PRO, SC5/Beds/Tower/1; *RH* ii. 321a–3a.
³ *RH* ii. 321a.
⁴ *RH* ii. 622b–3a; Youngs, *Guide*, i. 253.
⁵ PRO, SC5/Beds/Tower/2; *RH* ii. 323a–33b.

BUCKINGHAMSHIRE

Bunsty hundred[6]

The roll consists of eleven membranes, sewn at the head and varying greatly in size. The shortest is approximately 11 × 22.5 cm, while the first and longest is approximately 21 × 45 cm. This membrane, which has a further short membrane stitched to its foot, is the only one to be written on both sides. All are in the same, large, distinctive hand on ruled parchment. Each membrane has slits, or the remains of such slits, for twelve seals. The roll is a finished text with few corrections and no annotations. The short, final membrane, which deals with liberties, does not include all the vills for which there are manorial surveys. There are no returns of any sort for the vills of Castlethorpe, Cold Brayfield, Newton Blosssomville, or Olney.[7]

Lamua hundred[8]

The roll consists of three membranes, broader than average at approximately 30 cm and of varying length. The first and longest is written on both sides of the parchment. The final membrane, recording information about liberties, is the shortest and in a different hand. It nevertheless includes information for Twyford, Marsh Gibbon, Addington, and Adstock for which there are no manorial surveys. All three membranes are sewn at the head and have slits for seals: seven on the survey membranes, three on the liberties membrane. The roll appears to be a finished text, without correction or annotation. It contains a survey for Thornton and mentions Bourton on the liberties membrane, both of which were in Rowley hundred and associated with the earl of Cornwall.[9] There are no returns of any description for Charndon, Padbury, and Poundon.[10]

---

[6] PRO, SC5/Bucks/Tower/3; *RH* ii. 343b–50b.

[7] Warrington, which is also absent, was then part of Olney and only became a separate parish in 1866. Youngs, *Guide*, i. 42.

[8] PRO, SC5/Bucks/Tower/4; *RH* ii. 350b–3b.

[9] *RH* ii. 352a–b, 353b.

[10] Charndon and Poundon were then part of Twyford. Youngs, *Guide*, i. 32, 41.

Mursley hundred[11]

The roll consists of three membranes, approximately 20–22 cm wide and of varying length, sewn at the head. The first retains a single seal as well the slits which are to be found on all three membranes. The first two membranes record manorial surveys, the second of which has entries continued on the dorse. The third and smallest membrane, dealing with liberties, has a note about non-cooperation on the dorse. The roll appears to be a finished text without annotation or correction. A survey was included for Shenley and its hamlet of Westbury, which lay partly in Seckloe hundred. The obligation to pay one mark per annum to that hundred is recorded on both the manorial and liberties membranes. There is no mention of Nash on either.

Stodfold hundred[12]

The roll consists of four membranes approximately 28.5 cm wide and of varying length, sewn at the head. Returns run from vill to vill across membranes. The roll is a finished text without correction or annotation, but the last and shortest membrane, dealing with liberties, is noticeably less neat. Only the second membrane is written on both sides of the parchment and this is the only membrane not to have slits for seals. Lillingstone Lovell and Boycott, which became part of this hundred in the nineteenth century, appear on the roll for Ploughley hundred in Oxfordshire, probably because, as royal manors, they were originally associated with Kirtlington.[13] There is no mention of Shalstone among either the manorial surveys or the liberties.

Marlow borough[14]

The roll consists of two membranes approximately 19–20 cm wide. The second is fragmentary, leaving the return incomplete. The membranes are sewn end to end and are unusual in layout, with widely spaced lines. It is a neat, finished return.

[11] PRO, SC5/Bucks/Tower/1; *RH* ii. 334a–8b.
[12] PRO, SC5/Bucks/Tower/2; *RH* ii. 338b–43b.
[13] *VCH, Oxon.*, vi. 3; Youngs, *Guide*, i. 37.
[14] PRO, SC5/Bucks/Tower/5; *RH* ii. 353b–5b.

This circuit has the largest body of returns, which between them represent the whole span of the inquiry from initial verdicts to finished rolls. Additionally, the Cambridgeshire rolls have the distinction of including the largest amount of unpublished material belonging to returns in the National Archives. Rolls survive for fifteen hundreds—all fourteen of the hundreds in Cambridgeshire and a single manor at Witcham in the Isle of Ely, together with rolls for Cambridge itself and the suburb of Barnwell. Most appear to belong to the intermediate stages of compilation, being either original returns or fair copies and bear signs of editorial work. Some additions and interlineations are omitted from the Record Commission edition and, where they have been included, it is not possible to identify from the printed text which they are. There are rolls for all four hundreds in Huntingdonshire and the borough of Godmanchester, but nothing for Huntingdon itself. Unlike the Cambridgeshire rolls, they appear to belong to the final stages of the inquiry. The Huntingdon roll, of unknown provenance, in the Bodleian Library, Oxford, comprises further returns for the two Huntingdonshire hundreds of Leightonstone and Normancross, which are not part of the official corpus of returns in the National Archives. It consists of seventeen membranes, sewn end to end, with a schedule at m. 16. At its fullest, the roll is 19.5 cm wide, but up to 3 cm of the first three membranes have been lost through cropping on the left-hand side.[15]

CAMBRIDGESHIRE

Armingford hundred[16]

The unprinted roll was found among unsorted Chancery Miscellanea in 1926. It now consists of sixteen membranes, further fragments having been added since. One addition was made to m. 13, from E213/4/5 in 1938, and a second from Chancery

[15] Bodl., Huntingdon rolls 1; S. Raban, 'Fresh Light on the 1279 Hundred Rolls', *Historical Research*, 61 (1988), 105–6.
[16] PRO, SC5/Cambs/Tower/16.

Miscellanea in 1976, when m.16 was also added. It is so badly damaged that it is largely illegible, but appears to be a fair copy, neatly written in a single hand. Membranes are sewn at the head, with each vill beginning on a fresh membrane. Returns from Bassingbourn, Clopton, Croydon, Guilden Morden, Kneesworth, Litlington, Melbourn, Tadlow, Wendy, Whaddon, and also Royston (Herts.) can be identified and appear to follow the usual circuit formula of setting out the articles ahead of each response. Jurors are named on m. 8.

Chesterton hundred[17]

Two damaged fragments have been added to the roll which now comprises five membranes. Part of m. 2 was added from plea roll fragments in 1952 and the final membrane from Chancery Miscellanea in 1928. Neither is printed. Separate numbers have been allocated to the dorse of some membranes, with the result that there are discrepancies between the MS membrane numbers and those of the Record Commission text. The roll is a fair copy with signs of checking, but little editing. Membranes are sewn at the head, except for the first two membranes, which are sewn end to end and are therefore much longer than the rest. There are returns for all the vills in the hundred, except for Dry Drayton.

Cheveley hundred[18]

All that survives from this hundred is a single badly damaged membrane 18.5 × 57.5 cms which is not in print. There are no signs of stitch marks to indicate that it was once part of a larger roll. Details of tenancies are legible, but it is unclear to which vill they belonged. It appears to be a neatly written, final draft without obvious correction or annotation.

Chilford hundred[19]

The roll consists of nineteen membranes approximately 21 cm wide

[17] PRO, SC5/Cambs/Tower/3; *RH* ii. 402a–13b.
[18] PRO, SC5/Cambs/Tower/17.
[19] PRO, SC5/Cambs/Tower/4; *RH* ii. 413b–30b.

and of different lengths.[20] They are in a variety of hands and sewn together at the head. On some membranes, returns were made on both sides of the parchment. Each vill begins on a fresh membrane. Part of m. 2 was added from Miscellanea in 1975. This and m. 19 are unprinted. The roll appears to be a fair copy of edited returns. On several membranes the bounds of common land follow a short gap on the parchment.[21] Advowson information is included but, unusually for Cambridgeshire, there is no reference to the non-manorial articles. Every vill in the hundred is represented on the roll.

Flendish hundred[22]

The roll consists of seven membranes of varying size sewn together at the head. Three have further membranes added. Approximately 19 cm wide, some membranes are rather narrower than usual. All but m. 6 are written on both sides of the parchment. Jurors are named on the dorse of m. 2. It is neatly written, with few corrections or annotations and appears to be a finished return. All vills in the hundred are represented.

Longstow hundred[23]

The two-part roll consists of twenty-two membranes approximately 24–6 cm wide and sewn end to end. Written in several hands, some membranes have returns on both sides of the parchment. The damaged head of m. 22, which lists half of the hundredal jurors, has been omitted from the printed text. The dorse is marked 'totum hundred'. There are a good many insertions, annotations, and marginal symbols throughout this roll. These are either omitted from the Record Commission edition or not identifiable as such.[24] The returns for each vill begin on a separate membrane. The roll thus appears to consist of original verdicts, or possibly fair copies of original verdicts, which were then subject to editing. A copy of the Bourn return exists on mm.

---

[20] Eighteen membranes according to the PRO catalogue.
[21] e.g. on mm. 11[r], 11[d], 14.
[22] PRO, SC5/Cambs/Tower/5; *RH* ii. 430b–46b.
[23] PRO, SC5/Cambs/Tower/10 (2 pts); *RH* ii. 507a–42b.
[24] See above, Ch. 4.

7–13 of a sixteenth-century paper MS which probably belonged to Barnwell Priory. This does not differ significantly from the text in the National Archives, but it provides a complete list of jurors as well as the opening of the Caxton entry and part of the return for Caldecote.[25] Every vill in the hundred is represented on the roll.

Northstow hundred[26]

The roll consists of fourteen membranes of varying length and width, sewn together at the head.[27] It is a fair, but not final, copy with a number of annotations indicating checking. A number of entries are also flagged. Apart from m. 3, all membranes are written on one side of the parchment only. There is a separate membrane containing part of a return for Girton which differs considerably from that on the roll.[28] Every vill in the hundred is represented on the roll.

Papworth hundred[29]

The ten membranes of this roll of varying length and width are sewn together at the head. They are written on one side of the parchment only and several are worn and stained. Each vill occupies a separate membrane, seven of which are made up of two or three membranes in order to complete the return. Articles about liberties are addressed alongside estate surveys and some responses are flagged. Otherwise, the roll appears to be a fair, final draft without corrections or annotations. All the vills in the hundred are included, except for Willingham. There is also a return for Long Stanton which is normally regarded as part of Northstow hundred.

Radfield hundred[30]

The unprinted roll consists of two membranes only. One deals with

[25] Christ's College, Cambridge, MS Bourn aB, 7–22. A full account of the MS is in course of preparation by Stephen Baxter.
[26] PRO, SC5/Cambs/Tower/6; *RH* ii. 446b–66b.
[27] Thirteen membranes according to the PRO catalogue, but a short damaged final membrane is also present.
[28] PRO, SC5/8/5/6. See above, Ch. 4.
[29] PRO, SC5/Cambs/Tower/7; *RH* ii. 466b–83b.
[30] PRO, SC5/Cambs/Tower/15.

Dullingham, while the other, damaged, membrane, added from Miscellanea in 1975, deals with Weston Colville. Both are approximately 21 cm wide and written on one side of unruled parchment. They appear to be neat, final drafts without correction or annotation.

Staine hundred[31]

The roll consists of thirteen rather miscellaneous membranes in several hands, sewn together at the head. They are numbered one to twelve, with a further membrane at 7a. Membranes 4–5, the return for the earl of Gloucester's manor at Bottisham, are distinctively different in appearance. The first membrane deals with responses to the non-manorial articles for the whole hundred, but the returns for several vills also address these articles in addition to describing landholdings. The roll appears to be a neat final draft, with few corrections or annotations. Every vill is represented on the roll, except for Lode, which was not separated from Bottisham until 1894.[32]

Staploe hundred[33]

The roll consists of nine membranes of varying length and width, sewn together at the head. The return for each vill usually begins on a fresh membrane, continuing on the dorse where necessary. The final membrane consists of verdicts as to the bounds of commons and marshes for most vills in the hundred. The roll appears to be an edited text with few corrections or annotations. All vills in the hundred are represented on the roll.

Thriplow hundred[34]

The roll consists of eight membranes, approximately 23 cm wide and sewn together at the head. The return for each vill begins on a fresh membrane, with further membranes stitched at the foot to complete the return where necessary. The roll is written on one side

---

[31] PRO, SC5/Cambs/Tower/8; *RH* ii. 483b–97a.
[32] Youngs, *Guide*, i. 51.
[33] PRO, SC5/Cambs/Tower/9; *RH* ii. 497a–507a.
[34] PRO, SC5/Cambs/Tower/11; *RH* ii. 542b–54b.

of ruled parchment and appears to be a fully edited, finished text. Very few articles are explicitly mentioned and responses to the articles are generally subsumed into the manorial surveys, with a marginal note *Articul'*. There are signs of checking and a number of entries are flagged. A later note on the dorse of the return for Little Shelford implies that it had gone astray at some point before being returned to the roll. All vills are represented on the roll, except for Stapleford.

Wetherley hundred[35]

The nine-membrane roll is sewn end to end and written on one side of the parchment only. Returns for individual vills run from membrane to membrane and there are numerous interlineations, additions, and notes to indicate that the returns had been checked. Responses to the non-manorial articles have been incorporated into the manorial surveys with a marginated note *Articulum* alongside. A number of entries relating to liberties and tenure without warrant are flagged. It appears to be an edited, but not fair, finished roll.[36] All vills are represented on the roll, except for Coton.

Whittlesford hundred[37]

The fourteen-membrane roll, approximately 21 cm wide, is sewn at the head. Four membranes have returns on the dorse and several are damaged. The first membrane has the names of the jurors set out in two columns as in the Record Commission text. The roll is neatly written with virtually no corrections or annotations and appears to be a finished text. *Exam'* at the foot of several membranes indicates that the returns had been checked and a number of entries are flagged. Every vill in the hundred is represented on the roll.

---

[35] PRO, SC5/Cambs/Tower/12; *RH* ii. 554b–68a.
[36] See above, Ch. 4.
[37] PRO, SC5/Cambs/Tower/14; *RH* ii. 570a–90b.

Witcham hundred[38]

The only return for this hundred is contained on a single membrane 21.5 × 57 cm, written on both sides of the parchment. It is a finished text with few corrections or cancellations. The heading *Wycha'* is marginated as on fuller rolls, but there are no stitch marks to indicate that it was one part of a larger roll. There are no annotations. The membrane covers several manors belonging to the honour of Richmond in Witcham itself.

Cambridge borough[39]

The return for the borough of Cambridge consists of forty membranes of varying lengths, the last five of which, comprising part three, were omitted from the Record Commission edition. These contain returns *inter alia* for the parishes of St Sepulchre and All Saints in Judaismo, Holy Trinity and St Andrew. Part three does not appear to have been taken into account in the discussion of the Cambridge rolls by M. D. Lobel or by Helen Cam, although the latter observed that Cambridge has the only complete urban return.[40] The membranes on part three are mostly ruled, but not the others. None have material on the dorse. The three rolls are in a variety of hands, but with very few corrections or insertions. They are sewn end to end and seem to be finished rolls, although they are probably not in their original order. Part two ends with a distinctively different membrane dealing with advowsons, following two membranes giving the remaining non-manorial articles and the jurors' responses to them.[41] It was therefore probably the end of the return originally. The structure of the returns is discussed in Chapter 3.[42]

Barnwell suburb[43]

The roll consists of six membranes approximately 21.5–24 cm

---

[38] PRO, SC5/Cambs/Tower/13; *RH* ii. 568a–9b.

[39] PRO, SC5/Cambs/Tower/1 (3 pts); *RH* ii. 356a–93a.

[40] M. D. Lobel, *Cambridge* (The Historic Towns Trust; London, 1974), 8–12; *VCH, Cambs* iii. 7–8.

[41] PRO, SC5/Cambs/Tower/1, pt 2, mm. 33–5.   [42] Above, pp. 79–80.

[43] PRO, SC5/Cambs/Tower/2; *RH* ii. 393a–401b.

wide, sewn end to end and written on one side of the parchment only. The roll is a neat finished text with a few interlineations and corrections, but no marginalia. It is marked 'Barnwell suburb belonging to the borough of Cambridge' on the dorse of m. 1. The third membrane is a little stained and the fourth has two contemporary repairs.

Hurstingstone hundred[44]

It is a finished roll of ten membranes with minimal corrections and returns which run from membrane to membrane. The membranes, sewn end to end, are approximately 21 cm wide and of varying lengths. Only one side of the parchment is used. The final entry on m. 10 relating to the privileges of the bishop of Ely is in a different hand. The head of the roll is damaged, leading to the loss of the beginning of the return. This can be supplied from an unprinted sixteenth-century copy.[45] As it stands, the roll has no returns for King's Ripton or Ramsey together with Bury, Hartford, and Upwood in the abbey's banlieu.

Leightonstone hundred[46]

The return in the National Archives is a finished roll of fourteen membranes, sewn end to end. With one exception, only one side of the parchment has been used. The roll is in a much smaller hand than the Hurstingstone return. Membrane 14 is a separate membrane dealing with the non-manorial articles, which it takes in the same order as the Cambridgeshire hundreds. Several entries are flagged and information is inserted in response to queries.[47] There are also insertions relating to advowsons and the Gloucester fee. All vills are represented on the roll, as well as Swineshead, which was transferred to Bedfordshire in 1888, and Hargrave which is in Northamptonshire, adjacent to the border

---

44 PRO, SC5/Hunts/Tower/2; *RH* ii. 598a–607b.   45 PRO, SC12/8/56.
46 PRO, SC5/Hunts/Tower/3; *RH* ii. 607b–33b.   47 As on m. 10.

with Huntingdonshire.[48] A substantial portion of the returns can also be found on the Huntingdon roll.[49] Both rolls appear to be fair, final copies belonging to the last stages of the inquiry.

Normancross hundred[50]

Three unprinted membranes and a fragment of a fourth have been added to the beginning of the roll in the National Archives and the membranes renumbered to give a substantial roll of thirty-six membranes approximately 20 cm wide, with a schedule at m. 15. The added membranes are in poor condition and partly illegible, but *inter alia* cover the vills of Orton Longueville, Botolphbridge, Stilton, Ogerston, Morborne, and Folksworth. The membranes are sewn end to end with entries running from membrane to membrane. Most are written on one side of the parchment only, in several hands, and many have been cropped on the right-hand side. There are few annotations, but many minor additions and amendments, with a single hand predominating. Details of advowsons have been added at mm. 3, 6–7, 19, and 28. The roll is the least polished of the Huntingdonshire returns. The return preserved on the last eleven membranes of the Huntingdon roll is slightly earlier in date and significantly different in content, but nevertheless probably belongs to the inquiry.[51] Although it incorporates what appears to be a seigneurial return at m. 10, it is generally a fair copy with few annotations or insertions.

Toseland hundred[52]

The roll consists of nine membranes, approximately 25 cm wide, sewn at the head. They are neatly written in different hands on lined parchment and some have entries on the dorse. It appears to be a late draft or finished return, with some details about advowsons added. There are signs of queries and comments added by a checker and a little flagging, but otherwise few alterations or additions. The first membrane deals with the non-manorial questions

[48] *VCH, Beds.*, iii. 168; Youngs, *Guide*, i. 10.
[49] HR, mm. 1–6.
[50] PRO, SC5/Hunts/Tower/4; *RH* ii. 633b–65b.
[51] HR, mm. 7–17. See above, Ch. 3.
[52] PRO, SC5/Hunts/Tower/5; *RH* ii. 665b–87b.

and has a note at the foot about missing returns for the hamlets of Monks Hardwick, Tetworth, Stirtlow, and Hardwick. A number of vills which are mentioned on this section of the roll are missing from the estate surveys.[53]

Godmanchester borough[54]

The six-membrane roll is a neat, final version on ruled parchment approximately 21 cm in width. It is written on one side of the parchment only and the membranes are sewn end to end. A small schedule has been added to m. 6 in order to accommodate the last two articles.

EAST ANGLIAN CIRCUIT

Few returns survive for this circuit and none among the rolls preserved in the National Archives. The only contemporary returns of any description are the roll for part of Gallow hundred in the north of the county in the Fuller Collection of the University of London Library, identified by Diana Greenway in 1982, and a single membrane for Hevingham in South Erpingham hundred, edited by Bruce Campbell in 1986.[55] All the remaining material exists in the copies described below, often made by later lords, thereby making it impossible to assess whether the contents represent finished texts or the preliminary stages of information-gathering. The way in which these copies have been rearranged and culled in order to record what was needed for seigneurial purposes also means that some of the data and character of the original have been lost. Despite the fact that none of this material is explicitly attributed to the 1279 inquiry, the common structure and terminology of all but the urban text for King's Lynn greatly strengthens their claim to be survivors of the same set of proceeedings.[56]

---

[53] Buckden, St Neots, Yelling, Great Gransden, Waresley, and Tetworth.

[54] PRO, SC5/Hunts/Tower/1; *RH* ii. 591a–8a.

[55] D. E. Greenway, 'A Newly Discovered Fragment of the Hundred Rolls of 1279–80', *Journal of the Society of Archivists*, 7 (1982), 73–7; B. M. S. Campbell. 'The Complexity of Manorial Structure in Medieval Norfolk', *Norfolk Archaeology*, 39/3 (1986), 234–5, 256–61.

[56] See above, Ch. 4.

NORFOLK

Gallow hundred[57]

As well as being an original return of some sort, the roll for Gallow hundred is the most substantial Norfolk text surviving from the inquiry. First catalogued as a rental, its similarity to the other East Anglian returns for the same circuit, as well as its date, sometime between August 1279 and the beginning of March 1280, make an attribution to the 1279 inquiry virtually certain, especially as it shares all the characteristics peculiar to that enterprise.[58] As with the Huntingdon roll return for Normancross hundred in Huntingdonshire, it is hard to see what purpose such a compilation could have served had it simply been seigneurial in origin.[59] Nothing is known of its provenance before it entered the Fuller Collection, which was given to the University of London in 1965.[60] Although it is a substantial fifteen-membrane roll, it is incomplete. The head is damaged and begins part way through the return for Burnham Thorpe, while the final membrane bears stitch marks indicating the past existence of at least one further membrane. Since the roll covers only eight of the eighteen or so settlements in the hundred, one can reasonably assume that a considerable portion has been lost. The recorded settlements comprise Burnham Thorpe, Kettlestone with its hamlets of Fulmodeston and Croxton, North, East, and West Barsham, Sculthorpe, and Waterden. The membranes, approximately 19.5 cm wide and of varying length, are written on one side of the parchment only. They are sewn together end to end. Each vill begins on a fresh membrane and covers two or three membranes and the entries are in several hands. The entire compilation has the appearance of an intermediate stage between the raw verdicts of the jurors and a final fair copy.[61]

South Erpingham hundred

The single membrane comprising a survey for Hevingham is asso-

---

[57] ULL, Fuller Coll., 7/5.
[58] Greenway, 'Newly Discovered Fragment', 75–7.
[59] See above, Ch. 3.
[60] Greenway, 'Newly Discovered Fragment', 74 n.12.
[61] See above, Ch. 4.

ciated with the 1279 inquiry on the basis of internal evidence.[62] Similar in width to the Gallow roll and also written on one side of the parchment only, it shares the characteristic layout and terminology of the larger roll. The attribution is further supported by the presence of John le Mareschal, one of the manorial lords, who came of age in 1279 and had died by December 1282, thereby fixing the hearings within the relevant timeframe.[63] This single membrane offers no clue as to whether hearings were held elsewhere in the hundred. It bears none of the usual stitch marks to indicate that it was subsequently incorporated into a roll, only a single diamond-shaped cut at the centre of its head. The absence of such marks indicates that it was an early draft, but since no jurors are given it was probably not the original verdict.[64] Provenance throws no further light on the possible extent of the inquiry either. The membrane, now in Norfolk Record Office, was formerly part of the Hobart of Blicking collection.[65]

North Greenhoe hundred

A text, surviving in several copies, describing the holdings of the lords of Holkham, has been attributed to the inquiry. In addition to the version found in the fourteenth-century lay cartulary selected by Hassall and Beauroy for their edition of the Holkham documents, other copies were made by the abbey of West Dereham, the priory of Peterstone, and the lay lord of the manor of Burghall. It appears that Walsingham Priory also made a transcript, although this no longer exists. One of the copies is uniquely headed 'In the feodary of the hundred of North Greenhoe', suggesting that the text was once part of a document relating to the whole hundred.[66] If so, copies of other returns may be awaiting recognition in the lay and ecclesiastical cartularies of Norfolk. There is no clue as to how the North Greenhoe 'feodary' came into the hands of those who copied the Holkham return, nor is it clear whether it was a collection of jurors' returns or a final finished roll belonging to one of the

---

[62] Norfolk Rec. Off., NRS, 14761 29, D4; Campbell, 'Complexity', 234–5, 256–61.
[63] Campbell, 'Complexity', 232–6.
[64] Ibid. 234–6.   [65] Ibid. 232.
[66] *Lordship and Landscape in Norfolk 1250–1350*, ed. W. Hassall and J. Beauroy (Oxford, 1993), 66, 215–30, no. 253, 524.

commissioners. The way in which the return was edited by copy-ists in the different lordships has further obscured the picture.[67]

Smithdon hundred

A late thirteenth-century survey of Sedgeford in Smithdon hundred, from the muniments of the dean and chapter of Norwich, now kept in Norfolk Record Office, has been tentatively identified as a contemporary copy of one of the returns.[68] Assuming that the old reference DCN, 4437, can be identified with the document currently classified as DCN, 51/94, this is plausible though not beyond doubt. The single membrane, 20 × 59.5 cm and written on both sides of the parchment, is a fair copy of the verdict of 'the elders of the vill' (*seniores ville*) and contains many of the expres-sions characteristic of other East Anglian returns. The prior of Norwich is described as 'chief lord' and is recorded as having right of warren as well as the familiar seigneurial rights and obliga-tions.[69] There is no mention of the advowson, but since this was often omitted from the initial returns, it does not prove anything either way. Less convincing is the way in which villein holdings are recorded. Unlike the other returns, there is a long list of something over ninety named customary tenants with their holdings and rents. Tenants of free holdings written on the dorse have been entered in the left-hand margin, suggesting that, whatever the origin of the survey, it was probably copied to serve a seigneurial purpose.

King's Lynn borough

It has been suggested that a partial, fifteenth-century copy of a late thirteenth-century rental is in fact a return belonging to the inquiry.[70] This identification rests solely on internal evidence

---

[67] *Lordship and Landscape in Norfolk*, 524.

[68] Campbell, 'Complexity', 233, citing J. Williamson, 'Peasant Holdings in Medieval Norfolk: A Detailed Investigation into the Holdings of the Peasantry in Three Norfolk Villages in the Thirteenth Century', University of Reading Ph.D. thesis, 1976, 220.

[69] These comprised bull and boar, stray animals and fold right, pillory, tumbrel, and gallows. He owed suit to the hundred court and had the right to the amerce-ments of his men in any court. Norfolk Rec. Off., DCN, 51/94, dorse.

[70] *The Making of King's Lynn*, ed. D. M. Owen (Oxford, 1984), 156–7; E. and P. Rutledge, 'King's Lynn and Great Yarmouth', *Norfolk Archaeology*, 37 (1978), 92–3.

which dates it to 1267–83 and its similarity to other urban returns belonging to the inquiry. Since it only covers the northern part of the town belonging to the bishop of Norwich, it could alternatively be a seigneurial record. The information is recorded street by street, generally with a separate entry for each messuage. The text was edited by Dorothy Owen and the street frontages reconstructed by Elizabeth Rutledge.[71]

West Suffolk hundreds

Manuscripts once belonging to Bury St Edmunds contain copies of part of the returns for eight west Suffolk hundreds where the abbey held property (Babergh, Blackbourn, Cosford, Hartismere, Lackford, Risbridge, Thedwastre, Thingoe). An original verdict of the inquiry into knights' fees also survives for Hartismere hundred.[72] The two longest texts are in fourteenth-century registers compiled under Abbot Walter Pinchbeck (begun 1333) and Abbot John Lakenheath (d. 1381).[73] A third copy, comprising only the three hundreds of Babergh, Hartismere, and Thedwastre, is probably earlier but otherwise very similar.[74] The opening section of the return for Stanton in Blackbourn hundred, which is missing from the main texts, survives fortuitously in a late medieval terrier for the vill.[75] Although the transcripts are clearly headed as belonging to the eyre of Solomon Rochester and his associates in 1286, this attribution cannot be correct since internal evidence points to a date compatible with 1279–80. The most telling concerns Lidgate

---

[71] *Making*, ed. Owen, 156–81; Rutledge, 'King's Lynn', 94–101.

[72] PRO, E198/1/7.

[73] CUL, Ee, iii, 60, fos. 234ʳ–319ᵛ (Pinchbeck); printed in *The Pinchbeck Register*, ed. F. Hervey (Brighton, 1925), ii. 30–282. BL, Harl. MS 743, fos. 149ʳ–257ᵛ (Lakenheath). Blackbourn hundred is printed in E. Powell, *A Suffolk Hundred in the Year 1283* (Cambridge, 1919), 5–65. A note in CUL Add MS 3395 in a 17-cent. hand claims that there was a further copy of the inquiry at fo. 115 of 'The White Register of Bury'. However, the White Register of Abbot John of Northwold (1279–1301), which is otherwise plausible, now has neither 115 folios nor any trace of the inquiry in those which exist. BL, Add MS 14847.

[74] CUL, Add MS 3395. Dated to the late 13th cent. in J. H. Baker and J. S. Ringrose, *A Catalogue of English Legal Manuscripts in Cambridge University Library* (Woodbridge, 1996), 577.

[75] The terrier text ends shortly after the other texts for Stanton begin. BL, Add 4699, fos. 4ᵛ–6ʳ; BL, Harl. MS 743, fo. 239ʳ; CUL, Ee, iii, fo. 303ʳ. Powell incorporated it into his text otherwise drawn from BL, Harl. MS 743. *Suffolk Hundred*, 46–51.

in Risbridge hundred where the lord, John son of Henry of Hastings, was said to be 18 years of age. Since he was recorded as six years of age in his father's inquisition *post mortem* of 6 May 1268, he would have been eighteen within a year either side of 6 May 1280. The date of the hearing is narrowed down still further by the appearance of Alexander de Wridewelle at Wordwell and Sapiston in Blackbourn hundred, since he was dead by 1280 when his widow was negotiating with the abbey about her dower.[76] All the copies are very similar in spelling and format, but since the late Lakenheath register has material omitted from the other manuscripts, it is likely that all were copied from a common exemplar, perhaps based on an actual return.

MIDDLESEX AND LONDON CIRCUIT

Returns for this circuit are disappointing. In so far as they exist for Middlesex, they appear to deal exclusively with the order to inquire into distraint of knighthood issued at the same time as the hundred roll commission and treated as part of that inquiry in London. Although sewn together, only the first of the two membranes for Middlesex, preserved as PRO, Middx/Tower/1, dates from 1279. The second contains verdicts on estates in Ossulstone hundred confiscated following the Battle of Evesham. The first membrane has brief returns for all the hundreds in the county (Edmonton, Spelthorne, Elthorne, Isleworth, Gore, and Ossulstone), together with the liberty of Westminster. London itself has fared somewhat better with thirty-four surviving membranes recording verdicts on the special London articles, but even these represent only a fraction of what was originally envisaged.

LONDON

Some sort of return exists for all but Cordwainer Street and Lime Street wards, although they are fragmentary and extremely varied

---

[76] *Pinchbeck Register*, ed. Hervey, ii. 227–8; Powell, *Suffolk Hundred*, 2, 42, 44; CUL, Ee, iii, 60, fos. 301ᵛ–2ʳ; BL, Harl, MS 743, fos. 237ᵛ–8ʳ, 255ʳ.

in form.[77] It is tempting to identify the largely illegible membrane SC5/London/Tower/22, m. 30 (28) as a return for one of the missing wards, but there is no reason to do so. It contains a few lines only, relating to tenements, and could refer to any ward. It also seems to have been the outer membrane of the roll at some earlier stage in its existence.[78] Survival of the London returns has clearly been haphazard and incomplete. They are now sewn together at the head. The penultimate membrane is a later addition, as is the final membrane which was added from Chancery Miscellanea in 1929.[79] None of the returns are in print. The thirty-four membranes are either the raw verdicts of the jurors or fair copies rather than any sort of edited text.[80] With the exception of the return for Farringdon ward, responses were entered on one side of the parchment only.[81] The size of the membranes varies greatly. The first membrane, which is for Queenhithe ward and measures 19 × 52.5 cm, is the longest. Others are similar in width, but shorter. Among the smaller membranes, some like that for Vintry ward, are long and thin, while others like the 7.5 × 9 cm verdict for Tower ward are tiny.[82] Three of the membranes are in French, the remainder in Latin.[83]

NORTHAMPTONSHIRE AND RUTLAND CIRCUIT

The only return which may survive from this circuit is the single damaged membrane of a verdict for Hambleton and Normanton in

---

[77] PRO, SC5/London/Tower/1–26. Two numbers running across wards have been assigned to the face of each membrane. These are not always identical because of different conventions regarding the numbering of fragments and membranes with writing on the dorse. The catalogue gives separate piece numbers for each ward which sometimes, but not invariably, match the number on the dorse of membranes. For example, SC5/London/Tower/3, the return for Bridge ward, is m. 8 or, according to the number within a lozenge, m. 6. Both membrane numbers, as well as the piece number, are cited in footnotes below for the avoidance of confusion.

[78] The membrane is worn and had 'London' on the dorse in a large hand.

[79] PRO, SC5/London/Tower/1–26, mm. 33–4 (32–3).

[80] Thirty-three membranes according to the catalogue and the lozenge numbering.

[81] PRO, SC5/London/Tower/2, mm. 2–5 (2–3).

[82] PRO, SC5/London/Tower/8, m. 14 (12), 17, m. 25 (23). The Vintry ward membrane measures 9 × 27.5 cm.

[83] Those in French are PRO, SC5/London/Tower/15, 19–20, mm. 23, 27–8 (21, 25–6).

Martinsley hundred, Rutland.[84] Jurors are given, but the inquest is undated. It differs in order from other rolls in that the verdict begins with villeins and cottars rather than the usual survey of the demesne, which follows the entry for a knight's fee in Normanton. It is closest in form to the Normancross portion of the Huntingdon roll. The entries are short: 'there are thirty virgates and one bovate of land each of which owes works . . .' and valuations are provided at the end of each section. A checker can be seen making corrections and insertions, including an interlined total at the end of the villein entry.

OXFORDSHIRE AND BERKSHIRE CIRCUIT

There are no surviving rolls for Berkshire. Oxfordshire, by contrast is well provided with them. There is a roll for every hundred except those of Bloxham and Binfield. In this county thirteenth-century hundreds had evolved from large pre-Conquest groupings attached to manors belonging to the crown and bishop of Dorchester (later Lincoln), many with detached portions. The two and a half hundreds of Kirtlington had become Ploughley hundred, the three hundreds of Shipton had become Chadlington hundred, and the two hundreds of Headington had become Bullingdon hundred, associated with the recently developed suburban hundred outside the north gate of Oxford under the same lordship.[85] The four and a half hundreds originally connected with the royal manor of Benson had crystallized into the separate hundreds of Binfield, Langtree, Lewknor, Pyrton, and the half hundred of Ewelme. The triple hundred of Dorchester, Banbury, and Thame, belonging to the bishop of Lincoln, the triple hundred of Wootton, and the double hundred of Bampton remained as they were.[86] These diverse origins resulted in hundreds which varied greatly in size. This in turn meant that the rolls recording their returns to the inquiry range from thirty-five membranes for Wootton hundred to three membranes for Thame. The honorial groupings continued to dominate the hundredal structure of the county in the thirteenth century, overriding natural boundaries. Detached estates or vills can usually be ascribed to a seigneurial tie to the parent hundred.

[84] PRO, SC5/8/5/7.   [85] *VCH Oxon.*, v. 3.   [86] Ibid. viii. 2; xi. 3; xiii. 1.

Some of these geographical anomalies were rectified during the nineteenth century, but this only makes it the harder to decide which vills might be missing from any given roll.

OXFORDSHIRE

Bampton hundred[87]

Bampton is the only Oxfordshire roll for which there is a translation in English.[88] It was a large and complicated hundred, reflecting its origin as a double hundred dependent on the royal manor of Bampton. By 1279, it was in the hands of William de Valence, earl of Pembroke. The sixteen-membrane roll is a finished copy, with membranes sewn end to end and written on one side of ruled parchment. There is a note about distraint of knighthood on the dorse of m. 2.[89] Although the vills of Langford, Little Faringdon, and Shilton later became part of this hundred, in the thirteenth century they belonged to the Berkshire hundred of Faringdon and are therefore absent from the roll.[90] Upton and Signet, which were then part of Burford, are also absent.[91] Minster Lovell, Little Minster, and Northmoor, which fall into the geographical area covered by the hundred, were detached portions of Chadlington hundred, where their returns may be found.

Banbury hundred[92]

The returns for this hundred, one of the three belonging to the bishop of Lincoln, consist of four membranes. It is a finished roll, neatly written on one side of heavily ruled parchment. There is a modest amount of correction and cancellation and signs of checking. 'The roll of xij jurors' appears on the dorse of m. 4, together with an unprinted note that one of their number, Laurence of

---

[87] PRO, SC5/Oxon/Tower/1; *RH* ii. 688a–705a.
[88] *Oxfordshire Hundred Rolls of 1279*, ed. E. Stone and P. Hyde (Oxford, 1968), 7–87. The text has been 'drastically simplified'. Ibid. 16.
[89] *RH* ii. 689a.
[90] *VCH, Oxon.*, xiii. 1–2; Youngs, *Guide*, i. 397, 400, 405.
[91] Youngs, *Guide*, i. 407.
[92] PRO, SC5/Oxon/Tower/2; *RH* ii. 705a–10a.

Herdewyk' is in mercy. A separate two-membrane return for
Banbury vill is not in print.[93] The hundred comprised two separate
areas intermingled with Bloxham hundred in the north.
Northmoor, which lay geographically in Bampton hundred, was a
detached portion of Taynton and so its return is found on this roll.
Epwell only became part of the hundred in the nineteenth century.
It therefore appears on the roll of Dorchester hundred to which it
belonged at the time of the inquiry.[94]

Bullingdon hundred[95]

As one would expect from its origins as a double hundred, the
inquiry in Bullingdon hundred resulted in a long roll of twenty-one
membranes, which at approximately 21 cm wide were somewhat
narrower than those of most Oxfordshire rolls. They are sewn end
to end and are usually ruled, with writing in more than one hand
on one side of the parchment only. Neatly written and with very
few corrections or annotations, it appears to be a fair, final copy.
Among the annotations, the abbot of Osney's holdings are singled
out in several places and there are numerous marginal ink marks
which suggest that the roll had been read and its contents considered. The first membrane is endorsed 'Inquisition of Bullingdon
hundred. Year E. VII'. The final membrane ends with an important
note about further inquisitions concerning knights' fees and royal
forests ordered by Sampson Foliot.[96] Chilworth Musard,
Chilworth Valery, and Coombe, which mostly lay in the parish of
Great Milton in Thame hundred, were part of Bullingdon hundred
in the thirteenth century and therefore appear on this roll.[97] A note
at the end of the roll recorded that Draycot, part of the honour of
Wallingford, which belonged to the hundred was not included.
Instead it appears in the earl of Cornwall's hundred of Ewelme.[98]
The hundred was held by Hugh de Plessis, who also held the
Northgate hundred of Oxford, for which there is a separate eight

[93] See below, p. 171.
[94] *VCH, Oxon.*, x. 1–2; Youngs, *Guide*, i. 396.
[95] PRO, SC5/Oxon/Tower/3; *RH* ii. 710a–25b.
[96] *RH* ii. 725b. See above, Ch. 2.
[97] *VCH, Oxon*, v. 4.
[98] PRO, SC5/Oxon/Tower/3, m. 21; *RH* ii. 757a–b.

membrane return.[99] Returns for the manors of Iffley and Headington, with its hamlets of Wyke, Oldbarton, and Marston were included in Rose Graham's 1905 edition of the Oxford returns.[100]

Chadlington hundred[101]

Once the triple hundred of Shipton, the returns in 1279 amount to seventeen broad (*c*.32 cm), neatly written, and carefully laid out membranes, sewn end to end. The first membrane is damaged. In more than one hand, the roll has entries on one side of parchment only and a number of neatly stitched repairs. With very few corrections or annotations, it is clearly a finished roll. Summary valuations found at the end of each subsection throughout the hundred are an unusual and integral feature of the roll. Heythrop vill, which was later transferred to Wootton hundred where the rest of the parish lay, appears on neither roll, nor are there returns for Bruern, Cornbury, or Chipping Norton, which were subject to boundary changes in the nineteenth century.[102]

Dorchester hundred[103]

Like Banbury hundred, Dorchester belonged to the bishop of Lincoln. Although probably a finished roll, with little sign of emendation, annotation, or checking, the surviving eight membranes are damaged in places and have suffered losses. There is no heading to the roll, which opens in the middle of a return, which would almost certainly have included Dorchester. Whether it would also have included returns for Culham or Stadhampton, which do not appear elsewhere on the roll, is impossible to say. Over half the remaining membranes have also suffered from damage or cropping.[104] The roll is written on one side of the parchment and the membranes are unusually wide at approximately 30 cm. It appears to be a final

---

[99] PRO, SC5/Oxon/Tower/11; *RH* ii. 805a–11b.
[100] 'Description of Oxford from the Hundred Rolls', ed. R. Graham, in *Collectanea* (Oxford, 1905), 63–75.
[101] PRO, SC5/Oxon/Tower/5; *RH* ii. 725b–47b.
[102] *VCH, Oxon.*, xi. 3, 131; Youngs, *Guide*, i. 393, 395.
[103] PRO, SC5/Oxon/Tower/4b; *RH* ii. 747b–51b.
[104] Membranes 2, 3, 5, and 7.

text without annotation. Both Epwell, which was transferred to Banbury hundred in the nineteenth century and Fifield, which was later included in Ewelme hundred, belonged to this hundred in the thirteenth century and therefore have returns on this roll.[105] Conversely, returns for Brookhampton, which later became part of Dorchester hundred, can be found on the Ewelme roll.

Ewelme half hundred[106]

Originally one of the four and a half hundreds attached to the royal manor of Benson, by 1279 Ewelme hundred was in the hands of Edmund, earl of Cornwall. The roll has twenty membranes approximately 22 cm wide and sewn end to end. They are neatly written on one side of the parchment only with relatively few corrections. It appears to be a fair, finished copy, with slits for twelve seals. There are no significant annotations, but marginal pen marks in darker ink indicate that the returns were subsequently read. Brookhampton appears on this roll, although it was later transferred to Dorchester hundred.[107] Draycot was also included as part of the honour of Wallingford, although it belonged to Bullingdon hundred. There are no returns for Nettlebed or Nuffield (other than its hamlets of Gangsdown and Huntercombe).

Langtree hundred[108]

Formerly another of the four and a half hundreds of Benson, Langtree had likewise been granted by Henry III to the earldom of Cornwall. The roll has fourteen membranes sewn end to end. It is written on one side of fairly narrow parchment, approximately 19 cm wide. The eighth membrane is distinctive, in a different, less tidy, hand and in paler ink. There are few annotations or emendations, but additions were made to the beginning of the returns for Mongewell, Newnham Murren, Goring, Gatehampton, and Stoke Basset. In the case of Mongwell, these were quite extensive, incorporating information about the advowson, demesne appurtenances,

[105] VCH, Oxon., vii. 2, x. 3.
[106] PRO, SC5/Oxon/Tower/6; RH ii. 751b–74a.
[107] VCH, Oxon., vii. 81.
[108] PRO, SC5/Oxon/Tower/4a; RH ii. 774a–82a.

and scutage.[109] The entry for the warren at Whitchurch at m. 3 has been squeezed in. The roll appears to be a fair copy which had undergone some checking. The final membrane, which is badly damaged, has a seal tag. All vills in the hundred are represented.

Lewknor hundred[110]

Another of the four and a half hundreds of Benson, this hundred was also in the hands of Edmund, earl of Cornwall, hence the prominence of the honour of Wallingford on the last two membranes of the six-membrane roll.[111] The head of the roll is damaged, but it appears to be a reasonably neat, finished copy, with membranes sewn end to end and written on one side of ruled parchment. Some of the annotations may have been added after the roll was complete and there are also a number of later marginated symbols. Dated 10 April 7 Edward I, it is the earliest of the known returns.[112] It included descriptions of Tythrop, which is in Kingsey, and Stokenchurch, later in Buckinghamshire, and part of Wheatfield, later in Pyrton hundred.[113] No returns exist for Britwell and Cadmore End.

Pyrton hundred[114]

The last of the four and a half hundreds of Benson for which rolls survive, the Pyrton returns comprise eight broad membranes approximately 31 cm wide. Several, including the first and the last, are damaged. The membranes are sewn end to end and are neatly written on one side of the parchment. It appears to be a finished copy with no signs of checking or correction. There is an unprinted note on the dorse of the final membrane concerning 'those having land worth twenty pounds as found at the first inquisition'. All the vills known to have belonged to the hundred in the thirteenth century are represented on the roll.

---

[109] Membrane 2; 'Cum advocacione ecclesie' is interlined and 'Et idem habet xxx acras bosci et vj acras prati et de pastura iiij acras in dominico et j molendinum aquaticum. Et dat scutagium pro j feodo integro quando scutagium concederit a domino rege.' has been added to the end of the demesne entry, although this is not evident from the printed text. *RH*, ii. 774b–5a.

[110] PRO, SC5/Oxon/Tower/7; *RH* ii. 782a–8b.   [111] *RH* ii. 785a–8b.

[112] See above, Ch. 3.   [113] *VCH, Oxon.*, viii. 3.

[114] PRO, SC5/Oxon/Tower/12; *RH* ii. 812a–20a.

Ploughley hundred[115]

Formerly the two and a half hundreds attached to the royal manor of Kirtlington, the crown had retained control of the hundred although the manor itself was in the hands of Ela Longespée, countess of Warwick, as part of her dower.[116] It was a sizeable hundred which generated twenty membranes of returns. Approximately 23–4 cm wide, they are written on one side of the parchment and sewn end to end. It is the work of several scribes and there is evidence of correction and insertion. It is probably a final draft, although it appears messier than most of the Oxfordshire rolls. There are returns for Boycott and Lillingstone Lovell, which as royal manors may once have been attached to Kirtlington and were still part of the hundred at the time of the inquiry, although they were later transferred to Buckinghamshire. Similarly, Noke which lay physically in Bullingdon hundred, was included probably because, like the manor of Islip, it belonged to the abbot of Westminster. By contrast, Caversfield, which lay inside the hundredal boundary, was attached at that time to the Buckinghamshire hundred of Rowley for which no roll survives.[117]

Thame hundred[118]

The third of the bishop of Lincoln's hundreds, it was fragmented into three separate areas united by their links to the bishop's fee.[119] Its returns consist of a short roll of three narrow membranes, approximately 18 cm wide. They are neatly written on one side of the parchment and sewn end to end. There are a few corrections and cancellations, but no annotations. The vills of Ascot and Weston appear on this roll, although they were later transferred to Dorchester and Ploughley hundreds respectively.

---

[115] PRO, SC5/Oxon/Tower/13; *RH* ii. 822a–39b.
[116] *VCH, Oxon.*, vi. 5; *RH* ii. 822b.
[117] *VCH, Oxon.*, vi. 2–3.
[118] PRO, SC5/Oxon/Tower/14; *RH* ii. 820a–2a.
[119] *VCH, Oxon.*, vii. 115.

Wootton hundred[120]

The returns for Wootton hundred consist of thirty-five membranes in two rolls. A fragment from the head of the first roll, listing the jurors, was added from unsorted Miscellanea in 1974 and is therefore not in the Record Commission edition. Originally dependent on Wootton, by the thirteenth century the hundred was linked to the royal manor of Woodstock, for which there is a separate return.[121] The membranes are sewn end to end and appear to be a final version, although they contain a number of corrections and are in several hands. The second roll has slits for a seal tag at the end. There are no returns for Deddington, Clifton, Hempton, or Shipton-on-Cherwell.

Woodstock manor[122]

This is a unique return for a royal manor, complete with a single seal and slits for the seals of the remaining jurors. It comprises a single broad membrane 43 × 58 cm, neatly written in two columns.

Banbury borough[123]

The unprinted return of two membranes is neatly written on one side of lined parchment and sewn end to end. Jurors are named and the wording at the beginning of the return closely echoes that for Banbury hundred, which also belonged to the bishop of Lincoln. Burgage tenements are listed, but the format of the return is otherwise similar to that for manorial surveys.

Oxford borough, including the hundred of Hugh de Plessis (Northgate suburb)[124]

Returns for Oxford, amounting to twenty-one membranes, now

[120] PRO, SC5/Oxon/Tower/16/1–2; *RH* ii. 842a–77b.
[121] *VCH, Oxon.*, xi. 3; PRO, SC5/Oxon/Tower/15; *RH* ii. 839b–42a.
[122] PRO, SC5/Oxon/Tower/15; *RH* ii. 839b–42a.
[123] PRO, SC5/Oxon/Tower/17.
[124] PRO, SC5/Oxon/Tower/8 (SW ward), 9a and 18 (NW ward), 9b and 10 (NE ward), 9c (SE ward), 11 (Northgate suburb); *RH* ii. 788b–811b; 'The Hundred Rolls for the Parish of St Thomas, Oxford', ed. J. Cooper, *Oxoniensia*, 37 (1972), 165–76 (18).

contained in five rolls, were made on a ward-by-ward basis. A sixth roll of eight membranes in a distinctive hand contains returns for the suburb outside the north gate belonging to Hugh de Plessis. The membranes on each roll are sewn end to end in common with other returns for Oxfordshire. All but the second membrane of SC5/ Oxon/Tower/9b, which was added from Chancery Miscellanea in 1923, are in print, either in the Record Commission edition or, in the case of Oxon/Tower/18, in a modern edition by Janet Cooper. This latter is the second half of the roll for the NW ward which also became detached over time, only to be rediscovered long after the Record Commission edition was published.[125] Rose Graham's 1905 edition of all the then known texts for Oxford (including the Northgate suburb and the manors of Iffley and Headington, with its hamlets of Wyke, Oldbarton, and Marston from Bullingdon hundred), reorganized the returns into parishes for the convenience of local historians.[126] The Record Commission edition preserves the format of the rolls and is therefore more appropriate for those concerned with the inquiry itself.

Witney borough[127]

The return, found among Rentals and Surveys in the National Archives, consists of three membranes sewn end to end. It is a fair copy with a slit for a seal. Approximately 32 cm wide, it is larger in format than other Oxford returns, but the presence of the hundred roll commissioners for the circuit at the head of the roll makes its identification with the inquiry certain. Although burgesses are mentioned as having immunity from tolls, the return deals essentially with the tenants of the bishop of Winchester's manor.

SHROPSHIRE AND STAFFORDSHIRE CIRCUIT

There is no evidence that the inquiry was carried out in Staffordshire, but returns survive for the borough and liberty of

---

[125] 'Hundred Rolls', ed. Cooper, 165.
[126] 'Description', ed. Graham, 3–98.
[127] PRO, SC11/13; *Oxfordshire Hundred Rolls*, ed. Stone and Hyde, 91–105.

Shrewsbury and Pimhill hundred in Shropshire in the second of two volumes of transcripts of medieval documents made by Joseph Morris in the nineteenth century. They were subsequently purchased by Shrewsbury Public Library and are now in the Shropshire Archives.[128] Morris offered no observations about his exemplar and does not appear to have realized what he had copied.[129] Originally catalogued as an inquisition *Quo waranto*, the returns were first identified as belonging to the 1279 inquiry by W. J. Slack in a letter to the Public Record Office in 1950.[130] There can be little doubt that he was correct. In addition to twelve named jurors, the heading to the return for Pimhill hundred names Master Adam de Botinton and John de Chetewynde, more or less correctly, as the justices and dates the hearing to 24 August 1279, well within the expected timeframe. Although Chetewynd's forename is given as Adam on the patent roll, John could easily be an error of transmission. Nor is the absence of William Bagod, the third commissioner, a problem. Other hearings were conducted in the presence of two only. Slack's attribution was confirmed by Una Rees when she established that a rental in a fifteenth-century hand at the back of the Lilleshall Abbey cartulary BL Add. MS 50121 was almost certainly based in part on the Shrewsbury return.[131] A transcript for Bradford hundred follows that for Pimhill hundred in Morris's text. Its heading reads 'inquisition held before Lord John de Kirkby etc', which therefore makes it more likely that it was part of the inquiries known as Kirkby's Quest in 1284–5. It is impossible to be sure about this, however, since the entries are so truncated. In an intriguing footnote to the preface of his *Antiquities of Shropshire*, R. W. Eyton recorded that 'I have two original parchment rolls of tenures nearly contemporary but not identical with *Kirkby's Quest*. They extend only to the hundreds of Bradford and Pimhill.' Like Morris, Eyton does not appear to have been familiar with the

---

[128] Shropshire Archives, 6001/28, 21–62. For the history of Morris's transcripts, see R. A. Preston, 'George and Joseph Morris', *Shropshire Family History Journal*, 10 (1989), 103.

[129] He dated it 1278.

[130] W. G. D. Fletcher, Catalogue of Manuscripts of the Shrewsbury Free Library, 74. The Slack correspondence has proved untraceable, but is mentioned in a note to the catalogue entry for PRO, SC5/8/5/6.

[131] 'A Late-Thirteenth Century Rental of Tenements in Shrewsbury', ed. U. Rees, *Transactions of the Shropshire Archaeological and Historical Society'*, 66 (1989), 79–80.

1279–80 hundred rolls, so these may have been part of the material on which Morris drew. If so, the source for his Shrewsbury return remains unexplained and doubt must be cast on the identification of the Bradford roll with Kirkby's Quest.[132]

The Shrewsbury return is by far the fullest. It was edited in part by Una Rees alongside the Lilleshall rental.[133] Lists of tenants and their holdings in this extract do not catch the full flavour of the whole, even though it includes valuations and illustrates the way in which Morris reduced the entries to tabular form. The unprinted portion of the return shares many of the characteristics found in returns for other counties. Details of the grant of the fee farm and its annual render are rehearsed at the beginning of the return as in other urban returns. The following entry for the fee of the abbot of Buildwas at Meole Brace, one of the vills within the liberty, illustrates its affinity with rural returns elsewhere:

The abbot of Buildwas holds the grange of Meole with its appurtenances within the liberty and hundred of Shrewsbury by gift of Roger, once bishop of Chester, at the first foundation of the abbey of Buildwas and there are there in demesne five carucates of arable land and it is worth £41 per annum.
Item he has one acre of meadow which is worth half a mark per annum and there is there one water mill and one horse mill and it is worth £4.
Item he has a fish pond the size of half an acre of land and it is worth half a mark per annum.
Item the abbot holds the said grange by gift of the aforesaid bishop but it is not known by what warrant nor for what service.[134]

As one would expect of a grange, there were no tenants, but the peasantry are not well represented in other surveys. The eight villeins and their half virgate holdings, listed at the prior of Wenlock's manor at Sutton, are typical, but it is not clear how far the general paucity of this type of information reflects Morris's own lack of interest or whether it was a feature of the circuit. What is clear is that the Sutton return, like hundredal returns from other circuits, concludes with details about the parish church: 'There is

[132] *Inquisitio facta coram Domino Johanne de Kyrkekby etc.* Shropshire Archives, 6001/28, 63; R. W. Eyton, *Antiquities of Shropshire*, 12 vols. (London, 1854–60), i. 6 and 7, n. 10. I am grateful to Tony Carr for drawing my attention to this reference.
[133] 'Late-Thirteenth Century Rental', ed. Rees, 82–4.
[134] Shropshire Archives, 6001/28, 44.

there a church of which the prior is patron and it has in demesne 24 acres of land and the said church with the aforesaid land is worth 100s. per annum.'[135] In many ways the most interesting aspect of this problematic text is the full rendering of the articles of inquiry in the Shrewsbury return, which differ markedly from those set out on the Cambridgeshire rolls.[136]

WARWICKSHIRE AND LEICESTERSHIRE CIRCUIT

With one possible exception, no original returns survive for this circuit.[137] Copies preserve partial returns for two hundreds in each county, all of which suggest that the inquiry had either reached completion or a fairly advanced stage.

LEICESTERSHIRE

Two versions of returns for each of the two hundreds of Guthlaxton and Gartree were transcribed in the seventeenth century by William Burton, a Leicestershire antiquary.[138] One of the two versions for each hundred was subsequently printed in Nichols, *The History and Antiquities of the County of Leicester*.[139] Only the return for Kibworth Harcourt in Gartree hundred exists in modern editions.[140] Neither of the versions transcribed by Burton has returns for all the vills in these large hundreds. The texts are fully discussed in Chapter 4. There is no return for Leicester, although the two parishes of Evington and Aylestone, which are now part of the city, were recorded in the hundreds to

---

[135] Shropshire Archives, 6001/28, 48.   [136] See above, Ch. 2.

[137] See above, Ch. 4.

[138] Bodl. MS Rawlinson, B, 350, fos. 2–11, 11–31, 34 (Guthlaxton), 34–7, 42–51 (Gartree).

[139] J. Nichols, *The History and Antiquities of the County of Leicester* (Wakefield, 1971), i/1, pp. cx–xxi.

[140] R. H. Hilton, 'Kibworth Harcourt: A Merton College Manor in the Thirteenth and Fourteenth Centuries', in *Class Conflict and the Crisis of Feudalism: Essays in Medieval Social History* (London, 1985), 4, formerly published in W. G. Hoskins (ed.), *Studies in Leicestershire Agrarian History* (Leics. Archaeological Soc.; Leicester, 1949), 17–40; C. Howell, *Land, Family and Inheritance in Transition* (Cambridge, 1983), 271.

which they then belonged and the suburb outside the east gate was included in Gartree hundred.[141]

Gartree hundred

Nichols printed the shorter of Burton's two transcripts.[142] He omitted some forty-seven further places which were only to be found in the second transcript.[143] Evington, now part of Leicester, then belonged to this hundred.

Guthlaxton hundred

Nichols printed the fuller of the two transcripts.[144] He added a number of returns which originated in the shorter transcript to those already present at the end of Burton's transcription for Gartree hundred. These also included a return for Polesworth in Hemlingford hundred in Warwickshire and Aylestone which was then part of this hundred.

WARWICKSHIRE

Returns survive for Stoneleigh and Kineton hundreds and the boroughs of Coventry and Warwick.[145] The texts in which they are

---

[141] *VCH, Leics.*, iv. 415, 434.

[142] Bodl, MS Rawlinson, B, 350, fos. 34–7; Nichols, *History and Antiquities*, i/1, pp. cxix–cxxi.

[143] Bodl, MS Rawlinson, B, 350, fos. 42–51. The MS is tightly bound sometimes making it difficult to read marginated capitals. Names in italics are either tentatively identified or unidentified. In the order of the text, they are: Lubenham, Gumley, Saddington, Fleckney, Wistow, Newton, Theddingworth, Mowsley, Kibworth Harcourt, Kibworth Beauchamp, Smeeton, Westerby, Tur Langton, Thorpe Langton, East Langton, West Langton, Borough on the Hill (*Stocton*), North and South Marefield, Belgrave, Barton Overy, Ilston, Noseley, Stonton Wyville (*Staunton*), Cranoe, Welham, Stockerston, Old Keythorpe in Tugby, Glooston, Shangton, Easton, Bringhurst, Drayton, Prestgrave, Holt, Holyoaks, Blaston, Horninghold (*Horningwall*), Slawston, Gillesthorpe (*Selkthorpe*), Owston, Knossington, Pickwell, *Kinesthorpe*, Rolleston, Scraptoft, Ingorsby, Newbold. I am grateful to Harold Fox for his help with Leicestershire place names.

[144] Bodl, MS Rawlinson, B, 350, fos. 11–31, 34; Nichols, *History and Antiquities*, i/1, pp. cx–cxix.

[145] PRO, E164/15; University of Nottingham Library, MiO 14 (15c copy); Shakespeare Birthplace Trust, Stoneleigh MSS, DR 18/31/3 (14-cent. copy);

preserved are fully discussed in John's editions and the structure of the urban returns is discussed in Chapter 3.[146] Returns have survived for all parishes except Keresley in Stoneleigh hundred and seven parishes in the south of Kineton hundred. These comprised the five parishes of Stoneton, part of Barcheston, Burmington, Great Wolford, and Barton on the Heath, together with Little Compton and Sutton under Brailes which were part of Gloucestershire at this date. The detached parishes of Tanworth, Lapworth, and Stretton on Fosse are also missing.[147]

DR/10/1406, fos. 48–56; 'The Coventry Hundred Rolls', ed. T. John, in P. R. Coss (ed.), *Early Records of Medieval Coventry* (London, 1986), 365–94; *The Warwickshire Hundred Rolls of 1279–80*, ed. T. John (Oxford, 1992).

[146] *Warwickshire*, ed. John, 6–16; 'Coventry Hundred Rolls', 365.
[147] *Warwickshire*, ed. John, 20–1.

Conclusion

The early years of Edward I's reign saw an unprecedented series of major government inquiries. That of 1279–80 was in many ways the most ambitious. It was also the only one which was not called into being by some pressing need; the feudal recognitions collected in Gascony in 1273–4 gave the king-duke much needed information about the obligations of his vassals, while the first hundred roll inquiry in England in 1274–5, and its Channel Island equivalent, tackled the problem of corrupt officials and alienation of regalian rights.

Although not susceptible of proof, a plausible case can be made that Edward I conceived the 1279 inquiry as a second Domesday Book. It would be consistent with his character and his known taste for historical allusion. There are certainly striking parallels between the structure of the manorial findings of the two inquiries, even though Domesday Book is arranged by tenant-in-chief and the hundred rolls by vill. The principal difference between them is that the hundred rolls are far more detailed and the contents far more undisciplined, but this was probably not what Edward intended. The commission ordered information about tenures and liberties, in book form, to serve as an authoritative source for the crown and others. There is nothing in it to suggest that the king sought the extensive estate surveys which came to dominate the actual returns. Their inclusion seems to have been an incidental result of the translation of his will into the articles necessary for the inquiry to take place. They caused the scope of the proceedings to change and expand into something much more difficult to carry out.

The inquiry was apparently left unfinished, but the limited number of surviving returns, and their narrow geographical range, may be misleading. One can see from both the content and appearance of certain rolls that verdicts from some vills have gone astray. This, together with fragments identified over the years in the National Archives, and the more recent discovery of returns for parts of Norfolk, makes it highly probable that more rolls for parts of the Midlands and East Anglia once existed. There can be no doubt that hearings were planned for the whole country. Apart from the London and Shropshire returns, however, there is no solid evidence that they took place. This does not guarantee that no action was taken, as the extract rolls for the 1274–5 inquiry prove. Based on rolls, some of which no longer exist, they show that returns for large parts of the country could simply vanish without trace, even in such a well-preserved archive as that of the crown. Nevertheless, although the possibility of losses should always be borne in mind, the sheer immensity of the information required under the articles, and the unfinished state of many of the rolls returned to the exchequer, make it more likely that, outside London, the Midlands, the Marches, and East Anglia, proceedings ground to a halt before they could be brought to completion.

One of the most remarkable aspects of the Edwardian inquiries is the way that they passed with scarcely any contemporary comment. Despite their scale, they were apparently accepted as a normal part of government activity. Only the reports of obstruction on the Bedfordshire/Buckinghamshire circuit indicate that the pursuit of such detailed information about estates might have been regarded as unacceptably intrusive. One consequence of this silence is that most of the evidence for the conduct of the inquiry has to be internal. The commission and list of its addressees was entered on the patent roll, which is also a useful source of background information about the commissioners, but virtually everything else, including the articles, has to be deduced from the rolls themselves.

So far as one can judge, procedure followed the well-established practices of the general eyre and previous inquiries. Relatively few rolls open with a list of jurors, or details of when and where the hearings took place. However, there are a sufficient number of them to give an idea of the social composition of jurors and a time-frame for the inquiry. Where a date is mentioned, it is often confined to the regnal year. This enables us to fix the known limits of the inquiry to the eighteen months between 12 March 1279, when it was commissioned, and 19 November 1280, the last day of Edward I's eighth regal year. The earliest precisely dated hearings were those for the Oxfordshire hundred of Lewknor. Held on 10 April 1279, they had been conducted very expeditiously, perhaps because the hundred was comparatively small. The last known hearing, for Northstow hundred in Cambridgeshire, took place on

7 April 1280. Work was therefore still taking place over a year after the king set the inquiry in motion, but possibly not much thereafter.

Hearings before the commissioners seem to have taken place in county towns, with a hint that, in a small county like Huntingdonshire, all the hundreds might have been dealt with on the same occasion. Where there were too many hundreds for this to be practicable, as in neighbouring Cambridgeshire, the commissioners may have preferred to call representatives of the hundreds before them in groups. There is virtually no information about the preliminary investigations conducted by jurors on their own, apart from the geographical progression evident in returns for parts of Huntingdonshire and Warwickshire. This suggests that they may have travelled from one place to another, but is too tenuous to make it certain. Nor is it altogether clear how lords presented their evidence, although we are now far more aware of the importance of their contribution to the proceedings. On some rolls, the estates of ecclesiastical lords were all grouped together. In Lewknor hundred, the earl of Cornwall submitted a consolidated return for all his estates, rather than making surveys available at the hearings for each vill. No doubt other lords, both lay and ecclesiastical, did likewise, although the evidence for this has vanished as the surveys were subsequently sorted and entered under the appropriate vill. Occasionally, what appears to be the text or an echo of a seigneurial return can be detected among the jurors' verdicts, but the balance between oral and written submissions is no longer recoverable. There are, however, a handful of examples where the jurors carried out their cross-examination of seigneurial evidence.

As they stand, the surviving rolls are extremely varied both in what the jurors recorded and the extent to which superfluous information was later sifted out. It has been appreciated for some time that the rolls represent different stages by which verdicts were transformed into finished rolls, but although one can broadly distinguish between raw verdicts, returns on which editors and checkers were at work and fair, finished rolls, the distinctions between them were often blurred. In attempting to make sense of this, one has to guard against pressing the evidence into over-rigid categories. There was no reason why individuals working at a hundredal level should conform to a uniform pattern, while the checkers and editors who succeeded them created at most a circuit or county identity. There is no sense of a single organizing hand as in Exchequer Domesday. Part of the explanation for the disparate nature of the rolls may be that the final step of welding the returns into book form was never taken. Perhaps the time for the appointment of an overall editor never arrived because the inquiry remained unfinished. Indeed, but for the wording of the commission, one would not have expected the outcome to have been a book. By the later thirteenth century, the compilation of some form of extract roll would have been a more usual procedure. The exchequer text in which the Warwickshire returns have been preserved could be such a compilation although it is not heavily enough abbreviated for this to be convincing. There is also an outside chance that the original of Burton's first transcript for Guthlaxton hundred on the same circuit could have been such a roll. This is not enough, however, to support the idea that a sustained programme to make the rolls serviceable was ever undertaken. As they stand, they are an impressive monument to the capacity of Edwardian officialdom to collect, but not exploit, huge amounts of information. Had the government not been slowly working its way through the results of the 1274–5 inquiry, who is to say whether it might have made more of an effort to see the subsequent inquiry through to completion and to reduce its findings to a more useful form.

The question remains as to what use, if any, contemporaries made of the returns. Whatever the crown's intention, it was out of the question that the rolls could supplant the survey of 1086. Even digests would have been too limited in their geographical range to be worth much as a register of landholding and liberties, unless the inquiry ranged more widely than we believe. The number of returns providing valuations and information about scutage suggests that on some circuits officials understood that their findings were required for fiscal reasons. If this had also been in the king's mind, the uneven attention paid to the subject made the rolls wholly inadequate for the purpose. The long tenurial histories proffered by the lords of some great estates and the laborious recording of land and rights held without known warrant, which so often attracted the attention of annotators, imply that the findings were intended as a contribution to the *Quo waranto* proceedings. If so, it has left no trace. Although many of the returns were demonstrably checked and material of interest flagged, there is no evidence that they were subjected to anything other than careful reading.

The importance accorded to the church, both in the collection of evidence and its annotation, is one of the surprises of the inquiry, especially as it was not singled out in any way in the commission. Its profile may have been raised fortuitously by the inclusion of questions about alienations into mortmain among the articles. Mortmain tenure was an unusually sensitive issue at the time. The enactment of the Statute of Mortmain, just as the inquiry was beginning to reveal the sheer quantity of ecclesiastical property held without adequate written title, may indicate that its findings sharpened anxieties about ecclesiastical encroachment on lay fee. For all that, there is nothing to suggest that it was the only, or even most important, spur towards legislation.

The real afterlife of the 1279–80 inquiry began, not in the Middle Ages, but in the early nineteenth century, with the publication of the Record Commission edition. Since then the rolls have attracted the fitful but increasingly sophisticated attention of scholars as their potential has come to be realized. The future is exciting, with the expectation of more results stimulated by the resources of modern technology. It is also highly probable that further returns will be discovered, either misclassified like the Gallow roll, or awaiting recognition among unsorted manuscripts. Copies of more returns made by lords for their own records are almost certainly lurking in cartularies and registers under the guise of estate surveys. There may even be more discoveries to be made among the transcripts of antiquarians. There is now a framework within which these developments can take place, but it is essentially provisional. Too much depends on speculation, nice judgements, and local knowledge for it to be otherwise. Just as our understanding of Domesday Book has been a cumulative process, so the same is likely to be the case with the 1279–80 hundred rolls.

APPENDIX 1

Surviving Texts from the 1279–80 Hundred Roll Inquiry

Hundreds or towns	Manuscripts	Printed texts[a]
Bedfordshire		
Hundreds		
Stodden	PRO, SC5/Beds/Tower/1	*RH* ii. 321a–3a
Willey/Bucklow	PRO, SC5/Beds/Tower/2	*RH* ii. 323a–33b
Buckinghamshire		
Hundreds		
Bunsty	PRO, SC5/Bucks/Tower/3	*RH* ii. 343b–50b
Lamua	PRO, SC5/Bucks/Tower/4	*RH* ii. 350b–3b
Mursley	PRO, SC5/Bucks/Tower/1	*RH* ii. 334a–8b
Stodfold	PRO, SC5/Bucks/Tower/2	*RH* ii. 338b–43b
Towns		
Marlow	PRO, SC5/Bucks/Tower/5[b]	*RH* ii. 353b–5b
Cambridgeshire		
Hundreds		
Armingford	PRO, SC5/Cambs/Tower/16	15mm., unprinted

APPENDIX 1 *(continued)*

Hundreds or towns	Manuscripts	Printed texts[a]
Chesterton	PRO, SC5/Cambs/Tower/3	*RH* ii. 402a–13b; 2 fragments unprinted
Cheveley	PRO, SC5/Cambs/Tower/17	1m., unprinted
Chilford	PRO, SC5/Cambs/Tower/4	*RH* ii. 413b–30b; 2mm. unprinted
Flendish	PRO, SC5/Cambs/Tower/5	*RH* ii. 430b–46b
Longstow	PRO, SC5/Cambs/Tower/10, 2pts	*RH* ii. 507a–42b
	Christ's Coll., Cambridge, Bourn,	unprinted
	aB (16c partial copy)	
Northstow	PRO, SC5/Cambs/Tower/6	*RH* ii. 446b–66b; 2mm. unprinted
	SC5/8/5/5, m. 6[c]	1m. unprinted
Papworth	PRO, SC5/Cambs/Tower/7	*RH* ii. 466b–83b
Radfield	PRO, SC5/Cambs/Tower/15	2mm., unprinted
Staine	PRO, SC5/Cambs/Tower/8	*RH* ii. 483b–97a
Staploe	PRO, SC5/Cambs/Tower/9	*RH* ii. 497a–507a
Thriplow	PRO, SC5/Cambs/Tower/11	*RH* ii. 542b–54b
Wetherley	PRO, SC5/Cambs/Tower/12	*RH* ii. 554b–68a
Whittlesford	PRO, SC5/Cambs/Tower/14	*RH* ii. 570a–90b
Witcham	PRO, SC5/Cambs/Tower/13	*RH* ii. 568a–9b
Towns		
Cambridge	PRO, SC5/Cambs/Tower/1, 3pts	*RH* ii. 356a–93a, mm. 36–40 (pt 3)
		unprinted
Barnwell suburb	PRO, SC5/Cambs/Tower/2	*RH* ii. 393a–401b

Huntingdonshire		
Hundreds		
Hurstingstone	PRO, SC5/Hunts/Tower/2; SC12/8/56 (16c. copy[d])	RH ii. 598a–607b; copy unprinted
Leightonstone	PRO, SC5/Hunts/Tower/3; Bodl. Huntingdon rolls 1, mm. 1–6	RH ii. 607b–33b Huntingdon roll, unprinted
Normancross	PRO, SC5/Hunts/Tower/4. Bodl. Huntingdon rolls 1, mm. 7–17	RH ii. 633b–65b, first 4 mm. unprinted Huntingdon roll unprinted[e]
Toseland	PRO, SC5/Hunts/Tower/5	RH ii. 665b–87b
Towns		
Godmanchester	PRO, SC5/Hunts/Tower/1	RH ii. 591a–8a
Leicestershire		
Hundreds		
Gartree	Bodl. Rawlinson MS B, 350, 34–7, 42–51 (17c. copy)	fos. 34–7 printed in Nichols, *History and Antiquities*, i/1, pp. cxix–cxxi[f]
Guthlaxton	Bodl. Rawlinson MS B, 350, fos 2–11, 11–31, 34 (17c. copy)	fos. 11–31, 34 printed in Nichols, *History and Antiquities*, i/1, pp. cx–cxix
London	PRO, SC5/London/Tower, 1–26	33 mm., unprinted[g]
Norfolk		
Hundreds		
Gallow	ULL, Fuller Coll. 7/5	15 mm., unprinted *Lordship and Landscape*, ed. Hassall and Beauroy, 215–30, no. 253, 524
North Greenhoe—Holkham only		

Hundreds or towns	Manuscripts	Printed texts[a]
S. Erpingham—Hevingham only	Norfolk Rec. Off., NRS, 14761 29 D4	ed. and trs. Campbell, 'Complexity', 256–61
Smithdon—Sedgeford only	Norfolk Rec. Off., DCN, 51/94	1 m., unprinted
Towns		
King's Lynn	Borough Muniments Bc 1	*Making*, ed. Owen, 156–81, no. 174
Oxfordshire		
Hundreds		
Bampton	PRO, SC5/Oxon/Tower/1	*RH* ii. 688a–705a. Trans. in *Oxfordshire Hundred Rolls*, ed. Stone and Hyde, 17–77
Banbury	PRO, SC5/Oxon/Tower/2	*RH* ii. 705a–10a
Bullingdon	PRO, SC5/Oxon/Tower/3	*RH* ii. 710a–25b; 'Description', ed. R. Graham, 63–75 (part only)
	SC2/42/25 (16c. extract)	
Chadlington	PRO, SC5/Oxon/Tower/5	*RH* ii. 725b–47b
Dorchester	PRO, SC5/Oxon/Tower/4b	*RH* ii. 747b–51b
Ewelme half hundred	PRO, SC5/Oxon/Tower/6	*RH* ii. 751b–74a
Langtree	PRO, SC5/Oxon/Tower/4a	*RH* ii. 774a–82a
Lewknor	PRO, SC5/Oxon/Tower/7	*RH* ii. 782a–8b
Pyrton	PRO, SC5/Oxon/Tower/12	*RH* ii. 812a–20a
Ploughley	PRO, SC5/Oxon/Tower/13	*RH* ii. 822a–39b

Thame	PRO, SC5/Oxon/Tower/14	*RH* ii. 820a–2a
Woodstock—royal demesne manor	PRO, SC5/Oxon/Tower/15	*RH* ii, 839b–42a
Wootton	PRO, SC5/Oxon/Tower/16/1–2	*RH* ii. 842a–77b. Opening fragment unprinted
Towns		
Oxford	PRO, SC5/Oxon/Tower/8, 9 a–c, 10, 18[h]	*RH* ii. 788b–805a (8–10); 'Description', ed. Graham, 3–63 (8–10); 'Hundred Rolls', ed. Cooper, 165–76 (18); part of 9b unprinted
Hundred of Hugh de Plessis (Northgate suburb)	PRO, SC5/Oxon/Tower/11	*RH* ii. 805a–11b; 'Description', ed. Graham, 75–98
Banbury	PRO, SC5/Oxon/Tower/17	2 mm., unprinted
Witney	PRO, SC11/13	*Oxfordshire Hundred Rolls*, ed. and trs. Stone and Hyde, 91–105
Rutland		
Hundreds		
Martinsley—Hambleton and Normanton only	PRO, SC5/8/5/7	1 m., unprinted
Shropshire		
Hundreds		
Pimhill[1]	Shropshire Archives, 6001/28, 53–62 (19c. copy)	unprinted

APPENDIX 1 (continued)

Hundreds or towns	Manuscripts	Printed texts[a]
Towns		
Shrewsbury[j]	Shropshire Archives, 6001/28, 21–52 (19c. copy)	partly printed in 'Late-Thirteenth Century Rental', ed. Rees, 82–4
Suffolk		
Hundreds		
Babergh	BL, Harl.743, fos 149^r–257^v; CUL, Ee, iii, 60, fos 234^r–319^v; CUL, Add MS 3395 (Hartismere, Babergh, and Thedwastre only)	*Pinchbeck Register*, ed. Hervey, ii. 30–282; *Suffolk Hundred* ed. E Powell 5–65 (Blackbourn only)
Blackbourn[k]		
Cosford		
Hartismere		
Lackford		
Risbridge		
Thedwastre		
Thingoe		
Warwickshire		
Hundreds		
Kineton	PRO, E164/15; Univ. Nottingham Lib, MiO 14 (15c. copy); Shakespeare Birthplace Trust, Stoneleigh MSS, DR 18/31/3 (14c. copy[l]); DR/10/1406, fos 48–56[m]	*Warwickshire*, ed. John
Stoneleigh		

Towns		
Coventry	Shakespeare Birthplace Trust, Stoneleigh MSS, DR 18/31/3 (14c. copy)	'Coventry Hundred Rolls', ed. John, 365–94
Warwick	PRO, E164/15; Univ. Nottingham Lib, MiO 14 (15c. copy); Shakespeare Birthplace Trust, Stoneleigh MSS, DR 18/31/3 (14c. copy)	*Warwickshire*, ed. John, 25–38

a For full details, see Bibliography.

b The five-membrane return, PRO, SC5/8/5/4, once thought to be part of the 1279 inquiry, belongs to that of 1255. D. Roffe, 'The Hundred Rolls of 1255', *Historical Research*, 69 (1996), 202 n 4.

c The reference on the MS itself is SC5/8/5/1–6, m 6.

d Includes an otherwise lost return for King's Ripton.

e Extracts in S. Raban, 'Fresh Light on the 1279 Hundred Rolls', *Historical Research*, 61 (1988), 117 (Morborne and Caldecote); *Calendar of Charters and Rolls preserved in Bodleian Library*, ed. W. H. Turner and H. O. Coxe (Oxford, 1878), pp. xvi–xviii (Haddon and part of Folksworth).

f The entry for Kibworth Harcourt, which was not printed by Nichols, can be found in both Hilton, 'Kibworth Harcourt', in *Class Conflict and The Crisis of Feudalism* (London, 1985), 4, and C. Howell, *Land, Family and Inheritance in Transition* (Cambridge, 1983), 271.

g 34 mm. depending on how the membranes have been numbered. See above, Ch. 6 n. 77.

h Contains some of the same material as 9a.

i The transcript for Bradford hundred which follows may belong to Kirkby's Quest (1284–5).

j Including townships within the liberty.

k The opening part of the return for Stanton, which is missing from the main texts, survives in a late medieval terrier, BL, Add MS 4699, fos. 4^v–6^v.

l Coventry Priory estates only. Entries for Priors Hardwick and Priors Marston were also copied into the late 16th-cent. BL, Add MS 32100, fos. 13–17.

m Cartulary copies of returns for Stivichall, Chadshunt, Gaydon, Bishop's Ichington, and Bishop's Tachbrook only.

APPENDIX 2

Commission for the 1279–80 Hundred Roll Inquiry and the Oath Taken by the Commissioners[1]

THE COMMISSION

Rex dilectis et fidelibus suis Galfrido Aguylun' Johanni de Steynegreve et Godefrido de Alta Ripa salutem. Quia per diversas occupaciones super nos et super alios tam divites quam pauperes in regno nostro tam in dominicis feodis feodalibus et libertatibus quam rebus aliis diversimode factas nos et alii homines nonnulli jacturam sustinuimus et sustinemus ut nobis de hoc quod nostrum est et nostrum esse debet et aliis quod suum est et suum esse debet constare valeat in futuro assignavimus vos una cum hiis quos vobis associetis ad videndum omnes civitates burgos et villas mercatorias in comitatibus Warr' et Leic' tam infra libertates quam extra quorumcumque virorum fuerit sive fuerint divitum sive pauperum et ad inquirendum tam de dominicis nostris feodis feodalibus escaetis libertatibus ac rebus cunctis feodum et tenementa contingentibus quam aliorum quorumcumque et qui ea tenent scilicet in dominico ut in dominico in villanis ut in villanis in servis ut in servis in cotariis ut in cotariis et postmodo in liberis tenentibus ut in liberis tenentibus et in boscis in parcis in chaciis in warennis in aquis ripariis libertatibus feriis mercatis et aliis tenuris quibuscumque et quocumque modo et de quibus sive de mediis sive de aliis et de quibus feodis et aliis tenuris scutagium dari consuevit et dari debet et quantum de feodis honorum quorumcumque et qui feodalia illa tenent et qualiter et quomodo. Ita quod singule ville hameletta et alie tenure quocumque nomine censeantur distincte et aperte conscribantur in libris quos nobis per vos super hoc liberari volumus et ita quod nemini in aliquo parcatur[2] et

---

[1] PRO, C66/98, m. 21[d]. There are several printed texts, all drawn from this enrolment on the patent roll. In Latin, *Foedera Conventiones, Litterae et Acta Publica*, ed. T. Rymer (London, 1816–69), i/2. 567; *RH* ii, p. ix; *A Formula Book of English Official Historical Documents*, ed. H. Hall, 2 vols. (Cambridge, 1908–9), ii. 141–2. Commission in translation in *Cal Pat. 1272–81*, 343.

[2] The same commission appears to this point, tr. into the third person, at the head of the surviving copies of the Warwickshire returns. *The Warwickshire Hundred Rolls of 1279–80*, ed. T. John (Oxford, 1992), 25.

quod nobis et aliis constare possit ad plenum de premissis. Et ideo vobis
mandamus quod ad certos dies et loca etc. ad omnia et singula loca comitatum predictorum personaliter accedatis et per sacramentum tam militum
etc. de comitatibus illis et eciam per fidelem examinacionem quorumcumque de tenura et feodis suis premissa faciatis in forma predicta. Et ita
fideliter et diligenter vos habeatis in hac parte quod vestra fidelitas et
industria et circumspectio perpetuo debeant commendari et quod per iter-
atam inquisitionem seu attinctam pro necligencia vel insufficientia vestra
in hac parte super premissis faciend' merito redargui non debeatis.
Mandavimus enim vicecomiti nostro comitatum predictorum quod ad
certos dies et loca etc. venire faciatis coram vobis tot et tales tam milites
quam alios probos et legales homines de balliva sua per quos etc. ita quod
nichil omittatur in ullo loco. Mandavimus eciam universis et singulis tam
majoribus quam minoribus de comitatibus predictis tam infra libertates
quam extra quod vobis in premissis sint intendentes consulentes et
auxiliantes prout eis scire faciatis ex parte nostra. In cuius etc. Teste Rex
ut supra [apud Wodestoke xij die Marcii.]

THE OATH

Vos enquerrors jurrez qe bien et leaument servirez le Roy en le office qe
vos est enjoint e a tel office diligentement et leaument entenderez e leaument le freez pur le Roy et pur touz autres a vostre poer. Et ceo ne lerrez
pur puvre ne pur riche ne pur hautesce ne pur hayne ne pur favor ne pur
poer ne pur estat de nuli persone ne pur bien fet doun ne premesse de nulli
qe fet vos seit ou vos purra estre fet ne par art ne par engin ne lerrez qe les
dreiz le Roy leaument ne enquerrez e leaument freez escrivre et liverer al
Roy si com il vos ad enjoint. E qe benefice de seint eglise ne pensiun ne
autre bien fet ne receverez saunz conge le Roy si Deu vos aid e li seinz.

APPENDIX 3

The Cambridgeshire and London Articles of the 1279–80 Inquiry

A. CAMBRIDGESHIRE[1]

1. (1) *Que et quot maneria dominica rex habet in manu sua in comitatibus Cantabrigiensibus et Huntedoniis tam de antiquis dominicis corone quam de escaetis et perquisitis.*

Which and how many demesne manors the king has in his hand in the counties of Cambridgeshire and Huntingdonshire both as ancient demesne of the crown and as escheats and acquisitions.

2. (2) *Que maneria esse solent in manibus regum predecessorum regis et qui ea nunc tenent [et quo waranto et a quo tempore et per quem et quomodo fuerint alienata][2].*

Which manors used to be in the hands of the king's predecessors and who holds them now and by what warrant, since when, and by whom and how were they alienated.

3. (4) *Si aliquis liber sokemannus vel bondus de antiquo dominico alii sok*

---

[1] The text of the articles given to the jurors opened with the words *inquirere opportet. RH* ii. 688a, 822a. Where they are cited, they vary considerably as to whether all the articles were included, the degree to which they were abridged, their precise wording, and, sometimes, order. The present text is a composite reconstruction, from the Cambridgeshire returns among which those for Cambridge itself (ibid. 356a, 391a–2b), together with Kingston (ibid. 514a, 516a–17a) and Toft (ibid. 517a–b, 519b–20b) in Longstow hundred, are particularly comprehensive. An attempt has been made to provide the fullest and most intelligible text. Punctuation has been modernized and minor variations in wording have not been noted. Articles either similar or identical in form to those of the 1274–5 inquiry and the *nova capitula* of the general eyre have the article reference number from H. M. Cam, *The Hundred and the Hundred Rolls* (London, 1930), 248–56, in brackets. References to the articles of the 1255 hundred roll inquiry follow the numbering of D. Roffe, 'The Hundred Rolls of 1255', *Historical Research*, 69 (1996), 208–10, and those of *vetera capitula* of the general eyre, the numbering in H. M. Cam, *Studies in the Hundred Rolls* (Oxford, 1921), 92–4. For the variant articles in the 19-cent. transcript for Shrewsbury, see above, pp. 47–8.

[2] Text completed from the articles of the 1274–5 inquiry. Cam, *The Hundred*, 248–9.

emanno vel alicui libere tenenti seu bondo aliquid de terris aut tenementis suis vendiderit aut alio modo alienaverit³ aliquid tenendi libere per cartam.

Whether any free sokeman or bondman of the ancient demesne has sold any of his lands or tenements to another sokeman or to a free tenant or bondman, or has in any other way alienated anything so that it is held freely by charter.

4. *Quantum quilibet archiepiscopus episcopus abbas prior comes baro miles liber homo vel burgensis tenet in civitatibus burgis et villis mercatoriis aut omnibus aliis villis et hamelettis ut in castris forcelettis⁴ feodis militum terris tenementis⁵ dominicis honoribus boscis pratis parcis pasturis communibus aut separabilibus forestis chaciis warrennis feriis mercatis redditibus villenagiis cotagiis consuetudinibus serviciis operacionibus villanorum aquis piscariis separabilibus aut communibus ripariis vivariis molendinis gardinis brueriis marescis turbariis alnetis seu aliquibus aliis rebus ad castra forceletta feoda honores terras et tenementa quibuscumque pertinentibus et qui tenent in feodo et hereditarie et qui ad terminum vite vel annorum vel ad feodi firmam et utrum tenet de domino rege in capite vel de medio et de quibus mediis et per que servicia et per quas consuetudines et quantum pro feodi firma aut pro terminis vite vel annorum reddunt domino regi per annum aut dominis tenementorum predictorum.*

How much each archbishop, bishop, abbot, prior, earl, baron, knight, freeman or burgess holds in cities, boroughs and market towns or all other vills and hamlets, in castles, strongholds, knights' fees, lands, tenements, demesnes, honours, woods, meadows, parks, pastures common or several, forests, chaces, warrens, fairs, markets, rents, villeins, cottars, customs, services, villein works, waters, fisheries common or several, banks, fishponds, mills, gardens, heathland, marshes, turbaries, alder groves or anything else of any kind pertaining to castles, strongholds, fees, honours, lands and tenements, and who holds them in fee and hereditarily and who [holds] for life or a term of years or at fee farm and whether they are held of the king in chief or from a mesne lord, and from which mesne lords and for what service and by what customs and how much they render to the lord king or the aforementioned lords per annum in fee farm or for life or for a term of years.

5. *Quantum quilibet archiepiscopus episcopus abbas prior comes baro miles et liber homo habet in libere tenentibus ut in libere tenentibus in dominicis ut in dominicis⁶ in villanis ut in villanis in servis ut in servis in*

---

³ The Cambridge and Kingston articles end here.
⁴ *fortelaciis* at Kingston.
⁵ The Cambridge article ends here.
⁶ The Cambridge article ends here.

cotariis ut in cotariis et in omnibus aliis tenuris quibuscumque et quocumque modo et de quibus sive de medio sive de aliis eas tenent et per quas metas et divisas.

How much each archbishop, bishop, abbot, prior, earl, baron, knight and freeman has in free tenants, demesnes, villeins, serfs, cottars and in all other tenures whatever, and by whatever way and of whom do they hold them, either from a mesne lord or from others and within what bounds.

6. *De quibus feodis et aliis tenuris scutagium dari debet et consuevit[7] et quantum de feodis honorum quorumcumque et qui feoda illa tenent qualiter quo modo et a quo tempore.*

From which fees and other tenures scutage ought and used to be given and is customary and how much from the fees of whichever honour and who holds those fees, in what way, how and since when.

7. *Quantum terre vel tenementa quilibet liber homo villanus vel servus aut cotarius tenet in villis mercatoriis aut omnibus aliis villis ac hamelettis[8] et de quibus dominis et per que servicia et per quas consuetudines inde faciendas.*

How many lands and tenements each free tenant, villein or serf or cottar holds in market towns or all other vills and hamlets and from which lords and for what services and for rendering what customs.

8. *Qui habent piscariam communem aut separabilem in aquis vel ripariis domini regis quo waranto etc.[9]*

Who holds common or private fisheries in the rivers or banks of the lord king, by what warrant etc.

9. *Si aliqui tenentes de domino rege in capite de domino rege per baroniam vel serjauntiam magnam vel parvam terras aut tenementa sua alicui vendiderint vel aliquo alio modo alienaverint[10] quibus personis vendita seu alienata fuerint qui ea tenent nunc per quos etc.[11]*

Whether any tenants-in-chief of the king by barony or grand or petty serjeanty have sold lands or tenements to anyone, or alienated them in any other way, to whom they have been sold or alienated, who now hold them, by whom etc.

10. (9) *Qui clamant habere libertates qualiter et quo modo et quibus libertatibus hactenus usi fuerint et utrum habeant per cartas predecessorum regum aut potestate aut auctoritate propria vel favore aut permissione*

---

[7] The Cambridge article ends here.
[8] The Cambridge article ends here.
[9] *quo waranto etc* supplied from the Caldecote articles. *RH* ii. 529a. This article was omitted at Toft.
[10] The Cambridge article ends here.
[11] This article was omitted at Toft.

vicecomitum[12] *aut ballivorum seu ministrorum domini regis libertates illas habuerint vel non.*[13]

Who claims to have liberties, how and in what way, and which liberties have they exercised until now and whether they have these liberties by charter of the king's predecessors or by force or on their own authority or by favour or permission of the sheriff or the bailiffs or ministers of the lord king or not.

11. *Si aliquis super dominum regem vel aliquem alium majorem vel minorem per libertates illas aliqui occupaverint aut sibi attraxerint*[14] *qualiter quo modo per quem et a quo tempore.*[15]

Whether anyone has occupied or appropriated to himself those liberties against the lord king or anyone great or small, in what way, by whom and since when.

12.(8) *Qui habentes furcas tumberellum collistrigium vel alia que ad judicium perficiendum pertinent assisam panis et cervisie wreccum maris retorna brevium visum franci plegii et placitum vetiti namii extractas aut alia que ad regem pertinent quo waranto qualiter quo modo et a quo tempore et per quem.*[16]

Who, having gallows, tumbrels, pillories or other things pertaining to the exercise of judgement, assize of bread and ale, wreck of the sea, return of writs, view of frankpledge and plea of vee de naam, estreats or anything else belonging to the king, by what warrant, in what way, how and since when and by whom.

13.(11) *Qui ab antiquo liberas chacias et warennas ex concessione regis vel predecessorum suorum habuerint*[17] *fines et metas earum excesserint qualiter quo modo et a quo tempore et per quas metas et divisas chacias vel warennas illas habere debent per concessionem predictam.*[18]

Who from ancient times has had free chaces and warrens by grant of the king or his predecessors and has exceeded their metes and bounds, how, in what way, and since when, and within what metes and bounds ought they have those chaces and warrens by the aforesaid grant.

14. (11) *Qui de novo appropriaverint sibi*[19] *liberas chacias vel warennas quo waranto et per quas metas et divisas et a quo tempore.*[20]

---

[12] The Kingston article ends here.
[13] This article was omitted at Toft.
[14] The Cambridge article ends here.
[15] This article was omitted at Toft.
[16] The Cambridge article omits *visum franci plegii et placitum vetiti namii* and ends *pertinent etc.*
[17] The Cambridge article ends here.
[18] This article was omitted at Toft.
[19] The Cambridge article ends here.
[20] This article was omitted at Toft.

Who has newly appropriated to himself free chace and warren, by what warrant and within what metes and bounds and since when.

15. *Qui habentes chacias warennas ferias mercata vel alias libertates que ad dominum regem pertinent*[21] *utrum eas habuerint ex concessione regis vel predecessorum suorum aut eas potestate ac auctoritate propria vel potestate quorum antecessorum suorum aut favore et permissione vicecomitum seu ballivorum suorum vel aliorum ministrorum domini regis aut predecessorum suorum ea perquisierint; et si ex concessione regis vel predecessorum suorum quorum predecessorum suorum et a quo tempore; et si potestate propria vel potestate ballivorum suorum aut permissione vicecomitum vel aliorum ballivorum seu ministrorum regis vel predecessorum suorum.*[22]

Those having chaces, warrens, fairs, markets or other liberties which belong to the lord king, whether they have them by grant of the king or his predecessors or by force or on their own authority or by the force of their ancestors, or by favour or permission of the sheriff or his bailiffs or of other ministers of the lord king or his predecessors, and if by grant of the king or his predecessors, which of his predecessors and how long ago and if by his own authority or the authority of his bailiffs or by permission of the sheriff or other bailiffs or ministers of the king or his predecessors.

16. (13[23]) *Si qui aut eorum antecessores fecerint aliquas purpresturas super dominum regem vel regalem dignitatem*[24] *vel communem*[25] *vel aliquem alium majorem vel minorem de comitatibus predictis*[26] *qualiter quo modo et a quo tempore*

Whether anyone or their ancestors has made any purprestures against the king or royal dignity or crown or anyone great or small in the aforementioned counties, in what way, how and how long ago.

17. (45) *Si aliqui viri religiosi teneant aliquas ecclesias in usus proprios quarum advocaciones ad dominum regem de jure debeant pertinere*[27] *vel aliqui alii hujusmodi advocaciones teneant qualiter quo modo et a quo tempore.*

Whether any religious hold any appropriated churches whose advowsons ought properly belong to the lord king or anyone else who holds such advowsons, in what way, how and since when.

[21] The Cambridge article ends here.
[22] This article was omitted at Toft.
[23] See 1255, art. 7, and general eyre, art. 9 of the *vetera capitula* and 13 of the *nova capitula*.
[24] The Cambridge article ends here.
[25] Correctly, *coronam?*.
[26] The Kingston article ends here.
[27] The Cambridge article ends here.

18. *Si que terre vel tenementa que debent esse escaete domini regis vel in custodia sua sint in manu sua aut in manibus aliorum*[28] *et si in manibus aliorum in quorum manibus per quem qualiter quo modo quo waranto et a quo tempore.*[29]

Whether there are any lands or tenements which ought to be escheats of the lord king or in his wardships [which] are in his hand or in the hands of others and, if in the hands of others, by whom, how, in what way, by what warrant and since when.

19. (14) *Que feoda militaria cujuscumque feodi terre aut tenementa data sint aut vendita viris religiosis aut aliis in prejudicium domini regis ubi dominus rex amittit custodias vel maritagium heredum*[30] *per quos qualiter quo modo et a quo tempore.*

Which knights' fees from whichever fee, lands or tenements have been given or sold to religious or others to the prejudice of the lord king, whereby the lord king has lost the wardship or the marriage of heirs, by whom, in what way, how and since when.

20. (7) *De sectis antiquis consuetudinibus serviciis et aliis rebus domino rege et antecessoribus suis subtractis,*[31] *qui eas subtraxerint qualiter quo modo et a quo tempore; et qui hujusmodi etc.*[32]

Concerning ancient suits, customs, services and other things withdrawn from the lord king and his ancestors, who has withdrawn them, how, in what way, and since when; and who of this kind etc.

21. (3) *De feodis et feodalibus domini regis et tenementa ejus qui modo ea tenent nunc de ipso in capite*[33] *et quot feoda singuli eorum tenent et que feoda de domino rege tenere solent in capite et utrum tenentur per medium et per quem medium et a quo tempore alienata fuerint etc.*

Concerning fees and feudal rights of the lord king and his tenements, who now holds them from him in chief and how many fees each of them holds and which fees used to be held of the lord king in chief and which are held through mesne tenants and which mesne tenant and when were they alienated [and in what way and by whom].

22. (6) *Quot hundreda wapentacula sunt in manu domini regis et quot et que in manibus aliorum*[34] *et a quo tempore quo waranto et quantum quilibet hundredum wapentaculum valeat per annum.*

How many hundreds and wapentakes are now in the king's hand and

---

[28] The Cambridge article ends here.
[29] See 1255, art. 22, and general eyre, art. 7 of the *vetera capitula*.
[30] The Cambridge article ends here.
[31] The Cambridge article ends here.
[32] This article was repeated three times in the Kingston return.
[33] The Cambridge article ends here.
[34] The Cambridge article ends here.

which and how many are in the hands of others, since when and by what warrant and how much is each hundred [and] wapentake worth per annum.

23. *Si heres alicujus tenementorum*[35] *de domino rege in capite cujus custodia et maritagium ad ipsum regem de jure pertinent subtractus sit domino rege vel concellatus et alicui sine licentia domini regis maritatus per quem qualiter quo modo et a quo tempore.*[36]

Whether the heir of any tenement [held] of the lord king whose wardship or marriage rightly belongs to the said king has been withdrawn from the lord king or concealed and married to someone without the licence of the lord king, by whom, in what way and since when.

24. *Si aliqua domina vel puella que per dominum regem debet maritari gratis*[37] *alicui se maritaverit*[38] *sine licencia regis vel si rapta*[39] *fuerit et contra voluntatem propriam maritatur per quem*[40] *et cui qualiter quo modo.*[41]

Whether any lady or girl who should be married by the lord king has married someone free, without the licence of the lord king, or whether she has been abducted and married against her will, by whom, and to whom, in what way and how.

25. *Si alique terre vel tenementa que debent esse eschaete domini regis vel in custodia sua*[42] *concellata fuerint et in quorum manibus existant*[43] *et a quo tempore et per quem concelata sint.*[44]

Whether any lands or tenements which ought to be escheats of the lord king or in his wardship have been concealed and in whose hands they are to be found and since when and by whom they were concealed.

26. *Si aliqui de feodo domini regis baroniis seu serjantiis magnis vel parvis data vendita vel alio modo alienata fuerint quibus personis per quem et a quo tempore; et qui particulas inde alienatas tenent et quantum particule ille valent per annum.*

Whether any fee of the lord king baronies or serjeanties, grand or petty, have been granted, sold or in any way alienated, to which people, by whom and since when; and which alienated parcels do they hold and how much are those parcels worth per annum.

---

[35] *tenentis* at Cambridge. *RH* ii. 392a.
[36] See general eyre, art. 4 of the *vetera capitula.*
[37] *qualis* at Kingston. *RH* ii. 516b.
[38] The Toft article ends here.
[39] *capta* at Kingston. *RH* ii. 516b.
[40] The Cambridge article ends here.
[41] See general eyre, arts. 4–5 of the *vetera capitula.*
[42] The Toft article continues *sint in manu sua vel in manibus suorum etc.*
[43] The Cambridge article ends here.
[44] See also art. 18, and general eyre, art. 7 of the *vetera capitula.*

27. *Qui sunt illi qui tenentur ad wardas seu defensiones[45] ad castra domini regis faciendas[46] et si quid de wardis illis concelatum vel subtractum fuit per quos et a quo tempore et quantum pro wardis illis reddere debent.*

Who are those who are obliged to the performance of castle guard or defence of the castles of the lord king and whether anything concerning those wards has been concealed or withdrawn, by whom and since when and how much they ought to render for those castle guards.

28. *Si qui cursus aquarum riparum domini regis diverterint et molendina stagna seu gurgites in eisdem levaverint[47] quo waranto qualiter quo modo et a quo tempore.[48]*

Whether anyone has diverted the course of river banks of the lord king and has built mill-pools or weirs on them, by what warrant, how, in what way and since when.

29. *Qui patronatus abbathiarum prioratuum dignitatum prebendarum custodum hospitalium et liberarum capellarum domini regis qui ab antiquitus ad coronam domini regis pertinebant et qui sunt in manu domini regis et qui non[49] et qui eos tenent nunc qualiter quo modo et a quo tempore etc.[50]*

Which patronage of abbeys, priories, prebendal dignities, custody of hospitals and free chapels of the lord king used anciently to belong to the crown, and which are in the hands of the lord king and which not, and who holds them now, how, in what way and since when.

30. *De terris Normannorum felonum fugitivorum et aliorum que sunt et esse debent escaete domini regis[51] qui ea tenent qualiter quo modo et a quo tempore et utrum in feodo et hereditarie vel ad terminum vite vel annorum.[52]*

Concerning lands of the Normans, felons, fugitives and others which are and should be escheats of the lord king, who holds them, in what way, how and since when and whether [they are held] in fee and hereditarily or for life or for a term of years.

31. *Que et quot burgagia placeas et terras vacuas rex habet in civitatibus burgis villis mercatoriis et aliis villis et hamelettis[53] et qui ea tenent et quantum dominus rex inde perciperit per annum.[54]*

---

[45] The Toft article ends here.
[46] The Cambridge article ends here.
[47] The Cambridge article ends here.
[48] This article was omitted at Toft.
[49] The Cambridge article ends here.
[50] This article was omitted at Toft.
[51] The Cambridge article ends here.
[52] See general eyre, art. 37 of the *vetera capitula*. This article was omitted at Toft.
[53] The Cambridge article ends here.
[54] This article was omitted at Toft.

Which and how many burgages, plots and empty lands the king has in cities, boroughs, market towns and other vills and hamlets and who holds them and how much the lord king receives from them per annum.

32. *De firmariis domini regis tenentibus civitatibus burgis aut aliqua maneria domini regis ad feodi firmam qui occasione dicte firme capiunt escaetas domini regis et per illos alienatur aut ipsas retinent commodum inde proveniunt in usus proprios convertendo.*[55]

Concerning the farmers of the lord king, holding cities, boroughs or any manors of the lord king at fee farm, who by occasion of that farm take escheats and alienate them, or retain them, by which they come to convert [them] to their own use.

33. *Si qui viri religiosi intraverunt feodum domini regis in toto vel in parte ubi dominus rex amittit custodiam et maritagia heredum qualiter et quo modo et a quo tempore.*[56]

Whether religious have entered the fee of the lord king either wholly or in part so that the lord king loses custody and marriage of heirs, in what way, how and since when.

34. *Quantum quilibet tenet de essartis infra forestas domini regis et quantum terre et tenementa illa valent per annum et quantum rex percipit de assartis illis per annum ut in redditibus consuetudinibus serviciis et aliis. Et si aliquis plus inde subtraxit quam ad ipsum pertinent habendum etc.*[57]

How much anyone holds of assarts in the forest of the lord king and how much the lands and tenements are worth per annum and how much the king receives from those assarts per annum in rents, customs, services and others. And whether anyone has taken more than he should have for himself.

35. *Qui pontes et calcetas ubi regie et communes strate esse debent et parari solent et consueverunt et eos dirui permiserunt*[58] *et ibidem passagium per batellos passagium fecerint certum transeuntibus pro passagiis suis capientes et passagia illa ad firmam annuatim dimittentes in prejudicium et lesionem regis dignitatis et transeuntium grave dampnum quibus locis et a quo tempore passagia illa habuerint quid et quantum capiunt pro firma predicta et quantum quilibet transiens solvit pro passagio suo.*[59]

Who is and was accustomed to repair the bridges and causeways where the royal and common highways ought to be, and allowed them to decay and there made passage for the passage of boats, taking a sum from those

[55] This article was omitted at Toft.

[56] See also art. 19; 1255, art. 17, and general eyre, art. 14 of the *nova capitula*. This article was omitted at Toft.

[57] This article was omitted at Kingston and Toft.

[58] The Cambridge article ends here.

[59] This article was omitted at Toft.

travelling for their passage and granting those tolls for an annual farm to the prejudice and damage of royal dignity and the grave damage of travellers, in which places, and since when they have had those tolls, what and how much they take for the aforementioned farm and how much each traveller pays for his passage.

The following articles appear in isolated returns only:

36. *De advocacionibus ecclesiarum et qui sunt veri patroni ecclesiarum existencium in burgo Cantabr'.*[60]
Concerning the advowsons of churches and who are the true patrons of the churches in the borough of Cambridge.

37. *Quantum quilibet tenet ut in terris pratis croftis et gardinis et quantum continet si sit acra dimidia vel roda.*[61]
How much each hold in lands, meadows, crofts and gardens and how much it contains if it is half an acre or rod.

38. *Quantum opera villanorum valent etc.*[62]
How much the villein works are worth etc.

39. *De purpresturis factis quantum in latidudine et longitudine.*[63]
Concerning purprestures which have been made, what their size is in latitude and longitude.

40. *Qui tenent ad terminum vite vel annorum.*[64]
Who holds for life or for a term of years.

41. *De terris elemosinatis domibus religiosis.*[65]
Concerning the land given in alms to religious houses.

42. *Que et quantum quilibet libere tenens per cartam vel libere sokemannus aut bondus tenet in dictis maneriis de domino rege in capite vel per medium et per quod servicium.*[66]
What and how much each freeman, holding by charter, or free sokeman or bondman holds in chief in the aforesaid manors of the lord king, or through a mesne tenant and for what service.

---

[60] *RH* ii. 392b.
[61] Waterbeach (Northstow hund.) entry only. Ibid. 454b.
[62] Waterbeach (Northstow hund.) entry only.
[63] Waterbeach (Northstow hund.) entry only.
[64] Fowlmere and Hauxton (Thriplow hund.) entries only. *RH* ii. 547b, 550b.
[65] Fowlmere (Thriplow hund.) and Arrington (Wetherley hund.). *RH* ii. 547b, 556a.
[66] Godmanchester entry only. *RH* ii. 591a.

1. *De illis qui habent xx libratas terre etc.*
Concerning those who have twenty pounds worth of land etc.

2. *De hiis qui districti fuerunt ad arma militaria suscipienda etc.*
Concerning those who were distrained to take knighthood etc.

3. *De terris and tenementis eorum in quibus locis sunt per Anglie etc.*
Concerning the whereabouts of their land and tenements in England etc.

4. *De domibus et redditibus regis si quas vel quos habeant etc.*
Concerning the king's houses and rents, whether they have them etc.

5. *Et siquid inde super regem vel patrem suum fuerit occupatus etc.*
Whether anyone has occupied [property of the] king or his father etc.

6. *De libertatibus domini regis que sunt in manu sua etc.*
Concerning regalian rights which are in the king's hands etc.

7. *Et que alie sunt super ipsum occupate etc.*
And which others belonging to him have been occupied on etc.

8. *De eschaetis domini regis ubi sunt etc.*
Concerning the whereabouts of royal escheats etc.

9. *De aliis eschaetis de tempore patris sui et predecessorum suorum etc.*
Concerning other escheats from the time of his father and his predecessors etc.

10. *De dominicis regis etc.*
Concerning royal demesnes etc.

11. *De placeis regis[68] dudum vacuis et nunc edificatis etc.*
Concerning plots, formerly vacant, now built on etc.

12. *De placeis regis[69] nunc non edificatis etc.*
Concerning plots now without buildings etc.

13. *De redditibus super huiusmodi placeis levatis etc.*
Concerning rents levied on whatever plots etc.

14. *De feodis regis etc ut in advocationibus ecclesiarum etc.*
Concerning royal fees etc. as in ecclesiastical advowsons etc.

15. *De viis et semitis etc.*
Concerning roads and paths etc.

---

[67] Text compiled from PRO, SC5/London/Tower/1–26, mm. 8 (6), 10 (8), 14 (12).

[68] *regis* in PRO, SC5/London/Tower/5, m. 10 (8) only.

[69] *regis* in PRO, SC5/London/Tower/5, m. 10 (8) only.

16. *De cursu aque etc.*
Concerning watercourses etc.

17. *De aliis purpresturis etc.*
Concerning other encroachments etc.

18. *De occupationibus libertatum regis etc.*
Concerning encroachment on the king's liberties etc.

Bibliography

I. MANUSCRIPT SOURCES

Cambridge, Christ's College

Bourn aB   16c. copy of part of Longstow
            hundred roll

Cambridge, University Library

Add MS 3395   Bury St Edmunds register
Ee, iii, 60   Bury St Edmunds register
            (Pinchbeck)

London, British Library

Add MS 14847   Bury St Edmunds register
            (Northwold)
Add MS 4699   Bury St Edmunds terrier
Cott, Vesp. B xi   Hagnaby Chronicle
Harl. MS 743   Bury St Edmunds register
            (Lakenheath)

London, Public Record Office

C47   Chancery Miscellanea
C54   Close rolls
C66   Patent rolls
C133   Inquisitions *post mortem*
E164/15   Warwickshire hundred rolls
E198   Exchequer King's Remembrancer,
            records relating to distraint of
            knighthood
SC1   Ancient Correspondence of
            Chancery and Exchequer
SC5, Chapter House series   1255 and 1274–5 hundred rolls

SC5, Tower series	1279–80 hundred rolls
SC5/8/5/4–7	Fragments of hundred rolls
SC11/13	Return for Witney (Oxon)
SC12/8/56	Copy of hundred roll return for Hurstingstone hundred (Hunts)

London, University Library

| Fuller Coll., 7/5 | Gallow hundred roll |

Norwich, Norfolk Record Office

| DCN 4437 | Sedgeford survey |
| NRS 14761 29 D4 | Hevingham hundred roll |

Oxford, Bodleian Library

| Huntingdon rolls, 1 | Leightonstone and Normancross hundred roll |
| Rawlinson MS B, 350 | Transcripts of William Burton |

Shropshire Archives

| 6001/28 | Transcripts of Joseph Morris |

II. PRIMARY SOURCES

The Anglo-Saxon Chronicle, ed. D. Whitelock, D. C. Douglas, and S. I. Tucker (London, 1961, repr. Westport, Conn., 1986).

Annales F. Nicholai Triveti, ed. T. Hog (London, 1845).

Annales Monastici, ed. H. R. Luard, 5 vols. (Rolls Series; London, 1864–9).

Archives Historiques du département de la Gironde, 1 (1859), 3 (1861–2).

Book of Fees, 3 vols. (HMSO; London, 1920–31).

Calendar of Ancient Correspondence concerning Wales, ed. J. G. Edwards (Board of Celtic Studies, History and Law Series, 11, Cardiff, 1935).

Calendar of Charters and Rolls preserved in Bodleian Library, ed. W. H. Turner and H. O. Coxe (Oxford, 1878).

Calendar of Close Rolls, 1272–1509, 47 vols. (HMSO; London, 1900–63).

Calendar of Documents relating to Ireland 1252–1307, ed. H. S. Sweetman and G. F. Handcock, 4 vols. (HMSO; London, 1877–86).

Calendar of Inquisitions Post Mortem for Henry III, Edward I and Edward II, 6 vols. (HMSO; London, 1904–13).

Calendar of Patent Rolls, 1232–1582, 71 vols. (HMSO; London, 1906–86).

Calendar of Welsh Rolls in *Calendar of Chancery Rolls Various, 1277–1326* (HMSO; London, 1912).

Cartularium Monasterii de Rameseia, ed. W. H. Hart and P. A. Lyons, 3 vols. (Rolls Series; London, 1884–93).

Chronica Johannis de Oxenedes, ed. H. Ellis (Rolls Series; London, 1859).

The Chronicle of Bury St Edmunds, ed. A. Gransden (London, 1964).

The Chronicle of Pierre de Langtoft, ed. T. Wright, 2 vols. (Rolls Series; London, 1866–8).

Chronicon de Lanercost, ed. J. Stevenson (Edinburgh, 1839).

Chronicon ex Chronicis, ed. B. Thorpe (London, 1849).

Chronicon Petroburgense, ed. T. Stapleton (Camden Soc., 47; London, 1849).

Close Rolls, 1227–72, 14 vols. (HMSO; London, 1902–38).

Collections for a History of Staffordshire, ed. William Salt Archaeological Society, 5/1 (1884), 105–21 (Staffordshire hundred rolls).

The Course of the Exchequer by Richard, Son of Nigel, ed. C. Johnson (London, 1950).

'The Coventry Hundred Rolls', ed. T. John, in P. R. Coss (ed.), *The Early Records of Medieval Coventry* (British Academy Records of Social and Economic History, NS 11; London, 1986), 365–94.

'Description of Oxford from the Hundred Rolls AD 1279', ed. R. Graham, in *Collectanea*, 4th ser. (Oxford Historical Society, 47; Oxford, 1905), 1–98.

Documents of the Baronial Movement of Reform and Rebellion, 1258–1267, ed. R. F. Treharne and I. J. Sanders (Oxford, 1973).

Domesday Book, ed. A. Farley, 2 vols. (London, 1783).

Domesday Book, ed. J. Morris *et al.*, 40 vols (Chichester, 1974–86).

The Earliest English Law Reports, ed. P. A. Brand, 2 vols. (Selden Society, London, 1966).

Enquêtes administratives d'Alfonse de Poitiers: Arrêts de son Parlement Tenu à Toulouse 1249–1271, ed. P.-F. Fournier and P. Guébin (Paris, 1959).

'Extent of Merionethshire', ed. M. C. Jones, *Archaeologia Cambrensis*, 3rd ser. 51 (1867), 183–92.

Extente des Îles de Jersey, Guernesey, Aurigny et Serk; suivie des Inquisitions dans les Îles de Jersey et Guernesey, 1274 (Société Jersiaise, 2; Ste Helier, 1877).

Feudal Aids, 1284–1431, 6 vols. (HMSO; London, 1899–1920).

Flores Historiarum, ed. H. R. Luard, 3 vols. (Rolls Series; London, 1890).

Foedera, Conventiones, Litterae et Acta publica, ed. T. Rymer, 4 vols. (Rec. Comm.; London, 1816–69).

A Formula Book of English Official Historical Documents, ed. H. Hall, 2 vols. (Cambridge, 1908–9).

The Gascon Calendar of 1322, ed. G. P. Cuttino (Camden Soc., 3rd ser. 70; London, 1949).

Gascon Register A, ed. G. P. Cuttino, 3 vols. (British Academy; London, 1975–6).

Great Domesday, gen. ed. R. W. H. Erskine (London, 1987–92).

Historia Anglicana, ed. H. R. Luard (Rolls Series; London, 1859).

Historia Anglorum, ed. F. Madden, 3 vols. (Rolls Series; London, 1866–90).

'The Hundred Rolls for the Parish of St Thomas, Oxford', ed. J. Cooper, *Oxoniensia*, 37 (1972), 165–76.

Inquisitio Comitatus Cantabrigiensis, ed. N. E. S. A. Hamilton (London, 1876).

'A Late-Thirteenth Century Rental of Tenements in Shrewsbury', ed. U. Rees, *Transactions of the Shropshire Archaeological and Historical Society*, 66 (1989), 79–84.

Liber Memorandorum Ecclesie de Bernewelle, ed. J. W. Clark (Cambridge, 1907).

Le Livre d'Agenais, publié d'après le MS Bodley 917, ed. G. P. Cuttino (Cahiers de l'Association Marc Bloch de Toulouse: Documents d'Histoire Méridionale, 1; Toulouse, 1956).

Le Livre des hommages d'Aquitaine: Restitution du second Livre noir de la connétablie de Bordeaux, ed. J.-P. Trabut-Cussac (Société Archéologique de Bordeaux; Bordeaux, 1969).

The London Eyre of 1276, ed. M. Weinbaum (London Rec. Soc. 12; London, 1976).

Lordship and Landscape in Norfolk 1250–1350: The Early Records of Holkham, ed. W. Hassall and J. Beauroy (British Academy, Records of Social and Economic History, NS 20 Oxford, 1993).

The Making of King's Lynn, ed. D. M. Owen (British Academy, Records of Social and Economic History, NS 9; Oxford, 1984).

Oxfordshire Hundred Rolls of 1279, ed. E. Stone and P. Hyde (Oxfordshire Record Society, 46; Oxford, 1968).

The Pinchbeck Register, ed. F. Hervey, 2 vols. (Brighton, 1925).

Placita de Quo Warranto (Rec. Comm.; London, 1818).

Powell, E., *A Suffolk Hundred in the Year 1238* (Cambridge, 1910).

Réceuil d'Actes relatifs à l'administration des Rois d'Angleterre en Guyenne au XIIIᵉ siècle: Recogniciones feodorum in Aquitania, ed. C. Bémont (Paris, 1914).

Rôles Gascons, ed. F.-Michel and C. Bémont, 3 vols. (Paris, 1885–1906).

Rotuli Hundredorum, 2 vols. (Rec. Comm.; London, 1812–18).

Select Cases in the Court of King's Bench under Edward I, ed. G. O. Sayles, 3 vols. (Seldon Society; London, 1936–9).

Select Pleas in Manorial and Other Seignorial Courts, ed. F. W. Maitland (Selden Society, 2; London 1889).

Stamford in the Thirteenth Century: Two Inquisitions from the Reign of Edward I, ed. D. Roffe (Stamford, 1994).

Statutes of the Realm, 11 vols. (Rec. Comm.; London, 1810–28).

The Stoneleigh Leger Book, ed. R. H. Hilton (Dugdale Society, Oxford, 1960).

'An Unpublished Northumbrian Hundred Roll', ed. H. H. E. Craster, *Archaeologia Aeliana*, 3rd ser. 3 (1907), 187–90.

The Warwickshire Hundred Rolls of 1279–80: Stoneleigh and Kineton Hundreds, ed. T. John (British Academy, Records of Social and Economic History, NS 19; Oxford, 1992).

The Welsh Assize Roll 1277–84, ed. J. Conway Davies (Cardiff, 1940).

The White Book of Peterborough, ed. S. Raban (Northants Rec. Soc., Northampton, 2001).

Yorkshire Hundred and Quo Warranto Rolls, ed. B. English (The Yorkshire Archaeological Society, Record Ser., 151; Leeds, 1996).

III. SECONDARY SOURCES

Baker, J. H., and Ringrose, J. S., *A Catalogue of English Legal Manuscripts in Cambridge University Library* (Woodbridge, 1996).

Barg, M. A., 'The Social Structure of Manorial Freeholders: An Analysis of the Hundred Rolls of 1279', *Ag. HR* 39 (1991), 108–15.

Beresford, M. W., and Finberg, H. P. R., *English Medieval Boroughs: A Handlist* (Newton Abbot, 1973).

Brand, P., *The Making of the Common Law* (London, 1992).

—— *Kings, Barons and Justices: The Making and Enforcement of Legislation in Thirteenth-Century England* (Cambridge, 2003).

Britnell, R. H., *The Commercialisation of English Society 1000–1500* (Cambridge, 1993).

Buck, M., *Politics, Finance and the Church in the Reign of Edward II: Walter Stapeldon Treasurer of England* (Cambridge, 1983).

Cam, H. M., *Studies in the Hundred Rolls: Some Aspects of Thirteenth-Century Administration* (Oxford Studies in Social and Legal History, 6; Oxford, 1921).

—— *The Hundred and the Hundred Rolls* (London, 1930).

Campbell, B. M. S., 'The Complexity of Manorial Structure in Medieval Norfolk: A Case Study', *Norfolk Archaeology*, 39/3 (1986), 225–61.

—— *English Seigniorial Agriculture 1250–1450* (Cambridge, 2000).

Carpenter, D. A., 'Was there a Crisis of the Knightly Class in the Thirteenth Century? The Oxfordshire Evidence', *EHR* 95 (1980), 721–52.

Chew, H. M., 'Scutage under Edward I', *EHR* 37 (1922), 321–36.

Coss, P., 'Sir Geoffrey de Langley and the Crisis of the Knightly Class in Thirteenth Century England', in T. H. Aston (ed.), *Landlords, Peasants and Politics in Medieval England* (Cambridge, 1987), 166–202, formerly published in *Past and Present*, 68 (1975), 3–34.

—— *Lordship, Knighthood and Locality: A Study in English Society c.1180–c.1280* (Cambridge, 1991).

—— *The Origins of the English Gentry* (Cambridge, 2003).

Crook, D., *Records of the General Eyre* (PRO Handbook, 20; London, 1982).

Darby, H. C., *The Domesday Geography of Eastern England* (Cambridge, 1952).

—— and Campbell, E. M. J. (eds.), *The Domesday Geography of South-East England* (Cambridge, 1962).

—— *Domesday England* (Cambridge, 1977).

—— and Maxwell, I. S. (eds.), *The Domesday Geography of Northern England* (Cambridge, 1962).

—— and Terrett, I. B. (eds.), *The Domesday Geography of Midland England* (Cambridge, 1954).

—— and Welldon Finn, R. (eds.), *The Domesday Geography of South-West England* (Cambridge, 1967).

Davies, R. R., *Conquest, Coexistence, and Change: Wales 1063–1415* (Oxford, 1987).

—— *The First English Empire: Power and Identities in the British Isles 1093–1343* (Oxford, 2000).

Dodwell, B., 'The Free Tenantry of the Hundred Rolls', *Ec. HR* 14 (1944), 163–71.

Dunbabin, J., *Charles I of Anjou: Power, Kingship and State-Making in Thirteenth-Century Europe* (London, 1998).

Eyton, R. W., *Antiquities of Shropshire*, 12 vols. (London, 1854–60).

Faith, R., 'The "Great Rumour" of 1377 and Peasant Ideology', in R. H. Hilton and T. H. Aston (eds.), *The English Rising of 1381* (Cambridge, 1984), 43–73.

Fleming, R., *Domesday Book and the Law: Society and Legal Custom in Early-Medieval England* (Cambridge, 1998).

Galbraith, V. H., 'The Tower as an Exchequer Record Office in the Reign of Edward II', in A. G. Little and F. M. Powicke (eds.), *Essays in Medieval History Presented to Thomas Frederick Tout* (Manchester, 1925), 231–47.

—— *The Making of Domesday Book* (London, 1961).

G. E. C., *The Complete Peerage*, revised edn., 14 vols. (London, 1910–98).

Giuseppi, S., *Guide to the Records of the Public Record Office*, 3 vols. (London, 1963–8).

Glénisson, J., 'Les Enquêtes administratives en Europe Ocidentale aux XIIIᵉ et XIVᵉ siècles', in W. Paravicini and K. F. Werner (eds.), *Histoire comparée de l'administration* (Munich, 1980), 17–25.

Gransden, A., *Historical Writing in England*, 2 vols. (London, 1974–82).

Greenway, D. E., 'A Newly Discovered Fragment of the Hundred Rolls of 1279–80', *Journal of the Society of Archivists*, 7 (1982), 73–7.

Griffiths, R. A., *The Principality of Wales in the Later Middle Ages: The Structure and Personnel of Government*, i. (Board of Celtic Studies, History and Law, 26; Cardiff, 1972).

Hallam, E. M., *Domesday Book through Nine Centuries* (London, 1986).

—— and Bates, D. (eds.), *Domesday Book* (London, 2001).

Hamshere, J. D., 'Regressing Domesday Book: Tax Assessments of Domesday England', *Ec. HR*, 2nd ser. 40 (1987), 247–51.

Harley, J. B., 'Population Trends and Agricultural Developments from the Warwickshire Hundred Rolls of 1279', *Ec. HR*, 2nd ser. 11 (1958), 8–18.

—— 'The Hundred Rolls of 1279', *Amateur Historian*, 5 (1961), 9–16.

—— 'The Settlement Geography of Early Medieval Warwickshire', *Institute of British Geographers: Transactions and Papers*, 34 (1964), 115–30.

Harvey, B., *Westminster Abbey and its Estates in the Middle Ages* (Oxford, 1977).

Hatcher, J., 'English Serfdom and Villeinage: Towards a Reassessment', *Past and Present*, 90 (1981), 3–39.

Hilton, R. H., *The Economic Development of Some Leicestershire Estates in the Fourteenth and Fifteenth Centuries* (Oxford, 1947).

—— *A Medieval Society: The West Midlands at the End of the Thirteenth Century* (London, 1966).

—— 'Kibworth Harcourt: A Merton College Manor in the Thirteenth and Fourteenth Centuries', in *Class Conflict and the Crisis of Feudalism: Essays in Medieval History* (London, 1985), 1–17, formerly published in W. G. Hoskins (ed.), *Studies in Leicestershire Agrarian History* (Leics. Archaeological Soc.; Leicester, 1949), 17–40.

Holt, J. C. (ed.), *Domesday Studies* (Woodbridge, 1987).

Howell, C., *Land, Family and Inheritance in Transition: Kibworth Harcourt 1280–1700* (Cambridge, 1983).

Howell, M., *Eleanor of Provence: Queenship in Thirteenth-Century England* (Oxford, 1998).

Huscroft, R., 'The Political Career and Personal Life of Robert Burnell, Chancellor of Edward I' (London University, Ph.D. thesis, 2000).

Jacob, E. F., *Studies in the Period of Baronial Reform and Rebellion, 1258–1267* (Oxford Studies in Social and Legal History, 8; Oxford, 1925, repr. New York, 1974).

John, T., 'Population Change in Medieval Warwickshire: Domesday Book to the Hundred Rolls of 1279–80', *Local Population Studies*, 59 (1997), 41–53.

Johnstone, H., 'The County of Ponthieu 1279–1307', *EHR* 29 (1914), 435–52.

Jurkowski, M., Smith, C. L., and Crook, D., *Lay Taxes in England and Wales 1188–1688* (PRO Handbook, 31; London, 1998).

Kanzaka, J., 'Villein Rents in Thirteenth-Century England: An Analysis of the Hundred Rolls of 1279–80', *Ec. HR*, 55 (2002), 593–618.

Keene, D., 'A New Study of London before the Great Fire', *Urban History Yearbook* (1984), 11–21.

—— 'Medieval London and its Region', *London Journal*, 14 (1989), 99–111.

King, E., *Peterborough Abbey, 1086–1310* (Cambridge, 1973).

Kosminsky, E. A., 'The Hundred Rolls of 1279–80 as a Source for English Agrarain History', *Ec. HR* 3 (1931–2), 16–44.

—— *Studies in the Agrarian History of England in the Thirteenth Century* (Oxford, 1956).

Leaver, R. A., 'Five Hides in Ten Counties: A Contribution to the Domesday Regression Debate', *Ec. HR*, 2nd ser., 41 (1988), 525–42.

List of Ancient Correspondence of the Chancery and Exchequer (PRO, Lists and Indexes, 15, revised edn.; London, repr. 1968).

List of Escheators for England (PRO, Lists and Indexes Society, 72; London, compiled 1932, issued 1971).

List of Sheriffs for England and Wales (PRO, Lists and Indexes, 9; London, repr. 1963).

Lloyd, T. H., *The English Wool Trade in the Middle Ages* (Cambridge, 1977).

Lobel, M. D., *Cambridge* (The Historic Towns Trust; London, 1974).

Loomis, R. S., 'Edward I, Arthurian Enthusiast', *Speculum*, 28 (1953), 114–27.

McDonald, J. and Snooks, G. D., *Domesday Economy: A New Approach to Anglo-Norman History* (Oxford, 1986).

Maddicott, J. R., 'Edward I and the Lessons of Baronial Reform: Local Government 1258–80', in P. R. Coss and S. D. Lloyd (eds.), *Thirteenth Century England*, i (Woodbridge, 1986), 1–30.

—— *Simon de Montfort* (Cambridge, 1994).

Maitland, F. W., *Domesday Book and Beyond* (Cambridge, 1897, repr. 1987).

Mate, M., 'Monetary Policies in England, 1272–1307', *British Numismatic Journal*, 41 (1972), 34–79.

Miller, E., 'The State and Landed Interests in Thirteenth Century France and England', *TRHS*, 5th ser. 2 (1952), 109–29.

—— and Hatcher, J., *Medieval England: Rural Society and Economic Change, 1086–1348* (London, 1978).

—— *Medieval England: Towns, Commerce and Crafts, 1086–1348* (Harlow, 1995).

Moor, C., *Knights of Edward I*, 5 vols. (The Harleian Society, 80–4; London, 1929–32).

Mundill, R. R., *England's Jewish Solution: Experiment and Expulsion, 1262–1290* (Cambridge, 1998).

Nichols, J., *The History and Antiquities of the County of Leicester*, 4 vols. (London, 1795; repr. Wakefield, 1971).

Patourel, J. H. le, *The Medieval Administration of the Channel Islands, 1199–1399* (Oxford, 1937).

Pearson, H., 'The Alecto Domesday Project', in E. Hallam and D. Bates (eds.), *Domesday Book* (Stroud, 2001), 151–8.

Polden, A., 'A Crisis of the Knightly Class? Inheritance and Office among the Gentry of Thirteenth-Century Buckinghamshire', in P. Fleming, A. Gross, and J. R. Lander (eds.), *Regionalism and Revision: The Crown and its Provinces in England 1200–1650* (London, 1998), 29–57.

Preston, R. A., 'George and Joseph Morris: Genealogists of Shropshire', *Shropshire Family History Journal*, 10 (1989), 102–3.

Prestwich, M., *Edward I*, 2nd edn. (New Haven and London, 1997).

Raban, S., *The Estates of Thorney and Crowland* (University of Cambridge, Department of Land Economy, Occasional Paper, 7; Cambridge, 1977).

—— *Mortmain Legislation and the English Church 1279–1500* (Cambridge, 1982).

—— 'Fresh Light on the 1279 Hundred Rolls: Some Huntingdonshire Evidence', *Historical Research*, 61 (1988), 105–17.

—— 'Landlord Return on Villein Rents in North Huntingdonshire in the Thirteenth Century', *Historical Research*, 66 (1993), 21–34.

—— 'The Church in the 1279 Hundred Rolls', in M. J. Franklin and C. Harper-Bill (eds.), *Medieval Ecclesiastical Studies in Honour of Dorothy M. Owen* (Woodbridge, 1995), 185–200.

—— 'The Making of the 1279–80 Hundred Rolls', *Historical Research*, 70 (1997), 123–45.

—— 'Edward I's Other Inquiries', in M. Prestwich, R. Britnell, and R. Frame (eds.), *Thirteenth Century England*, ix (Woodbridge, 2003), 43–57.

Raftis, J. A., *The Estates of Ramsey Abbey: A Study in Economic Growth and Organisation* (Toronto, 1957).

Roffe, D., 'The Hundred Rolls and their Antecedents: Some Thoughts on the Inquisition in Thirteenth-Century England', *Haskins Society Journal*, 7 (1995), 179–87.

—— 'The Hundred Rolls of 1255', *Historical Research*, 69 (1996), 201–10.

—— *Domesday: The Inquest and the Book* (Oxford, 2000).

Rowlands, I., 'The Edwardian Conquest and its Military Consolidation', in T. Herbert and G. E. Jones (eds.), *Edward I and Wales* (Cardiff, 1988), 41–72.

Rutledge, E. and P., 'King's Lynn and Great Yarmouth: Two Thirteenth-Century Surveys', *Norfolk Archaeology*, 37 (1978), 92–114.

Sawyer, P. (ed.), *Domesday Book: A Reassessment* (London, 1985).

Scales, L., 'The Cambridgeshire Ragman Rolls', *EHR* 113 (1998), 553–79.

Stones, E. L. G., 'The Appeal to History in Anglo-Scottish Relations between 1291 and 1401', *Archives*, 9 (1969), 11–21.

—— and Simpson, G. G. (eds.), *Edward I and the Throne of Scotland, 1290–1296*, 2 vols. (Oxford, 1978).

A Summary Catalogue of Western Manuscripts in the Bodleian Library at Oxford, 6 vols. (Oxford, 1895–1953).

Sutherland, D. W., *Quo Warranto Proceedings in the Reign of Edward I, 1278–94* (Oxford, 1963).

Trabut-Cussac, J.-P., 'Les Cartulaires gascons d'Edouard II, d'Edouard III et de Charles VI', *Bibliothèque de l'École des Chartes*, 111 (1953), 65–106.

—— 'Le Livre d'Agenais: A propos d'une édition récente', *Bibliothèque de l'École des Chartes*, 115 (1957), 179–89.

—— *L'Administration anglaise en Gascogne sous Henry III et Edouard I de 1254 à 1307* (Société de l'École des Chartes, Mémoires et Documents, 20; Geneva, 1972).

Treharne, R. F., *The Baronial Plan of Reform, 1258–1263* (Manchester, 1932; revised repr. 1971).

Vale, M., *The Origins of the Hundred Years' War: The Angevin Legacy, 1250–1340* (Oxford, 1996).

Victoria County History: *Bedfordshire*, ed. W. Page, 3 vols. (London, 1901–12).

—— *Cambridgeshire*, ed. L. F. Salzman, R. B. Pugh, J. P. C. Roach, C. R. Elrington, P. M. Wright, and C. P. Lewis, 9 vols. (London and Oxford, 1938–).

—— *Huntingdonshire*, ed. W. Page, G. Proby, and S. Inskip Ladds, 3 vols. (London, 1926–36).

—— *Leicestershire*, ed. W. Page, W. G. Hoskins, R. A. McKinley, J. M. Lee, 5 vols. (London and Oxford, 1907–64).

—— *Northamptonshire*, ed. W. Ryland, D. Adkins, R. M. Serjeantson, W. Page, and L. F. Salzman, 4 vols. (London, 1902–).

—— *Oxfordshire*, ed. L. F. Salzman, W. Page, H. E. Salter, and M. D. Lobel, 13 vols. (Oxford and London, 1907–).

Watt, D. E. R., *A Biographical Dictionary of Scottish Graduates to AD 1410* (Oxford, 1977).

Williams, G. A., *Medieval London, from Commune to Capital* (London, 1963).

Williams, N. J., 'The Work of Peter le Neve at Chapter House, Westminster', *Journal of the Society of Archivists*, 1 (1955–9), 125–31.

Youngs, F. A., *Guide to the Local Administrative Units of England*, 2 vols. (Royal Historical Society; London, 1980–91).

Index

Note: English counties are those prior to local government reorganization in 1974